STUDIES IN JOHN GOWER

Maria Wickert

Translated by
Robert J. Meindl

UNIVERSITY
PRESS OF
AMERICA

Copyright © 1981 by
University Press of America,Inc.
P.O. Box 19101, Washington, D.C. 20036

All rights reserved

Printed in the United States of America

ISBN: 0-8191-1993-8 (Perfect)
0-8191-1992-X (Case)

Library of Congress Number: 81-40128

Maria Wickert
1915–1959

σοὶ δὲ ταῦτ' ἀρέστ' εἴη

iii

Translator's Acknowledgements

I am grateful to the many friends and colleagues who have assisted me in the course of my labors. Professors Charles Moore and Stuart Northam of California State University, Sacramento, Professor Francis Hubbard of the University of Wisconsin, Milwaukee, Karen Kossuth of Pomona College, and the late Maria Wickert's daughter, Frau Almut Opitz of Cologne, have looked at part or all of the translation and frequently pointed out the better way. Professors Marc Bertonasco, Mary Giles, Paul McGinnis, and Mark Riley of California State University, Sacramento, and Professor Charles Janssens of San Jose State University were kind enough to offer suggestions concerning Latin and Old French passages, the responsibility for which remains mine unless otherwise noted.

The translations of the VOX CLAMANTIS and THE CRONICA TRIPERTITA are by Eric Stockton, THE MAJOR LATIN WORKS OF JOHN GOWER (Seattle: University of Washington Press, 1962), and are used by permission of the University of Washington Press.

I owe special debts of gratitude to Professor Lothar Wickert of the University of Cologne and to his lovely wife, Gisela Wickert-Micknat, for the hospitality they showered upon me in Cologne during the summer of 1970.

My special debt is as always to my wife, this time for assembling the index.

Robert J. Meindl

California State University, Sacramento
Summer, 1981

Table of Contents

Preface

Gower's claim to a place in the literary history of the fourteenth century is based upon the poems MIROUR DE L'OMME (SPECULUM MEDITANTIS), VOX CLAMANTIS, and CONFESSIO AMANTIS. They are written in three different languages: the MIROUR in a dialect that the author designates, with the necessary proviso, as French,[1] the VOX CLAMANTIS in a tolerably correct Middle Latin, and the CONFESSIO in the Middle English of the London area that was destined to provide the basis for a standard written language.

The destiny of the three works is closely connected with the fate of the three languages on English soil. When Gower selected French at the beginning of his literary career, and when he returned to French at its end, he clearly did so with the intention of addressing the entire educated world in the cultural language of the time:

> Al université de tout le monde
> Johan Gower ceste Balade envoie.
> [To the universality of the whole world
> John Gower sends this ballad.]
> TRAITIE 18.22-23

In the LIVRES DOU TRESOR, Brunetto Latini had similarly preferred French, as the common language of the educated classes, to his mother tongue.[2] However, what might have been suitable for the thirteenth century in Italy as well as England became less and less so in England in the fourteenth. English replaced French as the language of education around the middle of the century, and by its end had already appeared in royal decrees and the deliberations of Parliament. Chaucer's humorous characterization of his Prioress' knowledge of French, and the wretched grammar of many private letters from so-called educated circles, show how French slowly died out as a living language in England. Gower deluded himself when he believed the language of the MIROUR capable of a broad consequence. The work stands at the end of Anglo-Norman literature. It was scarcely circulated in manuscript, and not printed until the end of the nineteenth century. Unrecognized, it survived in a single mutilated manuscript until Macaulay discovered and identified it as Gower's.

The opposite fate was allotted the CONFESSIO
AMANTIS. Here Gower's choice of English was an experiment to which he may have been stimulated by
Chaucer's example. Nevertheless, the attempt seemed
novel and daring, and for that reason Gower experi-
mented on a subject that was less important to him
than that of his earlier writings. The extent to
which the royal commission, which he himself so
charmingly describes in the Prologue,[3] was a determining factor for Gower's new course, and the
extent to which doubt in the success of his moral
mission occasioned the genesis of the CONFESSIO,[4]
can hardly be ascertained. Certainly the new work
was of lesser significance in the author's eyes
than everything that he had previously written.
Thus it may not have been very important to him to
address a national audience instead of the educated
world, and to increase the modest stock of literature in the vernacular:

> And for that fewe men endite
> In oure englissh, I thenke make
> A bok for king Richardes sake.[5]
>
> Prologue, 22-24

It seems an irony of fate that he thereby, and only
thereby, found entry into the history of his land's
literature, and was able to maintain his place as a
father of English poetry, full of honor alongside
Chaucer, into the early seventeenth century.

The VOX CLAMANTIS lies in time between the
MIROUR and the CONFESSIO. The choice of Latin points
to the importance of the subject, the passion of the
language to the intensity of the inner concern that
urged Gower to the composition of this work, and the
number of manuscripts is evidence of its circulation
up to the second half of the fifteenth century. It
is respectfully mentioned in the literary histories,
but seldom looked at closely. Two circumstances appear to me to have been involved. The first is the
opinion that the Latin works of an English author
do not belong to the history of English literature.
Then, of course, nothing remains but to parcel a
phenomenon like Gower out to the three disciplines

of Anglistics, Romanistics, and Middle Latin. The
notion seems to me absurd. One should seek to understand a poet from the totality of his work and,
indeed, one should begin there where he himself was
most strongly interested, not at the points that
have become important for a later development in
literary history. Gower can be understood in his
entirety only in the light of the VOX CLAMANTIS.

The second difficulty lies in the theme of the
VOX, which is barely accessible to modern taste.
Whatever Chaucer had in mind when he bestowed upon
Gower the epithet "moral,"[6] the word implies for
modern readers a stigma to which not only Gower,
but, moreover, almost all fifteenth-century poetry
is subject, for while the school of Chaucer followed
his form, its spirit was Gower's.

The present investigations endeavor to understand this spirit. They are concerned with the
technical problem of textual criticism because the
work's development, as it is revealed in the different recensions, is very closely interwoven with
its aim. Moreover, the connection with the tradition of sermon and devotional literature alluded to
in the title VOX CLAMANTIS needed clarification.
Since Gower considered the state to be first of all
a moral institution, his moral mission was at the
same time a political mission, and it was therefore
necessary, in at least one section, to show his political ideas. I have also attempted to form from
scattered statements the coherent conception of
man's place and duty within the creation that was
in the author's mind. In order not to overlook the
formal side of Gower's poetry, I have added a chapter concerning his narrative technique, and interpreted a few tales from that work in which it is
most powerfully developed, namely from the CONFESSIO
AMANTIS.

The work was accepted as an inaugural disser-
tation by the Faculty of Philosophy of the University of Cologne. To the German Research Society,
which made publication possible, I give my deepest
thanks. For untiring assistance, I thank the

librarians of the Bodleian. Paul G. Buchloh was
kind enough to read the proofs with me.

Notes to the Preface
    [1] Cf. TRAITIE 18.24-27 in George C. Macaulay,
ed. THE COMPLETE WORKS OF JOHN GOWER (Oxford, 1899-
1902), 4 vols., I, 391:
        Et si jeo n'ai de Francois la faconde,
        Pardonetz moi qe jeo de ceo forsvoie:
        Jeo sui Englois, si quier par tiele voie
        Estre excusé . . .
        [And if I lack a Frenchman's eloquence,
        Forgive me my straying from it:
        I am an Englishman and therefore
        Ask to be excused . . .]
The language of the MIROUR is a late literary form
of Anglo-Norman.
    [2] Et se aucuns demandoit por quoi cist livres
est escriz en romans selonc le langage des Francois,
puisque nos somes Ytaliens, je diroie que ce est
. . . porce que la parleure est plus delitable et
plus commune a toutes gens [And if any wonder why
this book is written in romanz according to the
language of the French, since we are Italian, I
would say that it is . . . because the parlance is
more delightful and more common to all people.]
Quoted in Charles Victor Langlois, LA VIE EN FRANCE
AU MOYEN AGE (Paris, 1924-28), III, 337.
    [3] Cf. 33 ff. of the earlier version of the
Prologue.
    [4] Cf. the CONFESSIO AMANTIS 1.1-10.
    [5] The later version has "A bok for Engelondes
sake."
    [6] Cf. TROILUS AND CRISEYDE 5.1856. [All Chaucer
citations are from F. N. Robinson, ed. THE WORKS OF
GEOFFREY CHAUCER, 2nd ed. (Boston, 1957). Trans.]

Explanation of Abbreviations

Visio	Gower, VOX CLAMANTIS, Book 1
VC	Gower, VOX CLAMANTIS, Books 2-7
EETS OS	Early English Text Society, Original Series
EETS ES	Early English Text Society, Extra Series
MLR	Modern Language Review
MP	Modern Philology
PMLA	Publications of the Modern Language Association of America

Chapter One
The Text and Development of the VOX CLAMANTIS

Gower's VOX CLAMANTIS has survived in eleven
manuscripts.[1] It was first printed in 1850,[2] and
since 1902 has been available in a critical edition[3]
that one may consider definitive in the event that
no new manuscript material of crucial importance
should come to light. The work comprises seven
books. The first deals in visionary fashion with
the events of the summer of 1381, and surpasses
the others in literary and historical significance.
The remainder of the VOX CLAMANTIS is an extensive
class critique framed by general observations about
the nature and destiny of mankind. The theme of
class critique had already emerged in an earlier
Anglo-Norman poem[4] of the author, and it recurs in
a compressed form in the prologue to that English
frame-narrative to which he owes his literary significance.[5] However, in neither the earlier nor
the later work is it induced by a contemporary political crisis. As a mirror image of the convulsion of 1381 and as an expression of a profound
moral and political awareness occasioned by the
Peasants' Rebellion, the VOX CLAMANTIS is thought
to be unique.[6]

The historical transmission of the work presents no difficulties. The four oldest manuscripts
appear to have originated during the poet's lifetime, perhaps under his supervision.[7] The rest are
easy to classify, with the exception of one manuscript which presents the poem in only six books.[8]
The first book is missing--except the prologue and
first chapter--and the remaining books are consequently numbered from one to six. As a result,
Macaulay questioned whether the first book, the
vision of the Peasants' Rebellion, was a part of
the poem's original design or whether the author had
actually added it belatedly.[9] Some inner criteria
appear to support the testimony of this manuscript
(L): Books II-VII seem totally independent of the
vision, and the prologue of the second book--with
its whole series of exordial topoi and with the
first mention of the title[10]--appears to introduce

an independent opus rather than join together two
parts of a larger work.[11] In any case, Macaulay
did not attach a great deal of importance to the
condition of the Laud manuscript because the family
relationship of the Latin Gower manuscripts suggests an omission rather than the preservation of
an older version. He did not pursue the inner
criteria further. Thus he left suspended the question of the original form of the VOX CLAMANTIS,
chiefly because the final redaction, which includes
the vision, unquestionably originated with Gower
himself.

The problem of the development of the VOX
CLAMANTIS appears to me worthy of investigation
not only on compositional grounds. For the question of the date of composition for the VC (Books
II-VII) would have to be raised anew in the event
that the Visio (Book I) was indeed added belatedly
either after or near the completion of the VC.
Macaulay failed to observe that the most important
key to dating the poem disappears when the Visio
is separated from the original assemblage of the
VOX CLAMANTIS. In that case the possibility
arises that the VC was written before the Peasants'
Rebellion.[12] It is not, however, advisable to
suppose a very lengthy span of time between the
early version of the VC and its enlargement through
the Visio, since no reliable separate manuscript
tradition of the VC has survived. It is, however,
conceivable that the events of 1381 surprised the
author during work on the VC or shortly after its
completion. In the event that the VC was planned
before 1381, and perhaps in the main already executed, that would indicate that the motives which
might have compelled the author to the composition
of this work are not derived from the shock felt
by a country squire of Kent whose property has been
threatened, that his pessimism did not spring from
the passing darkness on the political horizon, that
not sudden panic but tranquil reflection determined
his scathing critique of man and society. Thus the
much more important problem of the origin and object of the VOX CLAMANTIS arises from the question
of its date.

This chapter will investigate the origin of
the work; the one following, its object. We shall
handle the problem in reverse chronology, in order
to advance from the secure basis of the transmitted
redaction, or redactions, to the traces of an earlier
recension. The material for such an investigation
consists in the text, the prose summaries of the
individual chapters, and a brief notice of Gower's
literary productions that has been preserved in
four codices of the VOX CLAMANTIS and in most manuscripts of the first recension of the CONFESSIO
AMANTIS.[13] This notice occurs in three versions,
the earliest of which almost certainly, the latest
of which perhaps originated with the poet himself.[14]
For our purposes the middle version can be excluded.[15]
The other two, however, give divergent information
about the content and thesis of the VOX CLAMANTIS.

      The later version (hereafter designated B)
reads:
                . . . Secundus enim liber sermone
            Latino metrice compositus tractat
            de variis infortuniis tempore regis
            Ricardi secundi in Anglia contingent-
            ibus: vnde non solum regni proceres
            et communes tormenta passi sunt, set
            et ipse crudelissimus rex, suis ex
            demeritis ab alto corruens, in foueam
            quam fecit finaliter proiectus est.
            Nomenque voluminis huius VOX CLAMANTIS
            intitulatur.[16] [The second book, met-
            rically composed in the Latin language,
            treats of the various misfortunes
            occurring in England in the time of
            King Richard II. Whence, not only
            did the nobles and commons of the
            realm suffer torments, but even the
            most cruel king himself was finally
            laid low, falling because of his
            fault from on high into the pit which
            he had made. And the name of this
            book is called THE VOICE OF ONE CRYING.]

      This version mentions neither the Peasants'
Rebellion nor the class critique, but alludes tersely

3

to the unfortunate vicissitudes of Richard II's reign
that led to the monarch's deserved downfall. Were
the title VOX CLAMANTIS not given, one would assoc-
iate the summary with the CRONICA TRIPERTITA, which
treats English history from 1387 to the deposition
of Richard in 1399. Because the title is named,
it is clear that for the author of Notice B the VOX
CLAMANTIS was a work that included the CRONICA TRI-
PERTITA and that meant to specify the particular
symptoms of the king's fatal misrule that ended with
his downfall. In this view the Peasants' Rebellion
is only one among several symptoms, and so subordinate in the presentation of the whole trend that it
appears to merit no special emphasis.

On the other hand, one reads in the earlier
version (hereafter designated A):
. . . Secundus enim liber, sermone
latino versibus exametri et penta-
metri compositus, tractat super illo
mirabili euentu qui in Anglia tempore
domini Regis Ricardi secundi anno
regni sui quarto contigit, quando
seruiles rustici impetuose contra
nobiles et ingenuos regni insurrex-
erunt. Innocenciam tamen dicti domini Regis tunc minoris etatis cause
indi excusabilem pronuncians, culpas
aliunde, ex quibus et non a fortuna
talia inter homines contingunt enormia
euidencius declarat. Titulusque voluminis huius, cuius ordo Septem continet paginas, VOX CLAMANTIS nominatur.[17]
[The second book, composed in the
Latin language in hexameter and pentameter verses, treats of the astounding
event which took place in England during the time of King Richard II in the
fourth year of his reign, when the lowly
peasants violently revolted against the
freemen and nobles of the realm.
Nevertheless, pronouncing upon the
innocence of the said lord the king
as excusable in this matter because
of his minor age, the book declares

that the blame, because of which--
and not through Fortune--such enorm-
ities take place among men, clearly
lies elsewhere. And the name of
this book, which is arranged in
seven sections, is called THE VOICE
OF ONE CRYING.]

Version A reveals an entirely different conception of the contents of the VOX CLAMANTIS. It
places total emphasis on the Peasants' Rebellion--
everything else is subordinated to an investigation
of the question of blame and to a disclosure of the
causes that led to the monstrous event. The king
is absolved of responsibility because of his minority. This, plus the mention of the fact that the
book is divided into seven parts (paginae), ex-
cludes the CRONICA TRIPERTITA from consideration.[18]
Version A, therefore, sees in the VOX CLAMANTIS a
work in seven parts whose theme is the Peasants'
Rebellion and whose purpose is instruction in the
question of who must bear the blame for it. Nothing indicates a causal nexus between this event
and the collapse of Richard II's rule.

Version B appears in four manuscripts in which
the CRONICA TRIPERTITA follows the VOX CLAMANTIS,[19]
and in one manuscript of the last recension of the
CONFESSIO.[20] It can have originated, according to
its contents, only after the conclusion of the
CRONICA TRIPERTITA, that is, after 1400. Version
A does not occur in any Latin Gower manuscript,
but in numerous codices of the first recension of
the CONFESSIO AMANTIS, where it immediately follows
the CONFESSIO. It was probably written at the same
time that the CONFESSIO was completed or shortly
thereafter. The two versions of the notice indicate that Gower altered the political tendency of
the VOX CLAMANTIS in the course of a decade (ca.
1390-1400), and that the alteration was paralleled
by a quantitative modification, namely the inclusion
of the CRONICA TRIPERTITA.

The text of the VOX CLAMANTIS itself reveals
two redactions,[21] represented by the manuscript

5

groups SCEHGL (hereafter designated B-Text) and TH2 (designated A-Text).[22] The two redactions differ at the point in the class critique that deals with the special duties of the king, that is, at the beginning and end of the brief Mirror for a Prince in Book VI.[23] Here the A-Text agrees with the judgment of Richard in Version A of the notice, while the B-Text sounds a pessimistic tone and occasionally breaks out into open censure of the youthful ruler.[24] The passage in question at the beginning of the Mirror for a Prince occurs in the seventh chapter of Book VI. The Latin chapter heading reads the same in both recensions; however, since its content asserts Richard's innocence, it corresponds only with the A-Text:

> Hic loquitur quod sicut homines esse super terram necessario expedit, ita leges ad eorum regimen institui oportet, dummodo tamen legis custodes verum a falso discernentes vniquique quod suum est equo pondere distribuant. De erroribus tamen et iniuriis modo contingentibus innocenciam Regis nostri, minoris etatis causa, quantum ad presens excusat.[25] [Here he says that just as it is necessarily ordained for men to be on earth, so it is right that laws be instituted for governing them, provided, however, that the guardians of the law discern truth from falsehood and render every man his due with impartial authority. Yet up to the present he absolves our king's innocence of the sins and injustices now going on, because of his minor age.]

The redactor of the B-Text clearly performed his work carelessly and forgot to correct the headnote when he changed the chapter's ending. Furthermore, the headnote has influenced the wording of Version A of the notice of 1390. The literal correspondences are obvious;[26] only the sense is not the same. While the chapter headnote attests to Richard's innocence in the decay of the administra-

tion of justice, Version A of the notice absolves
him of responsibility for the Peasants' Rebellion.
Indeed, it is possible to establish a connection
indirectly by maintaining that the Peasants' Rebellion was a consequence of the intolerable state of
justice in the country; however, that contradicts
the whole tenor of the Visio. Nowhere, as will be
shown in the following chapter, does the Visio ad-
mit the possibility that the legis custodes or the
king are to blame; rather, it one-sidedly condemns
the insurgents as rebels against divine as well as
human law. One cannot escape the impression that
the reference in Version A is belated and artificial, and that the seventh chapter of Book VI of the
VOX CLAMANTIS originally had nothing to do with the
Peasants' Rebellion or the Visio. However, more
will be said on the subject later. For the time
being it suffices to establish that the A-Text of
the VOX CLAMANTIS furnished the basis for the A-
Version of the notice. Since the A-Version presupposes the existence of the CONFESSIO--it enum-
erates Gower's three major works--it cannot have
originated before 1390. Therefore, in 1390 the
A-Text is still the officially recognized form of
the VOX CLAMANTIS. Thus we obtain the year 1390
as the terminus ante quem non for the redaction of
the B-Text.

As soon as one attempts to arrive at a more
exact dating of the B-Text, however, one encounters
considerable difficulties. To place it at the time
of the composition of Version B of the notice, that
is, about 1400, will not do because Richard is also
still alive at the time of the B-Text. The direct
addresses and admonitions to the king would otherwise be pointless. Thus an authorial adjustment
to the altered political circumstances after Richard's fall does not appear to have been the cause
of the new recension. The textual history of the
CONFESSIO AMANTIS indicates a change in Gower's
attitude toward Richard II analogous to that in
the textual history of the VOX CLAMANTIS. Macaulay
had to fix this change of opinion in 1391/92, but
without being able to set forth a sound reason for
so doing. The estimate originates solely in the

7

constraint of the tight chronological sequence of
the three CONFESSIO recensions as Macaulay establishes it, and will become untenable as soon as an
editor resolves to date the third recension after
1393. But even if the assumption of a crisis in
Gower's political convictions for the year 1391/92
were more secure, the analogy of the CONFESSIO
is still to be used with caution. Richard was 25-
27 years old in 1391-93, and the designation "puer,"
which is applied to him conspicuously often and
emphatically in the divergent passages of the B-
Text, is not really appropriate to that age. It
would be difficult to justify at all after 1390,
the year of the A-Version of the notice and thus
of the authoritative A-Text. To be sure, statements of age of this kind are always relative,
and the use of "puer" alone proves nothing, especially when one considers that Gower himself may
have then been in his sixties.[27] However, Richard's
youthfulness does appear to have been so strongly
emphasized with a definite intention.

If one were to compare 6.555-80 in the A-
and B-Texts,[28] one would find the designations
"puer," "puerilis," "iuvenis," and "iuvenilis" five
times in the earlier version but no fewer than twelve
in the later. The reason for the increase is readily apparent. The A-Text absolves the boy of
all responsibility and directs its major attack
against the mature men who should educate and
counsel him.[29] They are heaped with reproaches
and represented in a very unflattering biblical
parallel.[30] The B-Text, however, mentions them
in only a few words. They are in their avarice
certainly an additional evil,[31] but not fons et
origo mali. The cancerous sore is, rather, the
concio iuvenilis, the king's corrupt and corrupt-
ing young associates. The B-Text enlarges upon
this theme, whereas the A-Text makes no mention
of youthful comrades. Thus the emphatic repetition of the word "puer" and its synonyms. This
attitude of the B-Text points to a political
position characteristic of the period between
1385 and 1387. Thus one arrives at a starting
date of somewhere around 1386-87 for the second
redaction of the VOX CLAMANTIS. Such an estimate,

however, is impossible unless one assumes a continual fluctuation in Gower's attitude toward Richard: initially positive (A-Text), pessimistic in 1386-87 (B-Text), hopeful in 1390 if not enthusiastic (CONFESSIO AMANTIS and the A-Version of the notice), and finally negative in 1391-92 (the third recension of the CONFESSIO).

A substantial simplification of the complicated chronological problem results if one assumes that Gower made post eventum corrections within the second recension of the VOX CLAMANTIS when he joined the work with the CRONICA TRIPERTITA after Richard's fall, and attempted an organic transition. The CRONICA begins with a statement of the year (1387),[32] which is followed by a passage of nine lines that in all of the manuscripts is written over an erasure.[33] What may have been there originally cannot be determined. What is there now represents a rather inept attempt to join the CRONICA TRIPERTITA to the chronicle of the Peasants' Rebellion,[34] that is, to the VOX CLAMANTIS. The CRONICA TRIPERTITA itself begins after the erasure with attacks upon the king's consilium iuuenile:

Rex induratum cor semper habet, neque fatum
Tale remordebat ipsum, qui iure carebat:
Stultorum vile sibi consilium iuuenile
Legerat, et sectam senium dedit esse reiectam:
Consilio iuuenum spirauerat ille venenum,
Quo bona predaret procerum, quos mortificaret:
Sic malus ipse malis adhesit, eisque sodalis
Efficitur, tota regis pietate remota. 1.13-20
[The King always had an obdurate heart, but
such an affliction provided no remorse for
one who was lacking in righteousness. He
took the base, immature counsel of fools to
himself, and caused the principles of older
men to be rejected. He absorbed the poisonous counsels of brash youths to the effect
that he was to prey upon the goods of his
nobles, whom he reduced to a state of weakness. In such fashion did the wicked King
cling to wicked men and become their ally,
since he had lost all piety.]
That is, in a somewhat sharper tone of voice, the

same complaint that the B-Text of the VOX CLAMANTIS substitutes for the accusation against the corrupt elders. At the same time the king is reproached for not having taken to heart the lesson of the Peasants' Rebellion--or should one say of the VOX CLAMANTIS? Gower appears to have proceeded in the following manner: when he realized that the history of Richard was a continuous development in the direction of catastrophe, the Peasants' Rebellion became for him the first symptom of irreversible decline. The VOX CLAMANTIS and the CRONICA TRIPERTITA formed in this new view of things a unity that was outwardly established by effacing a number of lines in the beginning of the CRONICA and substituting a reference to the VOX CLAMANTIS. At the same time Gower deleted his favorable statements about Richard in the VOX and inserted a passage that pointed to the beginning of the CRONICA. The result is that the reader of the B-Text receives the impression that the VOX CLAMANTIS is a last futile warning to the young king, the ignoring of which led to the situation of 1387. Perhaps several dark and oracular lines in the introduction to the Mirror for a Prince already allude to the ending of the CRONICA TRIPERTITA:

Nescit enim mater nato que fata parantur,
Fine set occultum clarius omne patet;
[A mother, to be sure, does not know what fate is designed for her child, but in the end every secret is clearly revealed] (B-Text, 6.575-76);
. . . set ei sors stat aborta doli;
[but his destiny does arise out of this wrongdoing] (6.572).

The keenness with which Gower criticizes the king personally also indicates that a reinterpretation of the motivation for the Mirror for a Prince, derived from the conditions of the 1380's, first appeared after the king's deposition. With the second and third recensions of the CONFESSIO AMANTIS, Gower unobtrusively replaced the lines concerning Richard II with a new version. This was all the less conspicuous since it was done--at least in the case of the third recension--in a private dedicatory copy, while the mass of codices continued to circulate the first recension. On the other hand, the second recension of the VOX CLAMANTIS appears, to judge from the number of codices, officially to have replaced the earlier version. It criticizes in a tone that would have, during Richard's lifetime, brought the author to the Tower instead of yielding him, shortly after its appearance, a royal commission for the composition of the CONFESSIO AMANTIS.

We arrive at the following conclusion: the latest recension of the VOX CLAMANTIS, that is, the B-Text, does indeed simulate the situation of ca. 1387, but is, as Notice A testifies, to be dated after 1390, and in all likelihood originated, as its political attitude shows, in the period after Richard's fall, when the VOX CLAMANTIS was joined to the CRONICA TRIPERTITA. It forms the basis for Notice B. The older recension, that is, the A-Text, underlies Notice A and was consequently concluded before 1390. The year 1381 provides the terminus post quem for the Visio; however, it would be valid for the remaining books only if they were not composed before the Visio.

If we return to our original concern, namely to the question of whether textual history is able to provide information concerning the relationship of the Visio to the VC, then we must consider the third book of the VOX CLAMANTIS. The alterations in Book VI have attracted such a strong interest because of their historical significance that a divergence in the textual tradition of the third book has remained practically unnoticed. It involves the first twenty-nine lines of Book III. They exist in three redactions, of which two are represented by the manuscript group of the B-Text,[35] while the third occurs only in the small manuscript group of the A-Text.[36] The two versions of the B-Text differ from each other only stylistically. They will hereafter be designated B^1 (CHGEDL) and B^2 (S). In contrast, the A-Text version differs distinctly in its contents from the B-Text group. The important lines in this context are 1-8:
A-Text:
Sunt clerus, miles, cultor, tres trina gerentes;
Hic docet, hic pugnat, alter et arua colit.

11

Quid sibi sit clerus primo videamus, et ecce
De reliquis fugiens mundus adheret eis.
Primo prelatos constat preferre sequendos,
Nam via doctorum tucior illa foret.
Morigeris verbis modo sunt quam plura docentes,
Facta tamen dictis dissona cerno suis.
[There are the cleric, the knight, and the peasant, the three carrying on three [different]
things. The one teaches, the other fights,
and the third tills the fields. First let
us see what the clergy are. Behold, the whole
world cleaves to them and shuns the rest of us.
Evidently, prelates prefer to be waited upon
first, for the pathway of learned men ought to
be quite secure. I observe how much they teach
with their moral words, but their deeds are not
in harmony with what they say.]
B-Text (B^1):
Sunt Clerus, Miles, Cultor, tres trina gerentes;
Hic docet, hic pugnat, alter et arua colit.
Quid sibi sit Clerus primo videamus, et ecce
Eius in exemplis iam stupet omnis humus.
Scisma patens hodie monstrat quod sunt duo pape,
Vnus scismaticus, alter et ille bonus:
Francia scismaticum colit et statuit venerandum,
Anglia sed rectam seruat vbique fidem.
Ergo meis scriptis super hoc vbicumque legendis
Sint bona dicta bonis, et mala linquo malis.
[There are the cleric, the knight, and the peas-
ant, the three carrying on three [different]
things. The one teaches, the other fights,
and the third tills the fields. First let us
see what the cleric is. Behold, the whole
world is now stunned by his example. The schism
of today shows plainly that there are two popes,
one a schismatic and the other the proper one.
France favors the schismatic and declares that
he ought to be revered, but England everywhere
preserves the right faith. I accordingly bequeath the good things said by my writings a-
bout this matter to good readers wherever they
may be, and I bequeath the bad things to the bad.]
B-Text (B^2):
Sunt Clerus, Miles, Cultor, tres trina gerentes,
Set de prelatis scribere tendo prius.

12

Scisma patens hodie monstrat quod sunt duo pape.
(from here identical with B[1])
[There are the cleric, the knight, and the peasant, the three carrying on three [different]
things. But I intend to write about the prelates first. The schism evident today shows
that there are two popes.]

The B-Text mentions the Schism; the A-Text,
like the prose summary of the chapter headnote, which
reads the same in all redactions,[37] says nothing
about it. Thus there is the same correspondence of
summary and A-Text as in the analogous passage of
Book VI. Should the A-Text of Book III therefore be
dated before the autumn of 1378? An argumentum ex
silentio is, naturally, hazardous; nevertheless, one
must clarify the situation at the beginning of Book
III in order to determine what the Schism signifies
for this part of the VOX CLAMANTIS.

In the second book Gower rejects the cheap ex-
cuse of the masses that Fortuna is responsible for
the decline of the times. Supported by the authority of the Bible, he advocates the view that man's
moral behavior defines his fate. Like the destiny
of the individual, the destiny of human society in
its organization in church and state is dependent
upon the moral integrity of its institutions. After
this general observation, the third book begins with
a moral inventory of the three estates of society.
The church has precedence. First the secular, then
the regular clergy are treated in hierarchical gradation from the top downwards. The Schism would
have constituted not only the natural point of departure for a criticism of the church in root and
branch, but at the same time an extraordinarily
effective beginning for a mercilessly negative
judgment such as Gower heavy-heartedly delivers.
Moreover, it would have provided, according to the
organic conception of the nature of the state as
well as of the church that the author shared with
his public, the natural explanation for all the
symptoms of disease in the body of the church, for
the branches too will suffer the disease of the root.
Gower himself speaks of this causal nexus in the

class critique of the MIROUR DE L'OMME, where it
is said of pope and cardinals:

> Ce dist qui sapience enfile,
> Du bonne mere bonne file,
> Et par contraire il est auci:
> Mais c'est tout voir, qant chief s'avile,
> La part des membres serra vile.
> Au Court de Rome il est ensi. 18841-46
> [The wise man says that good daughters
> come of good mothers, the reverse of
> which is also true. Certainly it is
> true that when the head becomes vile,
> so do the limbs. Thus things are at
> the court of Rome.]

It is scarcely credible, or rather improbable to a
high degree, that in the VOX CLAMANTIS Gower should
have voluntarily renounced the strongest and most
palpable argument for the necessity of a moral regeneration of the church. The belated insertion of
the Schism into the B-Text shows that he was well
aware of the significance of this event for his
class critique, even though from lack of space--he
was limited to the number of lines of the erasure--
he could not make full use of it but had to be satisfied with a brief reference. The redaction of
the A-Text, therefore, appears at this point to refer back to the time before the Schism. If this supposition is correct, the VC, or more precisely the
third book of the VOX CLAMANTIS, originated during
the span of time between Richard's accession and the
outbreak of the Schism, that is, during the period
from 1377 to the autumn of 1378.[38]

With that the series of textual-historical reference points for the development of the VOX CLAMANTIS
is exhausted. The internal criteria remain to be
investigated. There are in the VC neither direct
references to the Visio nor allusions to the events
of 1381. A reference to the Peasants' Rebellion in
the seventh chapter of Book VI, as shown above,[39]
was interpolated belatedly into the text from Version
B of the notice and cannot really be considered. The
compositional connection of the VC with the Visio is
very loose and indistinct. The last chapter of the
last book retrospectively mentions a dream inspira-

tion, but gives no details nor makes any clearly
recognizable reference to the Visio.[40] At the
point of transition between the Visio and the VC,
that is, in the prologue of the second book, in
which--if anywhere--the juncture ought to have become visible, a clear allusion is absent from the
text. Only the prose summary makes a connection to
the Visio, whereas one cannot be read into the text
without doing violence to the wording.[41]

The VC's only actual point of contact with the
Visio is its critique of the peasantry in the ninth
and tenth chapters of Book V. Macaulay even remarks in the notes his surprise that there is not
one word of mention in these chapters of the events
of 1381. He does not attempt an explanation. However, it is a matter not only of the absence of any
reference to the rebellion, but of Gower's attitude
toward the peasants. One is here in the fortunate
position of being able to compare, by means of the
Mirour and the Visio, Gower's attitude before and
after 1381. Of course, one does not expect sympa-
thies for the agricultural worker, be he bound or
free, in a country squire of the time--even before
the Peasants' Rebellion. The relationships between
the two classes had been strained to the utmost
since the Statute of Labourers: complaints in Parliament were the order of the day, warnings from
the pulpit numerous, and acts of violence frequent.
The state of affairs was equally intolerable for
both parties.[42] However, even for a biased onlooker--
as Gower probably was because of his station in life--
there is a difference between the critique of a class
that does not fulfill its duties and the condemnation
of a class that in organized rebellion endangers the
existence of the state. The Visio's judgment of
damnation will be treated extensively in the next
chapter. It is of a severity unmitigated by any
missionary endeavor, by any intercession on behalf
of the peasants. In the Visio the rebellious peasant is Satan incarnate. In the MIROUR, on the other
hand, and also in the VC, the peasantry ranks as one
among the various classes that in their totality
comprise the state, and that the poet calls upon to
come to their senses and return to their divinely

15

ordained duties. The blame for the decline of the
times rests with all the classes; the peasantry
are only partially responsible. Indeed, one could
conclude from the scant space that is granted the
failings of this class in the MIROUR and the VC,
and from the meager emphasis that is allotted to
their vices as opposed to those, for example, of
the clergy or jurists, that Gower assigns the main
guilt to the other classes. That may be in part
because the root of all evil is the disappearance
of justice, for which the upper classes are more
responsible than the lower, and it may be grounded
in part in the practice of the homily, which in
principle directed itself equally to all classes
and spared none,[43] but which in practice somewhat
overlooked the lower classes because they were
already expiating a part of their punishment
through difficulty and hardship--"tribulationes"
is the terminus technicus--in their mortal existence. One may read in the Book of Wisdom: Horrende
et cito apparebit vobis, quoniam iudicium durissi-
mum his, qui praesunt, fiet. Exiguo enim conced-
itur misericordia; potentes autem potenter tor-
menta patientur [Horribly and swiftly will he
appear to you, for a most severe judgment shall
be for them that bear rule. For to him that is
little, mercy is granted, but the mighty shall be
mightily tormented] (Wisdom 6.6-7). Gower, whose
class critique has to a considerable extent the
character of a homily,[44] could have made this his
guiding principle.

     In the details of the VC's argument, Gower
follows his own model from the MIROUR. The class
vices of the rural populace are sloth (MIROUR 26434;
VOX CLAMANTIS 5.573, 577, 581, 587 f.), excessive
wage demands (MIROUR 26435-48; VOX CLAMANTIS
5.579-82), gluttony (MIROUR 26449-58; VOX CLAMANTIS
5.637-48), and presumptuous dress (only in the
MIROUR 26458-64). The stylistic characters of
the two works are, however, different. In the
MIROUR, Gower sketches a melancholy description of
the old, simple, rustic, Horatian way of life,
which he contrasts to the evil present, finally
clothing the moral of his observations in the garb

of an epigram.[45] In the VC he provides a theological foundation for peasant labor. Common to both works are allusions that appear to refer to jacquerie;[46] common also is the tendency to symbolize the peasant malady through botanical comparisons.[47] In the MIROUR, the metaphor of the nettle provides the occasion for a prediction of impending catastrophe that is evidence of Gower's political sensitivity and that guarantees a pre-1381 date.[48]

However, it has not been observed until now that a similar premonition of the catastrophe occurs in the VC. The critique of the peasants in Book V ends with an urgent warning in the twelfth hour:
Hiis, nisi iusticia fuerit terrore parata,
Succumbent domini tempore credo breui. 5.653-54
[I believe that in a short time the lords will submit to them, unless justice shall have been obtained by means of fear.]
The time reference, "tempore breui," points clearly to the future, and indeed to the near future. The situation is still exactly the same as at the time of the MIROUR, strained to the utmost, the eruption immediately at hand. This part of the VC was obviously written before 1381. Gower's attitude toward the peasant question agrees in all respects with that of the MIROUR, as does his gaze into the political future. The tone has become somewhat sharper, but the catastrophe of 1381 is still to come.

For the time being we come to the following conclusion: beyond the fact that there are two redactions, the B- and A-Texts, certain inner criteria indicate a stage in the development of the VOX CLAMANTIS that is to be located before 1381. At that time the greater part of the class critique, that is Books II-V, already existed. Whether the Mirror for a Prince of Book VI[49] and the frame of Books II and VII were already a part of the nascent work cannot be ascertained by the hitherto employed means.[50] Book I, the Visio, was obviously missing because it presupposes the Peasants' Rebellion. It is probable that at least Book III was begun before the Great Schism. From this one can posit an ear-

17

liest redaction (a), which comprises Books III-V,
perhaps even Books II-VII, and which was written
in the years 1377-81.

It is, therefore, no longer possible for us
to view the convulsion of 1381 as the motive force
that aroused the author to political and moral
awareness and that found its expression in the VOX
CLAMANTIS. This convulsion can at most be held
responsible for the final form of the work. The
main part of the VOX CLAMANTIS, the VC, does not
describe Gower's contribution to the solution of
a current political problem. In order to recognize the purpose of the VC, one must exclude the
Visio. Therefore, in the following chapters Visio
and VC will be examined separately.

Notes to Chapter One
    1 S = All Souls College 98, Oxford; G = Hunterain
Museum T.2.17, Glasgow; C = Cotton Tib. A.4, British
Museum; H = Harleian 6291, British Museum; E = Ecton,
in 1902 in the possession of General Sotheby; D =
Digby 138, Bodleian, Oxford; L = Laud 719, Bodleian,
Oxford; L_2 = Lincoln Cathedral Library A.72; T =
Trinity College D.4.6, Dublin; H_2 = Hatfield Hall,
in 1902 in the possession of the Marquis of Salis-
bury; C_2 = Cotton Titus A.13, British Museum (incom-
plete). The symbols and manuscript descriptions
are from the edition of Macaulay (see note 3), IV,
lix-lxxi.
    2 By H. O. Coxe for the Roxburghe Club.
    3 George C. Macaulay, THE COMPLETE WORKS OF
JOHN GOWER (Oxford, 1899-1902), Vol. 4.
    4 MIROUR DE L'OMME, 18421-27480. Macaulay,
WORKS, Vol. 1.
    5 CONFESSIO AMANTIS, Prol.93-1088. Macaulay,
WORKS, Vol. 2.
    6 See Bernhard ten Brink, GESCHICHTE DER ENG-
LISCHEN LITERATUR (Strassburg, 1893), II, 102 f.:
"The peasants' insurrection of the year 1381 made
a powerful impression upon the poet, whose own lo-
cality was chiefly afflicted by the horrors of
those days . . . Thus he determined in his VOX
CLAMANTIS to hold up to the world at the same time
a picture of those days of terror, for the sake of

arousing a wholesome fear, and a mirror in which it had to see with shuddering its own form and innermost being." There is a similar evaluation of the work in Emile Legouis and Louis Cazamian, A HISTORY OF ENGLISH LITERATURE, rev. ed. (London, 1940), p. 125; and Walter Schirmer, KURZE GESCHICHTE DER ENGLISCHEN LITERATUR (Halle, 1945), p. 46.

[7] Cf. WORKS, IV, lix.

[8] L = Laud 719, Bodleian.

[9] Macaulay, WORKS, IV, xxi f., and also in the CHEL, II, 144.

[10] Book II, Prol.83: Vox clamantis erit nomenque voluminis huius.

[11] Hereafter the first book will be designated the Visio and Books II-VII the VC.

[12] Macaulay expresses himself very cautiously: ". . . As to the date of composition, all that we can say is that the work in its present form is later than the Peasants' rising . . . it was evidently composed while the memory of that event was fresh." He is inclined to establish it after, rather than before, Richard's wedding (the end of 1382), although he chooses to draw no compelling chronological conclusion from the admonition to marital fidelity in Book VI, 913 f. WORKS, IV, xxx.

[13] It is important for the dating of the VOX CLAMANTIS that the three recensions of the CONFESSIO AMANTIS, which are represented by three manuscript groups, be kept distinct. Macaulay's chronological estimate, until now unopposed, reads as follows:

CONFESSIO--1st Recension--concluded 1390;
CONFESSIO--2nd Recension--concluded 1390/91;
CONFESSIO--3rd Recension--concluded 1392/93.
Cf. WORKS, II, xxi-xxvi and cxxvii ff.

[14] Both appear in manuscripts that, according to Macaulay, were prepared under the eyes of the author. The earlier version, moreover, exhibits Gower's characteristic stylistic properties, for example, a predilection for the unwarranted use of the comparative of adverbs and an excessive use of particles.

[15] The middle version originates in a manuscript group of the CONFESSIO AMANTIS that contains a contaminated text, the so-called 2nd Recension. The

notice also appears to have been contaminated after Gower's death, if one can so understand the phrase, found only here, "in his lifetime" (. . . tres precipue libros per ipsum dum vixit . . . compositos). WORKS, III, 480.

[16] WORKS, IV, 360. Translations of the VOX CLAMANTIS and the CRONICA TRIPERTITA are throughout those of Eric W. Stockton, trans. THE MAJOR LATIN WORKS OF JOHN GOWER (Seattle, 1962). Translator's note.

[17] WORKS, III, 479 f. in the critical apparatus. The last sentence of the English version is the present translator's.

[18] Whether the seven "paginae" are identical with the seven books of the received text cannot be determined with absolute certainty. The mention of Richard's innocence points to Book VI, the allusion to Fortuna to Book II. One may infer the class critique from "culpas aliunde . . . declarat" (Books III-IV).

[19] SCHG

[20] F = Fairfax 3, Bodleian. See WORKS, II, clvii.

[21] Three versions appear in some few places. Only the two chief recensions are important for our purposes.

[22] See above, p. 18, note 1, for an explanation of the symbols.

[23] Book VI, 545-80 and 1159-1200. In the second passage D, a contaminated manuscript, follows the A-Text, while in the LL_2 group the A- and B-Texts follow consecutively.

[24] Cf. Book VI, 555 and 569-72 in the B-Text.

[25] WORKS, IV, 243. The comprehensive synopsis that precedes the work in some manuscripts has the same wording. Cf. WORKS, IV, 14.

[26] Version A: innocenciam tamen dicti domini Regis (tamen . . . innocenciam Regis nostri, A-Text); tunc minoris etatis causa (minoris etatis causa); excusabilem pronuncians (excusat).

[27] The date of his birth is unknown. The literary histories commonly place it in 1330.

[28] A-Text:
> Stat puer immunis culpe, set qui puerile
> Instruerent regimen, non sine labe manent:
> Sic non rex set consilium sunt causa doloris,

Quo quasi communi murmure plangit humus.
Tempora matura si rex etatis haberet,
560 Equaret libram que modo iure caret:
. . . . .
Hoc set eum tangit discretum quem probat etas,
Non puerum, quia tunc fit sibi culpa minor.
Non est nature lex nec racionis, vt illud
Quod mundum ledit sit puerile malum;
Non dolus, immo iocus, non fraus set gloria ludi,
Sunt pueris, nec ibi restat origo mali.
Dixit enim Daniel, quod de senioribus orta
Exiit impietas, quam furor orbis habet:
Omne quod est mundi vicium plantant veterani,
Et quasi de peste spersa venena serunt.
Horum namque scelus fertur maculare figuras
Tocius mundi, quo furit ira dei. 6.555-78
[The boy is free of blame, but those who have
instrumented this boyish reign shall not en-
dure without a fall. So not the king but his
council is the cause of our sorrow, for which
the land grieves as if with a general murmur.
If the king were of mature age, he would set
right the scale which now is without justice
. . . But this latter thought [that good kings
choose good counselors] pertains to one that
maturity demonstrates as able to choose, not
to a boy, since his blame is smaller then.
It is not the law of nature or of reason that
the evil which afflicts the world is that of
a boy. To boys, evils are not wrongdoing but
joking, not dishonor but glorious sport, and
the origin of evil is not there. For Daniel
has said that the impiety which the madness
of the world embraces has arisen from older
men. Elders implant all the vice which the
world has, and they sow poisons as if they
had been scattered by a plague. For it is
said that the wickedness of these men corrupts the thoughts of the whole world, for
which reason God's anger rages.]
B-Text:
Rex, puer indoctus, morales negligit actus,
In quibus a puero crescere possit homo:
Sic etenim puerum iuuenilis concio ducit,
Quod nichil expediens, sit nisi velle, sapit.

21

Que vult ille, volunt iuuenes sibi consociati,
560   Ille subintrat iter, hiique sequntur eum:
Vanus honor vanos iuuenes facit esse sodales,
Vnde magis vane regia tecta colunt.
Hii puerum regem puerili more subornant,
Pondera virtutum quo minus ipse gerit.
Sunt eciam veteres cupidi, qui lucra sequentes
Ad pueri placitum plura nephanda sinunt:
Cedunt morigeri, veniunt qui sunt viciosi,
Quicquid et est vicii Curia Regis habet.
Error ad omne latus pueri consurgit, et ille,
570   Qui satis est docilis, concpiit omne malum:
Non dolus immo iocus, non fraus set gloria ludi
Sunt pueris, set ei sors stat aborta doli.
Sunt tamen occulte cause, quas nullus in orbe
Scire potest, set eas scit magis ·ipse deus:
Nescit enim mater nato que fata parantur,
Fine set occultum clarius omne patet.
. . . . .
Sic ego condoleo super hiis que tedia cerno,
580   Quo Regi puero scripta sequenda fero.
[The king, an undisciplined boy, neglects the
moral behavior by which a man might grow up
from a boy. Indeed, youthful company so
sways the boy that he has a taste for nothing
practical, unless it be his whim. The young
men associated with him want what he wants;
he enters upon a course of action and they
follow him. Vainglory makes these youthful
comrades vain, for which reason they vainly
cultivate the royal quarters more and more.
They abet the boy king in his childish behavior whereby he wields the authority of
virtue the less.
   There are also the older men of greed who
in pursuing their gains tolerate many scandals
for the boy's pleasure. Men of good character
withdraw, those who are vicious come in, and
the king's court contains whatever vice exists. Sin springs up on every side of the
boy, and he, who is quite easily led, takes
to every evil. To boys, it is not wrongdoing
but joking, not dishonor but glorious sport;
but his destiny does arise out of this wrongdoing. There are, however, hidden causes

22

which no one on earth can know, yet God knows
them well. A mother, to be sure, does not
know what fate is designed for her child, but
in the end every secret is clearly revealed
. . . I accordingly grieve even more than
they over the disgusting things which I see,
for which reason I offer the following writings for the boy king.]
[29] Cf. 567: Hoc set eum tangit discretum quem
probat etas; 555-56: . . . set qui puerile/Instru-
erent regimen, non sine labe manent; 575; Omne quod
est mundi vicium plantant veterani; 577: Horum namque scelus.
[30] Cf. 573 ff.: they are the lascivious elders
from the story of Susanna in the Book of Daniel.
[31] 565 f.
[32] CRONICA TRIPERTITA, Pars I, 1 f. (WORKS, IV):
Tolle caput mundi, C ter et sex lustra fer illi,
Et decies quinque cum septem post super adde.
[Take the first letter of mundus and add to it
C three times repeated, and take six periods
of five years; and afterwards add ten times
five, plus seven.]
[33] 4-12.
Dum stat commotus Ricardus amore remotus,
Principio Regis oritur transgressio legis,
Quo fortuna cadit et humus retrograda vadit.
Quomodo surrexit populus, quem non bene rexit,
Tempus adhuc plangit super hoc, quod cronica
                              tangit.
Libro testante, stat cronica scripta per ante;
Est alibi dicta, transit nec ab aure relicta:
Audistis mira, vulgaris que tulit ira:
Omnibus in villis timuit vir iustus ab illis.
[When the turbulent Richard forsook loving-
kindness, there arose a transgression of the
law, originating with the King. For this
reason Fortune sank down and the land went
into a decline. The people which he did not
rule well therefore revolted; to this day the
times bemoan what this chronicle touches upon.
With this book as witness, the chronicle was
written beforehand; it was spoken at another
time, but it did not pass unheeded by the ear.
You shall hear the amazing deeds which the

wrath of the people committed. In every city
the just man was terrified by them.]
Lines 9-10 are a direct reference to the arrangement
of the manuscript.
    34 The VOX CLAMANTIS is called "cronica" in the
incipit of two manuscripts of the B-Text.
    35 SCHGEDL
    36 TH2
    37 Hic tractat qualiter status et ordo mundi
in tribus consistit gradibus, sunt enim, vt dicit,
Clerus, Milicies, et Agricultores, de quorum errore mundi infortunia nobis contingunt. Vnde primo
videndum est de errore cleri precipue in ordine
prelatorum, etc. [Here he treats of how the state
or order of the world consists of three estates.
They are, as he says, the clergy, knighthood, and
peasantry. Through their going astray, the misfortunes of the world befall us. Hence we must
first examine the waywardness of the clergy, especially among the rank of prelates, etc.] See WORKS,
IV, 105.
    38 In the MIROUR DE L'OMME, which nobody
doubts was composed before the accession of Richard
II, Gower has also inserted the Schism belatedly.
Because only one manuscript exists, no more can be
known about the original version.
    39 See above, p. 6.
    40 Cf. 7.1461 and, above all, 1443-44:
    Hos ego compegi versus, quos fuderat in me
    Spiritus in sompnis: nox erat illa grauis.
    [I have compiled these verses, which a spirit
    uttered within me during my sleep. That was
    a hard night.]
These lines are hardly compatible with those that
immediately follow (1445-48), in which the author
represents himself as the spokesman of public
opinion.
    41 The summary states: Hic dicit quod ipse iam
vigilans, secundum vocem quam in sompnis acceperat,
intendit scribere ea que de mundo vidit et audivit.
[Here he says that now that he is awake he intends
to write, in accordance with the voice which he
understood in his dreams, of the things which he
saw and heard concerning the world.] Then the text
begins:

24

Multa quidem vidi diuersaque multa notaui,
Que tibi vult meminens scribere penna sequens.
                                      2.Prol.1-2
[I have seen and noted many different things,
which my reminiscing pen is eager to write
down for you now.]
However, it mentions no dreams. Rather, it seems
to attempt to express the same material that is
more fully explained, with reference to a quotation
from Seneca, at the end of the Prologue, namely
the origin of the material in countless oral and
written sources:
Non tamen ex propriis dicam que verba sequntur,
Set velut instructus nuncius illa fero.
Lectus vt est variis florum de germine fauus,
Lectaque diuerso litore concha venit,
Sic michi diuersa tribuerunt hoc opus ora,
Et visus varii sunt michi causa libri.
                                      2.Prol.75-80
[I shall not, however, speak of my personal
affairs in the words which follow, but I
shall report them just like a well-informed
messenger. As the honeycomb is gathered
from the bud of various flowers and the sea
shell is found and gathered from many a shore,
so many different mouths have furnished me
with the matter of this work; and my several
visions are the reason for the book.]
    42 Cf. George Macaulay Trevelyan, ENGLAND IN
THE AGE OF WYCLIFFE (London, 1946), 4th ed., pp.
183 ff.
    43 According to the words of the Bible: Loquere
ad populum, et cunctis audientibus praedica [Judges
7.3: Speak to the people, and proclaim in the hear-
ing of all]. On this passage, cf. Bromyard, SUMMA
PRAEDICANTIUM (Venice edition, 1586), s.v. praedicatio: Et sicut praeco nulli parcit, nec diviti,
nec potenti, vel pauperi, sed omnes tangit, qui
contra illud quod clamat fecerunt, vel faciant,
ita vos praedicate evangelium omni creaturae [And
just as the herald spares none--neither the wealthy,
nor the powerful, nor the poor--but touches all who
have acted or who do act against that which he proclaims, thus must you preach the Gospel to all the
creation].

                      25

[44] See below, pp. 69 ff.

[45] MIROUR 16497-508.

[46] MIROUR 27229-34; VOX CLAMANTIS 5.599 f.

[47] MIROUR 16489 "urtie"; VOX CLAMANTIS 5.601 "cardo."

[48] MIROUR 26485-96:

> Me semble que la litargie
> Ad endormi la seignourie,
> Si qu'ils de la commune gent
> Ne pernont garde a la folie,
> Ainz souffront croistre celle urtie
> Quelle est du soy trop violent.
> Cil qui pourvoit le temps present
> Se puet doubter procheinement,
> Si dieus n'en face son aie,
> Qe celle urtie inpacient
> Nous poindra trop soudainement,
> Avant ce q'om la justefie.
> [It seems to me that lethargy has rocked
> the nobility to sleep, so that the com-
> moners are not on their guard against
> folly, and will rather allow this nettle
> to grow whose nature is too violent.
> Any man who observes the present time
> can only expect to see, in the near
> future, unless God helps him, this
> impatient nettle sting us all too
> suddenly, and before anyone has a
> chance to examine it with moderation.

[49] VI, Chapters 8-18.

[50] The question will be taken up once more after the interpretation of the Mirror for a Prince and after the discussion of Books II and VII; cf. below, pp. 197 ff.

Chapter Two
The Vision of the Peasants' Rebellion

The first book of the VOX CLAMANTIS reports the
events of the summer of 1381 in a series of dream
visions. The author avails himself of the conventional frame for allegorical tales. He describes a
spring morning in an awakening nature, a walk to a
locus amoenus, the onset of evening, and finally the
transition from day's weariness to a restless sleep
and dream. The prologue that introduces the scene
explains the four causae of the work: the causa materialis, that is, the subject of the book;[1] the causa efficiens, that is, the writer;[2] the causa finalis,
that is, the instruction or entertainment that is the
book's object;[3] and the causa formalis, that is, its
meter and arrangement.[4] The prologue also includes
a few of the regulae according to which the work
should be received and understood by the reader. It
does not include, however, a title for the book, any
reference to a direct divine commission,[5] or a mention of gloria dei among the causae finales. A formal analysis of the prologue will not be given here,
in order to avoid duplication with a later chapter.[6]
However, it is important to investigate the prologue
and the allegorical narrative frame as they establish
the mood for the vision.

The prologue begins with a pertinent discussion
of the question of whether or not dreams are invested
with a mantic character. The author declines to un-
ravel the problem in its total medieval complexity;
instead, he contrasts the testimony of Sacred Scripture with the communis opinio and concludes that
dream visions are bound to come true. The mood of
the passage is neutral, as is the mention of the auth-
or's name and the disclaimer of literary ambition.[7]
A mood-establishing element emerges for the first
time in ll. 31-42. It is of great, if not to say compelling, power and reveals gloomy perspectives:
Quod michi flere licet scribam lacrimabile tempus,
Sic quod in exemplum posteritatis eat.
Flebilis vt noster status est, ita flebile carmen,
Materie scripto conueniente sue.
Omne quod est huius operis lacrimabile, lector
Scriptum de lacrimis censeat esse meis:

Penna madet lacrimis hec me scribente profusis,
Dumque feror studiis, cor tremit atque manus.
Scribere cumque volo, michi pondere pressa laboris
Est manus, et vires subtrahit inde timor.
Qui magis inspiciet opus istud, tempus et instans,
Inueniet toto carmine dulce nichil.
[Although I may weep over it, I shall write of a
tearful time, so that it may go down as an example for posterity. Just as our condition is
mournful, so the poem is mournful, the writing
being in accord with its subject matter. The
reader may judge everything of this book which
is tearful to have been written with my own tears.
As I write these things my pen grows wet with pro-
fuse weeping, and while I am carried forward by
my zeal, my heart and hand tremble. And when I
wish to write, my hand is burdened by the weight
of the task, and anxiety takes away its strength.
One who looks further into this work and into
the present time will find nothing consoling in
the whole poem.]
The passage is absolutely tear-soaked, and with tears
that are in no small part borrowed.[8] Its forceful-
ness depends on the following stylistic means: 1) an
unexpected appearance in a neutral context; 2) the
repetition of emotionally suggestive words in stra-
tegic positions;[9] 3) a renunciation of analysis of
the emotions expressed; 4) an intensification through
the addition of further symptoms (cor tremit atque
manus) until finally the word _timor_ in conspicuous
end position names the emotion explicitly.[10] Thus
Gower establishes an important coupling of sorrow
and fear for the entire vision.

    Ovid's significance for the tears passage is
limited to providing convenient forms of expression.
The tears themselves are not of Ovidian extraction,
although there is a superficial similarity between
the situation of the exiled poet in Pontus and that
of the anxious author in mutinous London. Both have
a lively sense of threatened safety and of the decline
of law and order.[11] Ovid's barbarian hordes, which
fall like wolves upon the defenseless Roman citizens,[12]
resemble Gower's mob of peasants, who are transformed
into raging beasts. For the reader versed in Ovid

this potpourri from the TRISTIA doubtless calls up associations which prepare for the content of the Visio. However, Ovid's tears flow from fear and pity for his own situation and depend upon the reader's sympathetic identification. Gower's tears and those of his audience are intended, as rueful tears of the sacrament of penance, to lead to a reconciliation with God and to a regeneration of the individual as well as of the people.[13]

The fear and sorrow motif is intensified in its gloomy effect through contrast with the detailed description of the June morning that intervenes between the prologue and the start of the first vision. It is, despite certain lovely touches, scarcely more than a skillful treatment of topoi. It is also conventional insofar as the spring day is among the customary requisites of medieval allegorical poetry. It is interesting because of Gower's clever utilization of contrast and because of an awkwardness that seems to me important for the poem's interpretation. When the courtly love allegory describes a May morning and leads the poet into a meadow in bloom, it usually does so with the intention of having him fall asleep there, whereupon the dream apparatus is set in motion. So it is in the ROMAN DE LA ROSE, in Chaucer's LEGEND OF GOOD WOMEN, and in Gower's CONFESSIO AMANTIS, to name but a few examples. In the Visio, on the other hand, the spring morning serves no real purpose, since the dream first ensues at night and in bed. The author obviously had difficulty padding out the day until evening in order to be able, finally, to begin with the visions. Why he made the effort is not readily apparent. Couldn't he have fallen asleep to the song of the birds if the cliche was so important to him, or gone straight to bed--as Chaucer did in the BOOK OF THE DUCHESS--if he absolutely had to dream at night? I wish tentatively to propose the hypothesis that the awkwardness arises because on the one hand Gower did not wish to give up the traditional spring morning scheme, but on the other was obliged to place the dream at night in order to satisfy another tradition.

This tradition is not properly literary, stem-

ming rather from the practice of medieval biblical
exegesis. The four levels of interpretation--the
sensus historicus, tropologicus or moralis, alle-
goricus, and anagogicus[14]--were entrusted not only
to legitimate theologians, but to every sermon listener and every reader of edificational works.
Moreover, the method had taken possession, beyond
the limited sphere of the Scriptures, of secular
literature, for it offered a welcome means of re-
interpreting heathen authors in a Christian sense.
Bernardus Silvestris' interpretation of the AENEID,
the INTEGUMENTA OVIDII, and the OVIDE MORALISE are
testimony to the influence of this form of biblical
exegesis in the Middle Ages.[15]

There is one chapter in the MORALIA that treats
of the significance of the time of day in biblical
exordia.[16] The prologue in heaven from the Book of
Job provides the occasion. Gregory begins with 1.6:
Quadam die cum venissent filii Dei, ut assisterent
coram Domino, adfuit inter eos etiam Satan [On a
certain day when the sons of God came to stand before the Lord, Satan also was present among them].
He then shows how precisely the Scriptures indicate
through statements of time and place, especially in
the beginning of a narrative, a story's positive or
negative conclusion.[17] Thus it is night when Judas
goes out from the Last Supper to betray the Lord
(John 13.30). At noon the Lord comes to Abraham
when He promises him offspring (Genesis 18.1); in
the evening He sends His messengers to proclaim the
destruction of Sodom (Genesis 19.1). Since the
trials of Job will end in the victory of the good,
the prologue in heaven begins during the day.[18]
Gregory also applies to visions the rule that the
beginning of a story by day predetermines a good
ending, but by night a bad. Solomon figures among
the abovementioned examples in this respect. He
received the gift of wisdom from the Lord, but at
night while asleep, and that is a sign that it would
not last.[19] Now Gower's visions do not end with a
feeling of relief. We have escaped again, but with
the oppressive certainty that the Lord has once more
but delayed his wrath; therefore, we must repent and
do penance before it is too late.[20] Gower was accordingly obliged to dream by night in order to a-

void a contradiction.[21]

The vision proper begins with the third chapter of the first book. It is grouped around three successive central conceptions: 1) the rebellious peasant hordes, which change into raging beasts before the dreamer's eyes; 2) murder and arson in London, striking the dreamer as a second fall of Troy; 3) great distress and salvation at the last moment, experienced by the dreamer as an impending shipwreck and the sudden calming of a storm at sea.[22] For the sake of brevity they shall be designated in the following discussion as the Beast Vision, the Troy Vision, and the Ship Vision. The three visions do not represent independent stages of an historical occurrence, although one could date the Beast Vision in the first week of June, the Troy Vision on 13-14 June, and the chief events of the Ship Vision on 13-15 June, 1381. The first vision flows almost unnoticeably into the second, so that for a time beast symbolism and Troy myth are intermingled. A genuine pause does occur before the third vision, which is also clearly distinguished in narrative technique from the preceding vision. There are no imagistic overlappings between the second and third visions; instead there appear chronological overlappings, or at least obscurities, which are yet to be investigated. We shall begin with the Beast Vision.

The Beast Vision[23] reveals simultaneously the individuality and the limitation of Gower's talent. Artistically, the idea of describing the Peasants' Rebellion of 1381 as an animal uprising could have been extremely fruitful. Models to which a work of this sort can be oriented with little difficulty are found in French treatments of Reynard the Fox. Of course, the beast epic as an artistic vehicle for class satire was hardly developed in England at the time.[24] It is unimportant for our purposes whether the causes actually lie in the English national character, or in the fact that the reading public to whom the mentality of the Reynard epics was accessible still understood enough French to delight in the original. The introduction of a new genre would hardly have presented an insurmountable obstacle in a century of receptiveness for nearly all

31

branches of continental literature. The transformation of the beast allegory might have proved more
difficult, for by its nature it concretizes abstrac-
tions in an artistic statement that reproduces concrete events in a code language that utilizes animals.
But even if such requirements did not exceed Gower's
talent, they contradicted his intellectual posture.
He was not inclined to be ironic, but apocalyptic.
For him the intrusion of chaos into the divinely ordained order of the world was an experience that
could˅not be expressed by means of an ironic, aloof
estates satire. The force of moral outrage, the priority of morals over aesthetics, inhibited his artistic development throughout his life.

Therefore, Gower's first vision is not a beast
allegory. That is apparent even superficially from
the fact that, while the rebellious peasants do indeed assume animal forms, the harried free men (ingenui) do not. In this way Gower's Beast Vision
distinguishes itself at the same time from the genre
of political prophecy, which, however, is not to be
disregarded as background for the first book of the
VOX CLAMANTIS. Political prophecy comes, at least
quantitatively, into an astonishing heyday in England in the 14th century. For example, SIX KINGS
TO FOLLOW KING JOHN (probably composed before the
death of Edward II in 1327), THE PROPHECY OF THOMAS
A BECKET (Hatton version, shortly after 1356), THE
PROPHECY OF JOHN OF BRIDLINGTON (circa 1364), WHEN
ROME IS REMOVED INTO ENGLAND (oldest surviving version 1382), and THOMAS OF ERCELDOUNE (circa 1400),
to name only the most important.[25] Richard II is
said to have been especially receptive to this kind
of literature.[26] Towards the end of the century,
prophecy played such a role in the political bat-
tles of ethnic groups as well as factions that Henry
IV felt forced to take legal steps against it. Nevertheless, these prophecies were often not much more
than literary exercises that translated historical
events into a cryptic style of expression that had
become traditional, and cloaked the author's glance
into the political future in a similar prophetic
obscuritas.[27]

Now animal symbolism is typical of the English

32

form of political prophecy, which at first arbitrar-
ily, later according to fixed conventions, introduced
its chief figures in beast form:[28] thus the King of
Scotland usually appears as a crab, the Black Prince
as a cock. Gower's CRONICA TRIPERTITA is rife with
this characteristic style of the English political
prophecy: no names are mentioned at all in the first
part and all persons are concealed behind animal designations which, according to the tendency of the
14th century, are often taken from heraldry. Moreover, one finds traces of the so-called sibylline,
that is, the originally continental form of prophecy, when Gower employs initials as ciphers. Insofar as the Visio was influenced by the political
prophecy, it reveals the English type, as for example
when the author transforms the ringlerader of the rebels, Wat Tylor, into a jay (graculus). The total
conception of the uprising of the beasts, however,
is difficult to explain in terms of the political
prophecy. That becomes evident when one compares
the Visio with the prophecies that were circulated
under the name of John of Bridlington.[29]

At first glance, Gower and John of Bridlington
show a certain similarity. Both wrote post facto
prophetic visions of historical events. The JOHN OF
BRIDLINGTON author uses every means to maintain the
illusion of true prophecy. He professes to have
found and annotated a poem from the first years of
the reign of Edward III, a poem that predicts the
future in bleak words and images. That the prophet
and commentator are identical, there can be no doubt;
the aim of the artificial schizophrenia is altogether
too obvious. Both works make use of animal symbolism.
In the PROPHECY OF JOHN OF BRIDLINGTON it is a code
language, a form of prophetic obscuritas[30] without
artistic ambitions, conditioned by its purpose and
consistently maintained from start to finish. Gower uses it not for camouflage, but for elucidation.
The apocalyptic mood that is produced by this means
is only a secondary effect. Gower is not interested
in the cheap nimbus of alleged political prophecy.
His Beast Vision has the sole purpose of expressing
with almost mathematical precision an easily intel-
ligible, scathing value judgment.

This value judgment is theologically and philosophically founded and thus perhaps not as evident to the modern reader as to the contemporary public. The crucial passage upon which an understanding of the first vision depends occurs just at the beginning, when the peasant hordes are transformed into beasts before the astonished eyes of the dreamer:

Ecce dei subito malediccio fulsit in illos,
Et mutans formas fecerat esse feras.
Qui fuerant homines prius innate racionis,
Brutorum species irracionis habent.   1.175-78
[The curse of God suddenly flashed upon them,
and changing their shapes, it had made them
into wild beasts. They who had been men of
reason before had the look of unreasoning
brutes.]

The usual view of the divinely ordained hierarchy (ordo) of the creation underlies the passage. The plant stands one step above the stone by virtue of its anima, the beast one step higher than the plant by virtue of its animus, the man one step higher than the beast by virtue of his ratio. Reduced to a simple equation, man equals animal plus ratio. By a reversal of the equation, man, if his ratio loses control, becomes an animal. That is neither allegory nor poetic display, but a kind of theological mathematics. God bestowed reason upon man in order that it guide his life. If his animal instincts gain the upper hand, then man is degraded to beast and sins against the law of God and of Nature. Thus the Bible warns: Nolite fieri sicut equus et mulus, quibus non est intellectus (Psalms 31.9) [Do not become like the horse and the mule, who have no understanding]. Gower develops the same train of thought more fully in Book Seven of the VOX CLAMANTIS:

Et sic bruta quasi perit humanae racionis
Virtus, dum vicium corporis acta regit.
Est homo nunc animal dicam, set non racionis,
Dum viuit bruti condicione pari.
Nescia scripture brutum natura gubernat,
Iudicis arbitrium nec racionis habet:
Est igitur brutis homo peior, quando voluntas
Preter naturam sola gubernat eum.   7.1171-78
[And so the power of human reason perishes
as if it were that of a beast, so long as

vice governs the actions of the body. Now,
1 should say that man is an animal, but not
a rational animal, as long as he lives in a
condition like a brute beast's. A nature
ignorant of learning governs a beast, and
it has no power of judgment or reason. Man
is therefore worse than a beast when his will
alone governs him contrary to nature.]
The passage goes one step beyond what Gower says at
the beginning of the Visio. There man's sin and punishment consisted in his becoming like an animal;
here, on the other hand, he is animal-like in status
but beneath the beasts in morality. The thought is
wholly in accord with the orthodox exegesis of another passage from Psalms, often commented upon by
the church fathers. I quote from the chapter De
Homine of the pseudo-Bonaventura's PHARETRA the following citation from Johannes Chrysostomus:
        Comparatus est, ait propheta, homo iumentis
        insipientibus, et similis factus est eis.
        Peius est comparari quam nasci. Natural-
        iter non habere rationem tolerabile est,
        verum ratione decoratum irrationabili
        creature comparari voluntatis est crimen
        non nature. [Man is compared, says the pro-
        phet, to the foolish beasts of burden, and
        he became like them. It is worse to be lik-
        ened to one than to be born one. To lack
        reason by nature is bearable, but to liken
        a creature endowed with reason to a brute
        beast is to level an accusation against
        his will and not his nature.]31
If the Visio does not execute this second step dog-
matically, it nevertheless expresses it artistically
through a second metamorphosis, which I will now
discuss.

    The dream transforms speculative trains of thought
into lively, visible figures. The peasant horde also
become animals externally. The divine judgment is
that the voluntary inner degradation be followed by
an involuntary outer.32 It is natural enough that
the peasants and rural laborers are changed into domestic farm animals. However, the author goes further,
and the terror that he seeks to suggest to the reader--
and here and there is actually able to arouse--does

not originate in this simple metamorphosis but in
a further transformation. To the degeneration of
man into beast is joined a further degeneration
in which the domestic animals become untrue to
their nature and acquire the proprietates of wild
animals:

> Deuia natura sic errat ab ordine, mores
> Porcus quod porci non habet, immo lupi.
> [Nature wandered so far from her regular
> course that a pig did not keep to the be-
> havior of a pig, but rather of a wolf.]
> 1.319-20

The ox is not only an ox, but at the same time lion,
panther, and bear (293 f.); the rooster wears un-
lawfully the claws and beak of the falcon (521).
This transformation is more than a play of fancy
or a cheap artificial device employed in order to
produce an impression of the monstrous; it is the
artistic equivalent of the second part of the train
of thought from Book VII cited above. Gower designates the event now as retrogradus ordo, now as natura denaturans. When man surrenders his ratio and
becomes an animal, he sins against the divine and
natural ordo of the cosmos.[33] When the beast,
moreover, conducts himself contra naturam, therein
lies a superlative instance of parekbasis. The
phenomenon may be explained stylistically as metamorphosis plus adynaton, from the point of view
of literary history as an influence of Revelations.
However, such an explanation is unfair to the author,
who is principally interested in moral instruction.

Now the hierarchical order of the class-organized state is also anchored in a tightly-linked hierarchy of the entire creation. The church fathers
saw in the institution of the state--and for medieval man that denotes the state organized in classes--
either God's punishment or his instrument of education. In either case a social revolution is also a
rebellion against a divine institution. Accordingly,
Gower nowhere poses the question of social justice.
The ordo, the divine principle for the preservation
of the world, has been violated, as Gower most emphatically remarks:

> Perfida stulticia tunc temporis omne negauit,

Quod natura sibi vel deus ipse petit:
Non timet ipsa deum neque mundi iura veretur,
Set statuit licitum criminis omne malum:
Ordine retrogrado sic quilibet ordo recessit,
Nec status ipse sapit quid sit habere statum.
                                    1.1307-12[34]
[The perfidious folly of the time then refused
everything which God Himself or nature demanded.
It did not fear God nor did it respect the laws
of the world, but it declared that every crimin-
al wrong was permissible. Thus all orderliness
departed in disorder, and the state did not know
what state it was in.]
It is only a natural consequence that such a viola-
tion of the ordo summons the forces of chaos to battle. He who will not obey God must serve the devil:[35]
Demonibus homines subici culpis meruerunt,
Tunc quia non hominem nec timuere deum. 1.1319-20
[Since they feared neither God nor man, these
men deserved to be enslaved to devils for their
faults.]
Thus Gower achieves a final gloomy intensification by
causing the degenerate beasts to be possessed or in-
spired by Furies and Demons, and the swine, after the
example of the New Testament, by Satan in person.[36]
He compounds it by adding the plagues of Egypt (frogs
and flies) and Philistia (mice). Thus the bestial
rebel becomes the demonic, and the temporal as well
as the eternal judgment of damnation is sealed:
Scit deus hos homines siluestres igne perhenni
Dignos et reprobos a racione vagos. 1.1017-18
[God knows those wild men were deserving of
eternal fire and were unreasoning reprobates.]

The conclusion of the awakened poet's dream experience is the dogmatic counterpart to the value
judgment implicitly contained in the Beast Vision.
The peasantry lie once more in bondage. Satan's power has been broken with God's help; however, the
devil slumbers always in the peasants and can erupt
anew. He must be suppressed with relentless severity.[37] The antithesis of bondsmen and free men is
shown throughout the entire Visio with a crassness
that aligns Satan in person on the one side and the
Christian martyrs on the other. Gower is not writing

37

a class critique, which according to its nature is
always a criticism of the abuses within a social
group without thereby questioning its right to be,
but a harsh condemnation, unmitigated throughout,
which divinely sanctions every action against the
peasantry. This is understandable in light of the
unique situation of 1381; it in no way, however, accords with the attitude that Gower adopts in the
following books of the VOX CLAMANTIS and in the
MIROUR DE L'OMME.

The Troy Vision (Chapters 13-15) spotlights
the seizure of London with a peculiar, solemnly macabre light. The scene changes from country to
city, and the city is London, the new Troy:
A dextrisque nouam me tunc vidisse putabam
Troiam, que vidue languida more fuit. 1.879-80
[On my right I then thought I saw New Troy,
which was powerless as a widow.]
Over the events of June 13 is diffused the atmosphere
of the fall of ancient Troy, which forms the background to the looting, murder, arson, and drunken-
ness of the mob and rabble soldiery. Well-known
individuals, no longer recognizable to a modern
reader, are hidden behind a catalogue of Trojan
heroes.[38] The Queen Mother appears in the role of
Hecuba,[39] and the youthful Richard II must then bear
comparison with the hoary Priam.[40] The description
attains its climax with the execution of Archbishop
Simon Sudbury, who is identified with the high priest
Helenus.[41] Thus the historical events receive an
impressive epic heightening.[42] It remains to be
considered whether this was the sole or just the
most compelling concern that led the author to the
Troy theme. Once again it appears as if rational
rather than artistic considerations influenced him.
For the Trojan model brings into the production, besides the epic flavor, an important new element that
indicates Gower's position on the philosophy of history. The history of Britain began in a hazy pre-
history with the fall of Troy, which led via the
wandering of Aeneas and the exile and divine rescue
of his grandson Brutus to the founding of a New Troy
on the island of Brutus. Obviously, Gower's public
knew the legend of London's founding. Geoffrey of

Monmouth, Wace, Layamon, were considered historical authorities. Although critical spirits such as William of Newburgh had expressed doubts, the prevailing opinion was still far from willing to separate history from legend.

Perhaps the designation of London as New Troy was especially the fashion in court circles. It appears three times in a 1393 court poem by Richard de Maidstone.[43] In any case, the association of old with New Troy lay ready to hand. Going beyond their common name, Gower implies to the reader that they may share a common fate. Might not the New Troy be about to fall as did the old? Names have a fateful significance for medieval man; history can repeat itself. The Trojan destiny hovers menacingly over the city on the Thames. When one considers what significance historical or pseudo-historical analogies have had for English history, one cannot take Gower's Troy Vision too lightly. It is to a modest extent an equivalent of the Arthurian renaissance of Tudor times. In the prosperous days of Elizabeth the legendary analogy promised a golden future. In the times of class unrest and national insecurity under Richard II the historical parallel proclaimed imminent downfall. For Gower the case of Troy is a kind of dumb show that masks the English tragedy and makes clear what conclusion is to be expected; the play itself stands in the midst of the last act, and the anxiety that has gripped the author imparts itself to the reader:

Sic amor ecce vetus Troie mutatur in iram,
Cantus et ex planctu victus vbique silet:
In lacrimas risus, in dedecus est honor omnis
Versus, et in nichilum quod fuit ante satis.

1.1333-36

[So behold, the ancient charity of Troy was changed into anger, and song was silent everywhere, overcome with lamentation. All laughter was turned into tears, all honor into disgrace, and what had previously been enough into nothing.]

Here the Troy Vision ends. There follows Chapter Sixteen, which suddenly projects the figure of the dreamer into the foreground and forms a bridge to

a new series of visions. In Chapter Seventeen a
ship appears, and it is so unexpected and unmotivated
that the unity of the poem is seriously endangered.
According to the prose summary, it symbolizes the
Tower of London, the refuge of the royal party.[44]
The remainder of the vision revolves about the ship
and the fate of its passengers, above all of the
author. Of Troy, old or new, nothing more is said.

There are several questions to be clarified
here. The first concerns the imagistic sphere in
which Gower's visions move. First, there was the
picture of the uprising of the beasts, frighteningly
distorted by adynaton; then the vividly epic portrayal of a burning Troy; now a ship in greatest
danger on a storm-tossed sea. The factor of fear
is common to all three; otherwise they have little
in common. Why is a single historical episode
such as the Peasants' Rebellion divided into three
different images, the inner coherence of which remains vague?

The second question concerns the ship itself.
The historical occurrences are centered around the
Tower. It would have been natural to remain within the Trojan sphere and to identify the citadel
with Priam's stronghold. Instead, Gower forces
upon the reader the image of a ship, which is much
further from the matter. True, the Tower stands
on the Thames; one could imagine it as a ship.
But this ship puts at once to sea and has to battle
with an infernal storm. Thus Gower places considerable demands upon the reader's capacity for illusion and his willingness to submit to it. Why
was the ship so important to the author at this
moment? What process of the imagination transformed the Tower into a ship?

The third question concerns the chronology of
the events in their relationship to the chronology
of the visions. Until the end of the Troy Vision
both run parallel. Then they suddenly overlap.
The Troy Vision deals with the 13th and 14th of
June, 1381, that is, with the seizure of London,
the concessions of the king in Mile End (?),[45] the
storming of the Tower (?),[46] and the murder of

Sudbury.[47] Even if the allusions to Mile End and
the Tower are uncertain, the surrender of the Tower
in any case should precede the murder of the Archbishop, who had sought refuge there. At the beginning of the Ship Vision, which follows from the
Troy Vision according to the dream chronology, the
storming of the Tower has yet to occur. It is sym-
bolically accomplished before the eyes of the reader
in the shipwreck. What reasons compelled the author
to alter the sequence of events in the dream?

   The reasons for the abandonment of the Trojan
setting are easy to see. An accurate retelling of
the history of Troy would end with its complete
collapse and so would not match the facts of English
history. The analogy is maintained as closely as
possible until the moment of the catastrophe in
order to make clear the gravity of the situation
and the importance of the warning. Then it is a-
bandoned.

   The reasons for the choice of the ship met-
aphor--the word metaphor is used here as the col-
lective name for all the possibilities of figura-
tive usage--is to be sought in the area of the associations that the author could evoke in his public with it. The ship plays a not insignificant
role in literature and preaching. It appears per-
ipherally in the sphere of exordial topoi when
the composition of a work is compared to the perils
of a sea journey.[48] The ship gains varying degrees
of importance, however, when viewed as a symbol of
the human soul,[49] mankind,[50] the church,[51] or the
state. It would be tempting to trace the ship of
state in a straight line back to Horace[52] and regard the remaining ship metaphors as a development
from biblical origins. However, it will not do to
let the religious and secular ships steer neatly
separated courses. The isolation of individual
areas and their traditions is impossible for a
mentality that sees all classifications as expressions of the same divine principle of creation. Thus the concept of the world as an organic
whole clarifies the nature of the church as the
corpus Christi as well as the nature of the class-

41

organized state; it would be absurd to wish to
break it down into its classical and New Testament
origins. Likewise there are no separable religious
and secular traditions of the ship metaphor.

Take, for example, Gower's contemporary, the
anonymous author of the poem "Heu Quanta Desolatio."
Does he have Horace in mind when, in the first
stanza, he compares England to a menaced ship,[53] and
is he conscious of the ecclesiastical tradition
when, in a later verse, he extolls Wyclif and his
disciples as the divinely-sent saviors of St. Peter's
ship, that is, the church?[54] In this poem the ship
metaphors have only a peripheral significance.
There is, however, from the same time or shortly
before, in any case from the years of ·Richard's
minority, a political song in English that has the
ship of state as its chief theme. It is usually
named after its refrain, "Seldom Seen is Soon Forgot," and is found in the Vernon Manuscript,[55] a
commonplace book of the 15th century. It behooves
one to consider it if one wishes to recreate those
possibilities of association for his ship vision
that Gower could assume in his public.

The anonymous author carefully examines the
inner decay of and the foreign political menace to
England during the Regency. He awakens the memory
of the glorious past in order to exhort to concord,
and conjures up the figures of Edward III, the Black
Prince, and Henry of Lancaster in order to strengthen
loyal devotion to the young Richard. The poem goes
as follows: once England was a noble and seaworthy
ship that defied every storm. In the whole world
there was not her equal. She was steered by a
strong and steady rudder (Edward III). Nowadays,
however, ship and rudder have become separated.
The ship is the knighthood of the realm, citizens
and peasants are the mast, prayer the wind that
fills the sails. Alas, however, piety is no longer
in fashion, etc.

It is a typical medieval ship of state, whose
individual parts are interpreted with reference to
class,[56] akin to the comparison between the polit-

ical cosmos and the human body in all its individual limbs. The vague outlines of Gower's ship have
little in common with the systematic-rational enum-
eration of detail in the English poem. Moreover,
the anonymous poet celebrates, with a touch of historical romanticism, the ship in the times of its
glory, while Gower describes his near its decline.
On this point Gower is in accord with the sermon
of an unknown monk from the beginning of the 15th
century.[57] Its text is Ecclesiasticus 43.26: Qui
navigant mare, enarrent pericula ejus; et audientes
auribus nostris admirabimur [Let them that sail on
the sea tell the dangers thereof, and when we hear
with our ears, we shall wonder]. The preacher, too,
proceeds from a pessimistic view of the present,
that basic mood that had prevailed in England ever
since the last third of the 14th century. He, too,
casts his eyes backward to happier times, to when
England was a proud ship on the sea of prosperity
and fortune.[58] The clergy formed the bow; the nobility, the stern; the third estate, the hull of
the ship. As long as virtue was at the helm and
the three estates lived harmoniously in fulfillment
of their particular tasks, it sailed on a sea of
wealth and happiness. However, once Vice took command, the ship became frail and Fortuna averted her
face.

        Here, then, is the opportune moment for the
moralizer to begin. What interests us in his performance is that he cites the Peasants' Rebellion
as an historical example of an imminently threatening shipwreck. And what links him with Gower
beyond that is the conviction that such catastrophic
situations are the wages of sin:
        Thus, thoroo pride and synne, a prosperite
        navigavimus in to wo. Mech wo and tribu-
        lacion fuit in hoc regno for synne: many
        mishappys mownt up inter nos: stormes of
        debate and dissencioun piryyd up fast.
        Nostra navis was so hurlid and burlid inter
        ventos et freta quod erat in grandi periculo
        et sepe in puncto pereundi. Fuit in grandi
        periculo quando communes surrexerunt contra
        dominos. Fuit iterum in grandi periculo

quando domini litigabant inter se . . .
(further examples follow). Qwo-so hath seiled
the see and abidde thes bittur stormys, he may
sauele telle our schip hath be in perlis: fuit
in periculis withinne, in periculis without,
in perles of oure selue, in perlis hostium, in
periculis alti maris, in periculis portus.
[Thus through pride and sin we sailed from
prosperity into woe. There was much woe and
tribulation in this kindgom because of sin:
many mishaps mounted up among us: storms of
debate and dissension piled swiftly up. Our
ship was so hurled and burled among the winds
and seas that it was in great danger and often
on the point of perishing. It was in great
danger because the commons rose up against the
lords. It was in great danger because the
lords quarreled among themselves . . . Who-
soever has sailed the sea and endured these
bitter storms, he may safely tell that our
ship has been in perils: it was in danger
within, in danger without, in peril from
ourselves, in peril from the enemy, in danger on the high seas, in danger in port.]59
If this sermon derives from the time of Henry V, it
must, to conclude from the overall tenor, be dated
before Agincourt; its pessimism would otherwise
have been somewhat moderated. The preacher could
naturally have been influenced by Gower; that
would indicate that Gower's ship was understood
in the beginning of the 15th century as a ship of
state. More probable, however, is a common dependence upon an older tradition. The anonymous poet
may have followed a sermon convention that also
helped shape Gower's imagination, no longer nor yet
again evident to us, by which the secular (in any
case not noticeably ecclesiastical) author of
"Seldom Seen is Soon Forgot" was also stimulated.
One detail that appears in the poet as well as in
the preacher perhaps helps to explain Gower's transformation of the Tower into a ship. Both provide
the ship of state with a tower, and the tower appears to be the particular mark of its strength.
The English poem states:
        Sum tyme an Englisch Schip we had,
        Nobel hit was and heih of tour;

44

Thorw al cristendam hit was drad.[60]
The sermon implies the same thing with "ffuit etiam
adeo fortis quod fortissima nauis of toure super
mare non audebat nostram expectare" [the ship was
so strong that the strongest ship of tower upon
the sea did not dare to encounter us],[61] and further
on it names a type of ship "brave turyeres." If
"turyere" is not in this case a corruption of the
word "triere," which might have been unknown to the
scribe, one might assume it to be an otherwise un-
recorded synonym for "ship of tour" modeled after
the pattern of French. A ship designation of this
kind could have facilitated for Gower the transformation of the Tower into a ship.

Is Gower's visionary ship therefore the Tower
on the one hand and the English state on the other?
I suspect that both notions were current and that
Gower intended to evoke them both. However, I also
suspect that there dominates another conception,
which is easily brought into harmony with the idea
of the ship of state and which also ties the last
vision organically to the one preceding. If the
author saw the events up to 14 June as an Ilias
Anglicana, wouldn't it then be logical to seek in
the Ship Vision a counterpart to the ODYSSEY? The
ship, Scylla and Charybdis,[62] the wandering,[63] all
point in this direction. And yet the literary
tradition and the historical consciousness of those
times speak against such an assumption.[64] The matter of the ODYSSEY never acquired the same significance in the literature of the Middle Ages as the
Troy myth. The AENEID, not the ODYSSEY, was regarded
as the natural continuation of the ILIAD. In part
that was due to patriotic reasons. Britain meant
"the island of Brutus," and Brutus was a fictitious
descendent of Aeneas. The fall of Troy and the
wandering of Aeneas together formed a piece of the
English national past, or past perfect. When Gower
portrays the escape from a burning "Troja nova"
aboard a rescuing ship, his literary as well as his
historical model is the AENEID and not the ODYSSEY.
He derives even Scylla and Charybdis, Iris, and the
unruly winds not from Homer but from Virgil's third
book.[65] With the Ship Vision as a reflection of the

45

AENEID, Gower found an appropriate continuation
for his Troy Vision. It guarantees the continuity
of action as well as the epic elegance. At the
same time it shows the only possible way out of the
menacing analogy of the Trojan catastrophe that
still corresponds to the actual events.

In his visions Gower manipulates historical
account and allegorical interpretation in such a
manner that they never fully coincide. Everything fluctuates. The author leaps continuously
from one manner of presentation to the other.
Within the same series of visions the peasant hordes
are now animals, now men, without a transition
having been clearly marked. Likewise, the Trojan
analogy is a magical illumination in which events
are from time to time immersed, rather than a consistently carried out, pseudo-historical equation.
Gower thereby attains--perhaps without having intended it--a realism in his nightmare such as
otherwise seldom occurs in medieval dream allegor-
ies. In the third series of visions, however, the
author abandons this technique of presentation and
simultaneously undertakes a change in the role that
he plays as dreamer and as subject of the angst
dreams. Thus before we continue with the investigation of the vision as an interpretation of reality, we shall stop for a moment and turn to the
figure of the dreamer.

The genre of the dream-narrative requires
that the action focus upon the person of the dreamer
at the beginning and end. He is the medium through
which the dream is transmitted to the reader.
Whether he appears again at intervals in this medial function depends on how concerned the author is
with maintaining the unity of the dream illusion.
Continuity is the rule, interruption the exception. In the visionary prophecy that was in circulation under the name of John of Bridlington
in the second half of the 14th century, the dream
occurs in three waves that are interrupted by the
awakening of the dreamer exhausted from the tremors
of fever. Gower is careful not to endanger the
unity of the illusion through occasional inter-

46

ruptions of the dreams. He has found another means
of introducing realistic characteristics into his
dream: he distinguishes between somnus and somnium.
While the author's sleep, or halfsleep, maintains
unity, the individual dream stories rush along in
terrifying crescendo[66] until the whirlpool of e-
vents in London draws everything together into one
single nightmare. The figure of the dreamer becomes visible at the boundaries of the individual
dreams. He assumes the role of chorus in the tragedy and functions as audience and commentator.
He can be terrified (181 f.), paralyzed with fear
(240 and 505 f.), express dread and alarm in
lengthy lamentations;[67] above all, he can eval-
uate[68] and explicate. At first he is not drawn,
either actively or passively, into the events of
the dream itself.
     This role changes abruptly in Chapter 16,
which links the Troy Vision to the Ship Vision.
This chapter belatedly establishes the figure of
the author as having been active in the first two
visions and uses him as a transition to the last
vision, in which he becomes the central figure.
One may see the influence of the AENEID in the
dreamer's differing participation in the events
of the second and third visions. According to
the account of the Iliou persis, Aeneas is little
more than an onlooker and reporter, whereas the
flight and wandering appear in a concentrated
first person narrative. Yet this is only a problem of external form. More important is the question of the poetic ego's functional significance
for the vision. Because Gower actually experienced June 1381, it is logical to look for autobiographical reminiscences in visionary garb in
his appearance in Chapter 16.[69] Since next to
nothing is known of Gower's life, however, there
are no controls for such an effort. Moreover, the
chapter heading warns against hasty autobiographical inferences:
     Hic plangit secundum visionem sompnii quasi
     in propria persona dolores illorum, qui in
     siluis et speluncis pre timore temporis
     illius latitando se munierunt. [According
     to the vision of his dream, he here laments,

47

as if in his own person, for the suffering of
those who protected themselves by hiding in
the woods and caves because of that fearful
time.]
Whoever may have been the author of the prose summary, the formula quasi in propria persona makes
one thing clear: the will of the author or the
understanding of the contemporary editor speaks
against a concrete autobiographical interpretation.

The sixteenth chapter is in form a cento of
Ovidian citations in a density such as seldom occurs
in Gower. I count no fewer than fifty literal borrowings of different lengths in 233 verses;[70] pre-
sumably there are still more. Most derive from the
TRISTIA, which is indeed similar to Chapter 16 in
mood and content. The prose statement hic plangit
causes the chapter to appear as a planctus that is
resolved through action and reflection. Both con-
centrate on the figure of the dreamer, who is suddenly drawn from the periphery into the vortex of
events, thus compelling the attention of the reader.
Of course, what happens to the author is, as the
summary suggests, of a universal nature. The effect that the events produce is more important than
the events themselves. Gower thus requires a psychological mirror to reflect them and so he projects
his own ego as exponent of a universal experience.

What then is the relationship of the poet's
reportorial and entirely passive self to his active
dream self? In his essay on the poetic and empirical I in medieval authors, Leo Spitzer establishes
a hypothesis concerning the different significance
of the two egos that with a few modifications is
applicable to the Visio.[71] According to it, both
forms are necessary, the one (the poetic I) in
order to push beyond the limits of individuality
to an experience of universal, paradigmatic significance, the other (the empirical I) in order to
record and portray the subject of this experience.
Gower's poetic I does not serve to communicate
his personal sufferings and fears in the summer of
1381, but to convey metaphysical insights that arise
from these sufferings. The hitherto scattered frag-

mentary references to the transcendental significance of the events are summarized in Chapter 16;[72]
there is attained through painful individual experience the universally valid knowledge that life can
be death and death, life;[73] there is made possible
the meeting with the allegorical figure of Sophia,
who teaches the author about God's anger.[74]

Its accented stoic tendency distinguishes Chapter Sixteen from the experiences of the following
vision, in which Sophia in person is called upon to
console the anguished author with the banality that
everything has an end and that patience is the final consequence of wisdom. The question of guilt
nowhere attains great importance:

> Sic tibi fata volunt non crimina . . .
> (1.1547)
> [Fate does not want your reproaches . . .]

and

> Non merito penam pateris set numinis iram:
> Ne timeas, finem nam dolor omnis habet
> (1.1549-50)
> [You are not suffering this torment as due
> punishment, you are suffering the wrath of
> heaven. Do not be afraid, for every sorrow
> has an end],

assures Sophis in Ovid's words.[75]

The malediccio dei, which transformed the peasant horde into animals at the beginning of the Visio,
and the numinis ira, which the poet borrowed from
Ovid in order to characterize his undeserved suffering, have a certain epic magnitude that allows the
idea of human sacrifice in Chapter 19 to appear appropriate. They are, however, far distant from the
Christian interpretation of history in the sense of
sin, penitence, and forgiveness. In order to give
the events a significance in the full sense of the
Christian concept of salvation, Gower requires a
human being whose inner process of purification in
constant correspondence to events leads to the kairos,
in which the literal rescue, that is, the death of
the ringleader, occurs not as simple accident but
as inner necessity. The active dream I has the task
of developing from the pupil of Sophia into a like-

ness of the prodigal son. Thus, the last vision is
not so much a new stage of the historical events as
a new illumination of these events from another lev-
el of experience. If one wished to employ the medieval termini of biblical exegesis, one could call
the Ship Vision the anagogical interpretation of the
events of 1381. In an age permeated by the exemplary significance of all substances and all events,
such a method was the natural way to true understanding. How an historical event could be anagog-
ically interpreted in secular letters is shown by,
for example, Bernard Silvestris' interpretation of
the flight, wandering, and Italian landing of Aeneas
as the way of the soul to the heavenly fatherland.[76]
Now Gower clearly intended to deal with history in
the Visio. The word cronica in the incipit of three
manuscripts[77] and lines 29 f. of the prologue[78] permit no doubt about that. The first two visions
sketch events known to the contemporary reader, in
the course of which the Beast Vision renders a moral
value judgment, the Troy Vision a wide historical
perspective of these events. The presentation is
relatively objective; thus the role of the author
is reduced to a minimum, thus also any direct, personal relationship with God is absent.[79] The last
vision, on the other hand, departs from the historical events and is in all essential respects anagogical, that is, it places external events in relationship to inner psychological events.

The ship's journey begins with a prayer to
Christ, the master of wind and waves.[80] It is not
much more than a Christian substitute for classical
efforts to win Neptune's favor before the beginning
of a journey. The objective is physical assistance
in a physical emergency. At first the journey promises well, but the dreamer's optimism proves mis-
leading. A violent sea storm breaks out and dashes
all hopes, and a fantastic sea monster menaces ship
and passengers, whose behavior suits the markedly
epic-classical presentation:

Brachia cum palmis, oculos cum menteque tristi
In celum tendens, postulat omnis opem:
Non tenet hic lacrimas, stupet hic, vocat ille
                                          beatos,

Proque salute sua numina quisque vocat. 1.1733-
36
[Stretching out his arms and hands to the sky
and turning his eyes there in a spirit of de-
jection, each man asked for help. One man did
not hold back his tears, another was struck
dumb, still another called upon the saints;
and each invoked God for his deliverance.]
Apart from the mention of the beati, the passage distinguishes itself more through the quality of its
Latin than through a specifically Christian coloring
of classical parallels.

At first the author implicitly includes himself (omnis). However, that changes with the impression of the storming of the Tower, which he describes as follows:
Visa michi Cilla fuit et tunc visa Caribdis,
Deuoret vt nauem spirat utrumque latus.
1.1741-42
[First it seemed like Scylla to me, and then
Charybdis, as it was eager to devour the ship
from both sides.]
His soul achieves an insight into the relationship
of the outer and inner events; that is, it recog-
nizes its own sin and guilt. Instead of the formula of Chapter 16--conscia mensque michi fuerat,
culpe licet expers (1553) [my mind was conscious
of the fact that there nevertheless was no hope of
even doubtful safety]--there now follow reflection
and contemplation:
Talia fingebam misero michi fata parari,
Demeritoque meo rebar adesse malum.
Sic mecum meditans, tacito sub murmure dixi,
"Hec modo que pacior propria culpa tulit."
Non latuit quicquam culparum cordis in antro,
Quin magis ad mentem singula facta refert:
Cor michi commemorat scelerum commissa meorum,
Vt magis exacuat cordis ymago preces. 1.1781-88
[Wretchedly I pictured the fate contrived for
myself, and I judged that misfortune was at
hand because of my own unworthiness. Medi-
tating to myself in this way, I said in a low
murmur, "My own guilt has brought the things
I am now suffering." None of my faults lay

51

hidden in the recesses of my heart, but instead
my deeds brought everything to mind. My heart
remembered the crimes I had committed, so that
the picture in my heart stimulated my prayers.]
It is the parable of the prodigal son that the author
experiences, just as Augustine had seen it, in two
principal phases of self-contemplation and return to
God.[81] Gower accomplishes the first phase in phrases
such as mecum meditans, cordis ymago; the second in
the prayer,

Peccaui, redeo, miserere precor miserendi! 1.1823
[I have sinned, I return, I implore thee to have
pity upon me who am to be pitied!]

Thus is discovered the meaning of earthly suffering,
which is to divorce the soul from the world and guide
it back to God:

Iam prope depositus sum mundo, frigidus, eger,
Seruatus per te, si modo seruer, ego. 1.1829-30
[Now cold, sick, almost buried in the earth, I
shall be saved by Thee, if I may now be saved.]

The historical events have taken on a metaphysical
significance--become anagogical in the true sense of
the word. The moment has arrived when the contention
that catastrophe can be averted through a process of
spiritual purification appears prepared and substantiated. God has mercy on the contrite sinners, removes his judgment of damnation, and the uprising
collapses.

At this point the epic cast of the story leads
to a striking mixture of heathen and Christian mo-
tifs that makes interpretation difficult. Chapter
18, in which the author had become introspective,
ended with the word preces. Chapter 19 accordingly
begins with the effectiveness of the prayer:

Clamor in excelsis, lacrime gemitusque frequentes,
Non veniam cassi preteriere dei. 1.1851-52
[There was an outcry in the skies, there were
tears and frequent groans, and the gods did
not neglect to show mercy.]

However, divine forgiveness is attached to a condition.
The Ovidian-Virgilian description of the uproar of the
elements had brought into the fray Aeolus and the four
winds, and especially Neptune. The calming of the sea
falls in his province and he demands a sacrifice (1853-
56). The concept of a sacrifice of expiation, and in-

deed of a human sacrifice, places a heavy demand on
the reader and stands in sharpest contrast to the
preceding chapter's perception of sin. The epic
solemnity may perhaps require it. However, hadn't
the offering of human sacrifice been forbidden by
Jehovah on Mount Moriah and by the Greek goddess at
Aulis? Of course, Gower tones the matter down by
speaking of requital (1867), and by suggesting the
possibility that the guilty can atone themselves
through death (1872). However, that is not to deny
that in the beginning, without any consideration of
moral justification, God is offered a sacrifice, a
bribe, as it were:
> Dona valent precibus commixta, per hec deus audit
> Micius, et votis annuit ipse precum. 1.1855-56
> [Our gifts in conjunction with our prayers pre-
> vailed; because of the gifts the god listened
> more kindly, and he gave approval to the solemn
> promises of our prayers.]
The sacrifice to Neptune as an epic reminiscence is
an alien element in Gower's story, as is evident at
the point where the account returns to the Christian
God. As far as Neptune is concerned, the sacrifice
has the desired consequence, for it is a holocaustum
sufficiens (1883). The storm abates and the elements
return to their accustomed courses. The dreamer
breathes easily, for the hour of rescue has come.
A smooth and clear denouement appears to have been
achieved.

However, at this moment sounds a voice ab excelso,
and God speaks of a postponement, not an appeasement,
of his anger. The sufficiens holocaustum appears to
have been forgotten; the settled account is reopened
in all its Christian dubiousness. After God's promise the already solaced author (1881) awakens to a
new life (1899), and only then does the already calmed
storm first cease. Such repetitions and overlappings
persist.[82] And as though he intended to make the confusion complete, Gower fails to distinguish clearly
between Neptune and God. At the beginning of the
chapter he gives the impression that there are two
gods, whose relationship to each other remains un-
clear.[83] When, however, the sacrifice is over and
Neptune has played his role, sounds the unspecified
heavenly voice. There is no perceptible transition.

53

In the event that two gods are still intended, the
general concept deus covers both. Probably it is
one and the same deity, now seen under classical,
now under Old Testament aspects.

Between the muddled development of Chapter 19
and its accompanying prose summary occurs an instructive contradiction. The summary reverses the
sequence of events. It begins with the heavenly
voice, and then God, appeased by prayer, restrains
the elements. Only then occurs the death of the
ringleader, quasi in holocaustum.[84] The human sacrifice is not avoided, but any possiblity of considering it as an attempt to influence God is excluded, since it occurs subsequently and seems
designated, through the addition of the words pro
delicto, as punishment. The sense of such a sacrifice after appeasement must be sought in Genesis.
When the Lord pacified the waters of the deluge
and bade him go from the ark, Noah constructed an
altar and offered a sacrifice:
> . . . et tollens de cunctis pecoribus et
> volucribus mundis, obtulit holocausta super
> altare (Genesis 8.20) [. . . and taking of
> all cattle and fowls that were clean, of-
> fered holocausts upon the altar].

And the Lord took pleasure in the sacrifice and
made his covenant of peace with mankind. The analogy does not hold true in all respects, but the
basic features of the Noah story are evident in
Gower. The situation of the few ingenui who succeed in fleeing aboard the rescuing ship corresponds to the fate of the ark's occupants. The
sea storm, which Gower industriously intensifies
into a colossus, shows a similarity to the deluge.
The sacrifice of thanksgiving, the choice of the
word holocaustum (instead of sacrificium), which
is inappropriate because there is no fiery sacrifice, point to the Genesis account. Perhaps
there is also a connection between the birds of
Noah's sacrifice and the statement of 1863 (Vna
peribat avis--a single bird perished), referring
to Wat Tylor, the jay. The most important in-
dication of the Noah story, however, probably lies
in the accentuation of pax restored.[85]

Seen in this way, Chapter 19 dovetails organically with the train of thought of the preceding chapter. The inner story suffers no interruption, the outer adjusts itself without too much difficulty. Both attain their climax and provisional conclusion at the same moment. One is tempted to view the summary as Gower's outline, from which he unintentionally departed (to the disadvantage of the narrative) in working out the details.[86]

The summary of Chapter 20 identifies the ship, vainly seeking a calm horbor, with the mens turbata of the dreamer.[87] Finally it lands in Great Britain, an island where, as a worthy old man informs the author upon interrogation, peace never reigns.[88] The shock is so severe that the dreamer loses consciousness. When he awakens, the heavenly voice instructs him for the last time.

From a compositional point of view, it is the task of this last chapter to justify the writing of the work and to sanction its content. That is accomplished in 2047 ff. with a divine commission, as is customary in allegorical dream narratives. Notwithstanding, Gower takes advantage of the opportunity to have the heavenly voice proclaim a considerable amount of banal practical wisdom[89] which reads like a selection from the DISTICHA CATONIS and which is entirely out of place. Even taking into consideration that maxims had to form the ornament of any refined literary work, it is difficult to come to terms with the fact that the trite stoicism recommended here gives the lie to the experiences of the last chapter. It sounds like Chapter 16 with Sophia all over again. Even the Fortuna concept, which the author elsewhere opposed on ethical grounds,[90] surfaces again. Gower was not enough of a mystic himself to portray convincingly a difficult anagogical theme within the framework of a concrete historical event. He used a meditation and sermon motif without having fully assimilated it. That such an assimilation of outer and inner experience was possible within the metaphor of a dangerous sea journey, and remained possible, is demonstrated by the example of Donne two and one-half centuries later.[91] The de-

corative value of the ship metaphor appears to have
been more important to Gower than its content.

The voyage through the stormy sea of life does
not end in the quiet harbor of God's peace, but in
a temporary landing place full of unrest and strife
that one has to endure with stoic equanimity. Everything remains in suspenso. Law and order, or, as
the author would say, pax et concordia, are still
endangered after the collapse of the Peasants' Rebellion. Gower's attitude is ambivalent throughout.
On the one hand he cannot very well say that God's
intervention was inadequate, so he joyfully shouts
his thanks[92] and designates himself a new man.[93]
On the other hand, his worries on his own and his
nation's behalf remain:
    Non tamen ad plenum fateor mea corda redisse,
    Qui mala tam subito tanta per ante tuli.
    Qui semel est lesus fallaci piscis ab hamo,
    Sepe putat reliquis arma subesse cibis. 1.2069-72
    [Nevertheless, I confess my strength did not
    fully return--I who had previously suffered
    such great harm so unexpectedly. The fish
    that has once been wounded by the treacherous
    hook often thinks that weapons lie hidden in
    the rest of its food.]
The conflict of moods is reflected in the wish for
England with which the Visio concludes:
    O mea si tellus, quam non absorbuit equor,
    Debita sciret eo reddere vota deo!
    Castigauit eam dominus, nec in vlcera mortis
    Tunc tradidit, set adhuc distulit ira manum. 1.2125
                                                    -28
    [O if my country, which the sea did not swal-
    low up, might also know it should render de-
    votion to God! The Lord punished it and then
    did not deliver it to the pangs of death, but
    stayed His hand from wrath.]
The feeling of liberation is coupled with a feeling
of continuing menace: adhuc distulit ira manum. The
author's pessimism is unequivocal. Gower was all too
cognizant of the significance of the events of 1381.
Sermons and devotional literature leave no doubts
about the significance of such tribulationes, and
it is no accident that the passage on tribulatio is

one of the longest in Bromyard's SUMMA. Let me cite
but one passage:
    . . . prosperitas multos a se seu a cogni-
    tione sua et a statu proprie salutis alienat;
    ideo deus tribulationes eis inmittit, ut ad
    se redeant [. . . prosperity separates many
    people from themselves or from self-knowledge
    and from a proper state of health; therefore
    God afflicts them with tribulations, that
    they might return to him].[94]

    Did Gower achieve his goal? Did the shock of
the Peasants' Rebellion point the English nation to
the way of the prodigal son? "O mea si tellus, quam
non absorbuit equor,/Debita sciret eo reddere vota
deo!" is a real wish, even though Gower expresses it
in an imaginary situation. In the MIROUR DE L'OMME
he had called for soul-searching, and in the class
critique of the VC he had attempted to explain the
signs of the times. Now in 1381, he believed the
catastrophe had begun and God had granted a reprieve
from his wrath only at the twelfth hour. No conver-
sion, however, ensued. The country slid back into
the same old rut. The angst dream, which had landed
the poet "in medio pravae et perversae nationis,"
proved in the end to have been correct and, after
the removal of the immediate danger, the homilist
exhorted deaf ears.

Notes to Chapter Two
    [1] 13-18 and 29 f.
    [2] 19-24.
    [3] 25-28 and 47-52.
    [4] 53 f.
    [5] The guardian angel in 9 ff. is meant to guar-
antee the credibility of the vision; however, it is
clearly not the causa efficiens of the work.
    [6] Cf. below, pp. 91 ff.
    [7] Cf. 19-24 and 25-28, respectively.
    [8] The loan derives from Ovid's TRISTIA. Macaulay
points out the following parallels in his notes: VOX
CLAMANTIS 1.Prol.33 f. (TRISTIA 5.1.5 f.); 36 (TRISTIA
1.1.14); 37 f. in the tradition of GDL TH$_2$ (TRISTIA
4.1.95 ff.). He overlooked 42 (TRISTIA 5.1.4). One
wonders involuntarily whether the choice of elegiac

meter instead of epic hexameters could perhaps have anything to do with the lacrimose material and the Ovidian model. However, the influence of the SPEC-ULUM STULTORUM and the AURORA may have been the determining factor.

9 Twice "lacrimis" before a caesura (36 and 37); once "flebilis" at the beginning of a line (33); "lacrimabile tempus" (31) and "flebile carmen" (33) at the ends of lines; also "flere" (31) and another "lacrimabile" (38).

10 If one wishes, one can view 39-40 as an exordial topos of trepidation before the matter which lies ahead; see E. R. Curtius, EUROPAISCHE LITERATUR UND LATEINISCHES MITTELALTER (Bern, 1948), pp. 91 f. However, the trepidation topos appears again shortly afterwards in a more extensive form (43-52).

11 Cf. TRISTIA 4.1 and 5.10.15-28.

12 TRISTIA 5.7.45-48 [Translations of the TRISTIA are throughout those of Arthur Leslie Wheeler (Cambridge, Mass., 1924). Trans.]:

Sive homines, vix sunt homines hoc nomine digni,
Quamque lupi saevae plus feritatis habent.
Non metuunt leges, sed cedit viribus aequum,
Victaque pugnaci iura sub ense iacent.
[If I look upon the men, they are scarce
men worthy the name; they have more of cruel
savagery than wolves. They fear not laws;
right gives way to force, and justice lies
conquered beneath the aggressive sword.]

13 This development is not yet fully clear in the prologue. However, the end of the first book, as well as that of the entire work, permits no uncertainty; cf. 1.1885 ff.; 7.1121 ff. and above all 7.1417-42.

14 They are most concisely explained in the first prologue of Nicolaus de Lyras' EXPOSITIO IN BIBLIA:

Littera gesta docet, quid credas allegoria,
Moralis quid agas, quo tendas anagogia.
[The letter teaches the deed, the allegory
what you should believe, the moral what you
should do, the anagogue what you should aim
for.]

Cited from the five volume edition (Rome, 1471).

15 Migne, PL 75.

16 MORALIA IN JOB, lib. II, cap. II.

[17] Historicus sensus. Quam accurate S. Scriptura facta describat.--Intueri libet quomodo sacra eloquia in exordiis narrationum qualitates exprimant, terminosque causarum. Aliquando namque a positione loci, . . . aliquando a qualitate temporis signant, quid de ventura actione subjiciant. [Historical sense. How Sacred Scripture describes events exactly. It is pleasing to behold how the sacred writings give expression to the circumstances, the conditions under which things take place when a narrative begins. For sometimes the setting and sometimes the date are given as a significant element in the forthcoming action.] Migne, PL 75:555.
[18] So Gregory in any case understands "quadam die."
[19] Hinc est quod Salomon, qui sapientiam non perseveraturus accepit, in somnis hanc et nocte accepisse describitur (3 Kings 3.11) [Hence it is that Salomon, who received wisdom but was not destined to persevere, is said to have received it in sleep and at night]. Loc. cit., col. 556.
[20] 1885-92.
[21] One is tempted to connect the night dream in Chaucer's BOOK OF THE DUCHESS with the elegiac character of the work, which treats of the death of Blanche. Unfortunately, the parallel does not work out completely in Chaucer. THE HOUSE OF FAME begins at night for no apparent reason.
[22] After the rescue, of course, there follows a second gloomy sea voyage, the motivation of which is insufficient and the interpretation of which is difficult, since clearly it has little to do with the historical event. See below, pp. 55-56.
[23] VOX CLAMANTIS I, Chapters 3-12. There is a summary in Macaulay's introduction to Vol. 4 and in Henry Morley, ENGLISH WRITERS (London, 1864-67), IV, 177-92.
[24] Caxton first translated and printed a Reynard tale in 1481. Previously there had existed in England only the story of "The Fox and the Wolf" and Chaucer's "Nun's Priest's Tale." Nevertheless, Chaucer's tale presupposes his public's familiarity with the Reynard story.
[25] The dates are from Rupert Taylor, THE POLITICAL PROPHECY IN ENGLAND (New York, 1911), pp. 48 ff. For WHEN ROME, etc. cf. Reinhard Haferkorn, WHEN ROME

IS REMOVED INTO ENGLAND, BEITRAEGE ZUR ENGLISCHE
PHILOLOGIE, 19 (1932).
    26 Cf. Taylor, loc. cit., p. 83.
    27 Ibid., pp. 89 f.
    28 Taylor names this type "Galfridian" because
it first appears in Geoffrey of Monmouth.
    29 Edited by Thomas Wright, POLITICAL POEMS
AND SONGS, Rolls Series (London, 1859), I, 123-215.
    30 The commentator knows ten forms of obscur-
itas, which he conscientiously introduces and explains in the second prologue of the work.
    31 Pseudo-Bonaventura, PHARETRA, lib. I, cap. 7.
The passage from Psalms referred to [48.13] reads in
the Vulgate: Et homo, cum in honore esset, non intel-
lexit; comparatus est jumentis insipientibus, et si-
milis factus est illis [And man when he was in honor
did not understand; he is compared to senseless
beasts, and is become like to them]. Cited from
Berthold Rembolt's edition of the PHARETRA (Paris,
1518).
    32 The standard biblical example is Nebuched-
nezzar, who, as punishment for his arrogance, was
turned into a grass-eating ox (Daniel 4.25 ff.).
Gregory comments in the MORALIA: . . . quia elatione
cogitationis se super homines extulit, ipsum, quem
communem cum hominibus habuit, sensum hominis amisit
[. . . because he exalted himself, puffed up in
thought, above men, he lost that very thing--the
human faculty--which he had in common with men].
Migne, PL 75:688. Gower describes the episode vividly and a bit touchingly in the CONFESSIO AMANTIS
1.2785-3042.
    33 In this connection Gower often mentions God
and Nature in the same breath; see 1092 and 1308.
The relationship of God and Nature, of the lex dei
and the lex naturae, will be discussed later.
    34 Cf. also 979-82:
O denaturans vrbis natura prioris,
Que vulgi furias arma mouere sinis!
O quam retrograda res est, quod miles inermis
Expauit, que ferus vulgus ad arma vacat!
[O the degenerate nature of our former city,
which allowed the madly raging rabble to take
up arms. O what a backward state of affairs it
is that the unarmed knight shakes with fear and

the barbarous mob has the leisure for fighting!]
[35] John 8.34.
[36] Cf. 377 f.:
Hii fuerant porci, maledictus spiritus in quos
Intravit, sicut leccio sancta refert.
[They were swine into which a cursed spirit
had entered, just as Holy Writ tells of.]
[37] 2093-2106:
Sic cum rusticitas fuerat religata cathenis,
Et paciens nostro subiacet illa pede,
Ad iuga bos rediit, . . .
Sic ope diuina Sathane iacet obruta virtus,
Que tamen indomita rusticitate latet;
Semper ad interitum nam rusticus insidiatur,
Si genus ingenuum subdere forte queat.
. . . . . .
Forcius ergo timor stimulans acuatur in ipsos,
Et premat hos grauitas quos furit illa quies.
[So when the peasantry had been bound in
chains and lay patiently under our foot, the
ox returned to its yoke, . . . Similarly,
Satan's power lay prostrate, overwhelmed by
divine might; but nevertheless it lurked in
hiding among the ungovernable peasantry.
For the peasant always lay in wait [to see]
whether he by chance could bring the noble
class to destruction.
. . . . . .
So that this goading fear became more sharply
whetted in them and their burden weighed
heavily upon them.]
[38] Lines 961-70 comprise a curious catalogue,
for it names only Greek victors, whereas one would
expect representatives of the conquered Trojans.
Clearly Gower is not overly concerned with the precision of the historical analogy. A second catalog
of mixed derivation, which is probably to be taken
as an outdoing topos, appears in 985-94.
[39] 997 f.
[40] 995 f. and 1115.
[41] Chapter Fourteen.
[42] The Beast Vision, in order that it might be
brought to the same stylistic plane, was studded
throughout with frequent classical tropes, often
in the form of outdoing topoi; cf. 263-76; 349-58;

61

441-60; 579 f.

43 "The Reconciliation of Richard II with the City of London," Wright, POLITICAL POEMS AND SONGS, I, 282, "Trenovantes"; 283, "Troia" and "Nova Troia"; 286, "Troia novella."

44 Hic eciam secundum visionem sompnii describit quasi in propria persona angustias varias que contingebant hiis qui tunc pro securitate optinenda in Turrim Londoniarum se miserunt, et de ruptura eiusdem turris: figurat enim dictam turrim similem esse naui prope voraginem Cille periclitanti. [According to the vision of his dream he likewise describes here, as if in his own person, the different troubles which befell those who went to the Tower of London to find safety. And he describes the breaching of the same tower. Indeed, he pictures the said tower to be like a ship near the whirlpool of the perilous Scylla.] In the text the comparison first appears in the next chapter, 1743-70.

45 995 f. appear to be a reference:
Nec solito Priamus fulsit tunc liber honore,
Set patitur dominus quid sibi seruus agat.
[Priam did not shine then with his usual honor; instead, the master put up with whatever the servant did to him.]

46 It is probably implicit in 997 ff.; Froissart also mentions the molestation of the Queen Mother.

47 Chapter Fourteen.

48 Curtius, loc. cit., pp. 136-38, gives an abundance of examples that indicate a continuity of the topos from classical antiquity to the Renaissance. I would add from my limited knowledge of the material the very detailed ship metaphor in the prologue of the eighth book of the POLICRATICUS. John of Salisbury renews the topos by using it to justify his writing. Gower is less original; cf. VOX CLAMANTIS 3.Prol.105 f. and perhaps 81 f.

49 For example, Hugo of St. Victor, DE ARCA NOE MORALI, Migne, PL 176. The relationship has already been reduced to a short formula in the second book, "De Vanitate Mundi": . . . Mundus diluvium est, cor autem hominis, si per amorem mundanorum se deorsum inclinat, naufragatur inter fluctus saeculi. [The world is a flood. The heart of man, if it prostrate

itself for love of the world, will be shipwrecked
among the waves of the world.] Migne, PL 176:715.
[50] For instance, Sebastian Brant, NARRENSCHIFF.
[51] For example, Hugo of St. Victor, DE ARCA NOE
MYSTICA, Migne, PL 176.
[52] CARMINA, 1.14.
[53] Wright, POLITICAL POEMS AND SONGS, I, 253:
Heu! quanta desolatio Angliae praestatur,
Cujus regnum quodlibet hinc inde minatur,
Et cujus navigium pene conquassatur.
[Alas! how much desolation there is in England,
Whose throne for this reason is threatened,
And whose ship is nearly wrecked.]
[54] Ibid., p. 258:
Tantos motus intuens Dominus in mari,
Quosdam viros nobiles fecit magistrari,
Ut fides ecclesiae possit restaurari,
Wyclif et discipulos voluit vocari,
    With an O and I, hi sunt viri nautae,
    Ducentes a Domino navem Petri caute.
[God observes the great motions upon the sea,
And also the great men by whom he intends it to
                                be governed;
That the faith of the church may be restored,
The church chooses to be summoned by Wyclif
                            and his disciples.
    With an O and I, these are the mariners,
    Carefully led by God to Peter's ship.]
[55] EETS OS 117, pp. 715 ff.
[56] The ecclesiastical estate is probably omitted
because the vessil is a man-of-war. The accommodation of the Black Prince and his uncle in the class
organization obviously proved difficult. Thus Henry
of Lancaster is a bark that escorts the ship, while
the Black Prince is aboard the ship but not identified with any part.
[57] MS. Bodl. 649, fol. 129[v] f. G. R. Owst,
LITERATURE AND PULPIT IN MEDIEVAL ENGLAND (Cambridge,
1933), pp. 72 f., gives a lengthy excerpt; however,
he does not preserve the macaronic character of the
original but translates the Latin parts.
[58] Magna nauis que navigauit multos dies in
mari prosperitatis est illud copiosum regnum, regnum
anglie. Deus per suam passionem saluet illud et con-
seruet. [That great kingdom, the kingdom of England,

is a great ship that has sailed for many days on the sea of prosperity. May God save and preserve it through his passion and death.] Ibid., fol. 129[V].

59 MS. Bodl. 649, fol. 130.

60 EETS OS 117, p. 716, ll. 17-19.

61 MS. Bodl. 649, fol. 129[V].

62 They are both named in 1723 and 1741. Scylla alone appears in 1768, 1842, 1951 f., 2085.

63 It begins with 1945.

64 Cf. A. B. Taylor, AN INTRODUCTION TO MEDIEVAL ROMANCE (London, 1930), pp. 120 ff.

65 Gower's sea storm is of course not purely Virgilian, but a mixture of Ovid (METAMORPHOSES 11. 410 ff., "Ceyx and Halcyone") and Virgil. Whether Gower came to Ovid independently, drawn by his personal preference, or whether he followed the Troy romances of Benoit de Sainte Maure and Guido delle Colonne--who had used Ovid liberally--cannot be determined for sure.

66 Cf. 299; 461 f.; 565 f.; 1595 f.; each is at the beginning of a new chapter.

67 Cf. the variation on the theme of the sequence "Dies irae, dies illa" in 635-78. The impetus for this passage may derive from the SPECULUM STULTORUM; see Macaulay's note on 635. However, Macaulay did not consider the sequence, to which Gower is much nearer in mood than to an ironic paraphrase of Wireker. That is especially clear toward the end, where verbal and contentual reminiscences of Thomas of Celano prevail. Another lamentation passage is the six elegiac distiches with the anaphora "O res mira nimis" [O what an astonishing thing], 623-34.

68 The numerous outdoing topoi (263-76; 349-58; 441-60, etc.) are primarily scathing value judgments, not only solemn hyperboles.

69 For example, in 1381-98 or 1585-90.

70 1359, 1363 ff., 1369, 1379 f., 1385 f, 1387, 1395, 1397 f., 1401 f., 1403, 1413 f., 1420, 1424, 1425 f., 1429 f., 1433, 1442, 1445-48, 1453, 1459, 1465, 1467 f., 1469, 1473, 1475, 1485, 1496, 1501 f., 1503 f., 1506, 1512, 1514, 1517 f., 1519, 1521, 1534, 1535 ff., 1539, 1549, 1564, 1565 f., 1569, 1571, 1573, 1575, 1585, 1589; cf. Macaulay's comments on these verses in the notes. Macaulay did not register the dependence of 1534 (TRISTIA 5.4.4), 1537 (TRIS-

TIA 1.5.11) and 1538 (freely after TRISTIA 3.3.44).
[71] "Note on the Poetic and the Empirical 'I'
in Medieval Authors," TRADITIO, 4 (1946), 414-22.
[72] 1369-78.
[73] 1583 f.
[74] 1545-56. The theme was already raised in
1455 f.
[75] Cf. FASTI 1.483.
[76] COMMENTUM BERNARDI SILVESTRIS SUPER SEX
LIBROS ENEIDOS VIRGILII, ed. R. Riedel (Greifswald,
1924).
[77] SCE according to Macaulay's designations.
[78] Quos mea terra dedit casus nouitatis adibo,
Nam pius est patrie facta referre labor.
[I shall enter into the recent misfortunes
that my country has exhibited, for it is a
worthy labor to report the deeds of one's
native land.]
[79] It is striking that the Visio contains no
prayer in a Christian sense until Chapter 16. All
starts in this direction are epically traditional
and religiously neutral; cf. 1471 f., 1555 f.
[80] It is unimportant for our purposes whether
the prayer has Christ in mind with the designation
"stella maris" and appeals to him alone, or whether
it is a double prayer to Christ and Mary. Cf.
Macaulay, Notes.
[81] In nobis ipsis dei imaginem contuentes
tanquam iunior ille evangelicus filius ad nosmet
reversi surgamus et ad illum redeamus a quo peccando
recesseramus. [Bearing the mark of God within us,
let us rise up like that younger son in the gospel,
reverse our course, and return to Him from Whom
through our sins we have departed.] In Pseudo-
Bonaventura, PHARETRA, Book IV, Chapter Fifty,
cited as a quote from DE CIVITATE DEI.
[82] Compare 1884-86 with 1927 f.; 1899 f. with
1933 f.; the conduct of the sailors in 1901 ff.
with 1935 ff.
[83] The forgiving God is simply designated
"deus" (in 1851 f.), while Neptune is introduced in
the following line as "deus maris." Because the two
distiches are contrasted through an adversative
particle, there appear to be two gods:
Clamor in excelsis, lacrime gemitusque frequentes

Non veniam cassi preteriere dei;
Attamen ipse maris Neptunus qui deus extat,
At [sc. ut] mare pacificet, tunc holocausta
                              petit. 1.1851-54
[There was an outcry in the skies, there
were tears and frequent groans, and the gods
did not neglect to show mercy. But Neptune,
who is god of the sea, demanded sacrificial
offerings to calm the sea.]
84 Hic fingit secundum visionem sompnii de quadam voce diuina in excelsis clamante, et quomodo
deus placatus tandem precibus tempestates sedauit,
et quomodo quasi in holocaustum pro delicto occisus
fuit ille Graculus, id est Walterus, furiarum
Capitaneus. [Here he depicts, according to the
vision of his dream, a certain voice calling on
high, and how God was finally placated by prayers
and calmed the storms. And he depicts how the
Jay, that is, Walter the captain of the madmen,
was killed as if for a sacrificial offering because
of his transgressions.]
85 1920: Pax redit, atque probis fit renouata
salus [Peace returned, and safety was restored to
the just].
86 It would be possible to hold a careless redactor responsible for the discrepancy. Yet, differences between the summary and the text occur re-
peatedly and the explanation does not account for
several instances where the summary is more knowledgeable than the text, while the supposition that
the summary accords with a rough draft accounts for
all instance.
87 Hic loquitur adhuc de naui visa in sompnis,
id est de mente sua adhuc turbata . . . [Here he
speaks of the ship he still saw in his sleep, that
is, he speaks of his confusion of mind].
88 The idea of peace as the unrealized and un-
realizable longing of the poet suffuses the entire
Visio. It is expressed by pax, concordia, amor.
This yearning for peace cannot be satisfied because
for the Christian author the soul can never find
peace in this world. Nor does he find solace in
the sense of John 14.27 and 16.33. What Gower has
the heavenly voice say in 2025 ff. is strikingly
inadequate and can in no way stand as a solution to
the problem.

[89] 2021-46.

[90] VOX CLAMANTIS, Book II passim.

[91] Cf. DEVOTIONS UPON EMERGENT OCCASIONS, ed. John Sparrow (Cambridge, 1923), pp. 114 ff. (Expostulation 19).

[92] Cf. 2064: exultans; 2082: Cum laudis iubilo cantica soluo deo [I joyfully render songs of praise to God].

[93] 2067: Tunc prius ad dominum cordis nouitate reviuens [Revived by fresh courage, then first to the Lord]; 2112: Et velut a sompno sum renouatus homo [And I was like a man refreshed by sleep].

[94] The last clause alludes to the parable of the prodigal son; see Luke 15.17.

Chapter Three
The VOX CLAMANTIS and the Medieval Sermon

A. The Homilist and the Archer

The contents of the VC, that is, the VOX CLAM-
ANTIS with the exclusion of the Visio, are most
often described as class critique or estates satire.
The concept of estates satire is unfortunate and mis-
leading,[1] and, furthermore, classification of the
poem in the category of class critique is justified
only to a limited extent. While it is satisfactory
for most of the material, it ignores or overlooks
the countless philosophical and theological dis-
cussions which suffuse and surround the VC. They
are not simply erudite ballast, strewn about at
random, but show the firm outlines of a system, the
essence of which is popular theology, that gives the
class critique sense and significance. The title
and the accompanying lines about an archer with
which Gower sends his poem into the world together
point in the direction of theology--or, more properly,
in the direction of the medieval sermon.

The title VOX CLAMANTIS first appears in the
prologue of the second book and thus refers with
certainty to the VC. What did the author wish to
express with this title? With what expectations
did the contemporary reader approach such a work?
Did Gower perhaps attempt a sensational "headline"
with his Voice of One Crying in the Wilderness?
Definitely not. For Gower, as for his reader, the
figure of John the Baptist signified a concrete
program. John was celebrated in three different
aspects in the course of the church year: in Feb-
ruary as the greatest among the prophets (according to Matthew 11.11), in June as the first Christian martyr, and in Advent and Lent as the preacher
who made ready the way of the Lord. In this his
chief characteristic, he became the epitome of the
vox clamantis.

In desiring his work to be understood according to the formula vox clamantis in deserto, Gower
made a statement about his own function, about the

69

form and content of the book, and about the contemporary situation. VOX CLAMANTIS is a coinage which the Gospels apply to John alone; however, they take it from Isaiah.[2] It has, therefore, an impersonal, functional significance in addition to its personal and thus unique connection with John the Baptist. Now alongside the current medieval comparisons of the preacher with the medicus, the piscator, and the miles--each of whom displays one of his functions--there appears a comparison with the praeco, the herald, who forcefully expresses the weight of divine authority and the medial nature of the preacher's position.[3] In this characteristic the preacher is the instrument, the voice of the Lord, the vox clamantis. So says John Waldeby in one of his baptismal sermons:

> . . . sicut sol in medio planetarum illuminat
> omnia celestia luminaria et sicut dux in
> medio exercitus dirigit omnes tirones in
> pungna [sic], sic Christus infra, id est in
> anima cuiuslibet predicatoris stans in eo
> loquitur tamquam in instrumento. Luc. 12[0]
> Ego dabo vobis os et sapientiam etc. Ed
> ideo joh. respondit de seipso: Ego vox clam-
> antis in deserto. Non solum joh. sed qui-
> libet predicator ydoneus vox Christi per
> ipsum clamantis dicitur; alias non dixisset;
> qui vox audit me audit? [. . . just as the
> sun in the midst of the planets illuminates
> all the heavenly lights, and just as a gen-
> eral in the midst of an army directs all the
> soldiers in battle, thus Christ here below,
> that is, standing within the soul of what-
> soever preacher he wishes, speaks as if
> through an instrument. Luke 12, I shall
> give you mouth and wisdom, etc. And thus
> John answered in like manner concerning him-
> self: I am the voice of one crying in the
> wilderness. Not only John, but whatsoever
> preacher who wishes is said to be the suitable
> voice of Christ which speaks through him;
> elsewhere has he not said: who hears you
> hears me?][4]

The right with which Gower, a layman, took upon himself the role of preacher and thus the designation

vox clamantis will be discussed later.[5] We must now
come to our second point, the form and content of
the Johannine homily.

Among the synoptic Gospels, Luke (3.1-14) provides the most detailed account of the Baptist's
sermon. I wish to show how it was understood by
reference to one of Bonaventura's commentaries,[6]
more suitable as an illustration than a contemporary sermon would be because it interprets the chapter as a whole. The late medieval sermon, rarely
treating a biblical text as a unity, instead real-
izes its own divisions and subdivisions, with appropriate citations, upon a short verse or verse
part. The result is that it seldom goes further
than vox--clamantis--in deserto.[7] Bonaventura, on
the other hand, discusses the tone, content, and
form of the Baptist's sermon in detail. The tone
he characterizes as zealous severity: Praedicatio
Joannis commendatur a zeli severitate.[8] The content he divides into three parts:
    a) Invective (increpatio)--Luke 3.7: "He [John
the Baptist] said therefore to the crowds that went
out to be baptized by him, 'Brood of vipers! Who
has shown you how to flee from the wrath to come?'"
    b) Exhortation (exhortatio)--Luke 3.8: "Bring
forth therefore fruits befitting repentance, and
do not begin to say, 'We have Abraham for our
father'; for I say to you that God is able out of
these stones to raise up children to Abraham."
    c) Threat of Punishment (comminatio)--Luke
3.9: "For even now the axe is laid at the root of
the trees; every tree, therefore, that is not
bringing forth fruit is to be cut down and thrown
into the fire."[9]
As for its form, Bonaventura labels the Baptist's
a class sermon.[10] The audience is not just a random collection, but is organized by estates. Whereas in ecclesiastical practice, however, the class
sermon usually focused on one class--for example,
on merchants or soldiers, the wedded or the widowed--
the Baptist's sermon laid hold of all parts of a
class-organized community. Bonaventura praises
the care with which John satisfied the particular
needs of the individual classes, which he reinter-
preted as subditi, ministri, and rectores:

Praedicatio Joannis commendatur primo quoad exigentiam populi tripliciter. Quantum ad primum notandum, quod secundum triplicem differentiam personarum audientium diversas instructiones administrat: primo, ad turbas, quae gerunt personam subditorum; secundo, ad publicanos, qui gerunt personam ministrorum; tertio, ad milites, qui gerunt personam rectorum sive praepositorum. [The preaching of John is recommended insofar as he takes into account the needs of a three-part populace. In dealing with this first point, that the audience contains three differentiated classes of people, he directs different instructions: first, to the mob, who act the role of the governed; second, to the publicans, who act the role of administrators; third, to the knights, who act the role of rulers or leaders.][11]

Inclusive and at the same time detailed class criticism is, therefore, characteristic of the Johannine homily.

Bonaventura is, of course, only one instance of the interpretation of Luke 3. But he brings together, without really adding a new point of view, the components that occur only individually in other ecclesiastical authors and in sermons. One may thus assume that he renders approximately the conceptions and associations that Gower could presuppose in his reading audience when he named his work VOX CLAMANTIS. In fact, all the mentioned characteristics of the Baptist's sermon recur in Gower's poem. He claims for his person the function of divine spokesman. He pitches the tone of his performance to zealous severity, although on occasion he shifts suddenly to sarcasm or sentimentality. In its essence[12] the poem is a critique of a class-organized society sub specie aeternitatis with the goal of its moral regeneration; therefore, it is not satire or class criticism, but increpatio after the manner of John. Its prelude is Book II, which speaks chiefly of the earlier fortune of the chosen people, of the English.[13] This is clearly a variation on the Father Abraham theme (Luke 3.8) in the Baptists's sermon, hence exhortatio. That they are the elect is no guarantee for either the children of Abraham or "God's own people" that the Lord will waive judgment for the sins of the present. There then follows a description of the bitterness and danger in the present situation.[14] It matches the Johannine threat that the axe has already been put to the root of the tree and is, according to Bonaventura, comminatio--actually comminatio de praesenti. To it Gower attaches a discussion of the question of blame that forms a natural transition to the class critique of Book III.[15] At the end of the work, in the 24th chapter of Book VII, the national theme returns, first in the poet's affirmation of his involvement in the national misfortune--one of the most beautiful sections of the work--[16] then in the threat of divine judgment upon the English people.[17] Thus one encounters here the Johannine comminatio de futuro, corresponding to the second half of Luke 3.9. Gower concludes with an exhortation to remorse and repentance that ends with a prayer for the forgiveness of sin.

Such are, in very concise fashion, the contents of the VOX CLAMANTIS with the exclusion of Book I. Such a content, tied to such a title, clearly refers the poem to the area of devotional literature. That in a total of approximately 8,000 verses there are other subjects woven in is obvious. There is, for instance, an exposition of the doctrine of the Trinity and an account of the creation of the world; the Last Judgment, Paradise, and Hell emerge in their turn, accompanied by an inspection of the deadly sins viewed sub specie mortis. It is a property of all these themes that they fit organically into the main theme when one views the poem as a Johannine homily. They are in no way digressions in which the author displays theological knowledge in unbridled liberality, without regard for his subject. They loosen the tightness of the structure, but they do not blur the clarity of the outline.

C. S. Lewis has pointed in another context to Gower's striking compositional talent.[18] His judgment is substantiated by the VOX CLAMANTIS. For a medieval work of its scope, the structure is astonishingly tight. Of course, this is not to Gower's credit alone. One must bear in mind that a centuries-old ecclesiastical tradition had made the material available to the author in a well thought out and orderly form. While the usually brief Sunday sermon allowed only modest possibilities, Lent, with its duty of a daily sermon, provided the great opportunity for clerics and monks to develop their oratorical gifts. Since the object of their efforts was to arouse remorse and penitence as preparation for the receiving of the Easter sacraments, they thoroughly and exhaustively developed the penitential theme, more intensively than almost any other part of Christian religious dogma with the possible exception of the Credo and Paternoster.

There were two basic forms of penitential sermon, which recur over and over in countless variations. Either the preacher chose the Seven Deadly Sins as a point of departure and treated them, be it concisely together with their complementary virtues, be it separately in their forms of appearance along with their earthly and heavenly consequences, or he used mankind as a point of departure and showed the classes with their special vices: the merchant in his avarice, the lawyer in his corruptibility, the soldier in his unbridled sensuality. Thus, for instance, all the examples which Alanus de Insulis attaches to his manual on the art of preaching break down into two groups: Sermones de Vitiis et Virtutibus and Sermones ad Status. The literature de vitiis et virtutibus receives a strong impetus in the thirteenth and fourteenth centuries,[19] perhaps because it became especially important when auricular confession was officially introduced as an obligation for both confessor and penitent.

Gower employed both sermon types literarily. His MIROUR DE L'OMME first deals de vitiis et virtutibus (1-18420), and then addresses itself to the individual classes (18421-26604). The VC, as we saw, is in the form of a Johannine class sermon. Certainly that is not to say that the VC is nothing but a versified sermon or sermon collection, although it seems conceivable that the appearance of versified sermons in the 14th century--they first became the fashion in England in the 15th--may have encouraged literary attempts in this direction. For our purposes it is sufficient to note that the VC conforms in content as well as in structure to the program that the title VOX CLAMANTIS promised to the contemporary reader.

Before we pass from the title of the work to the accompanying verses, we must again stop for a moment. An unexpected difficulty emerges when one follows the complex of the vox clamantis and its associations further, pursuing its appearance in the VOX CLAMANTIS and, beyond that, in Gower's total work. Its religious coloring seems to fade occasionally and instead there appears a distinct political shading. Often one cannot ascertain with certainty whether the author perceives himself, in his function as vox clamantis, as the spokesman of God or of the public opinion. He leaves it up to the reader to discern periodically, out of the ambivalence of the set phrase, the deciding component. This uncertainty has a very disturbing effect. It is not unreasonable to require of an author that he proclaim clearly whether he wishes to be understood as a homilist (the vox clamantis in a biblical sense) or as a political spokesman (the vox clamantis as representative of the public opinion). However, one forgets in making such a demand that there was no such alternative for Gower and his contemporaries.

For the modern reader the dilemma begins with the first mention of the book's title, that is, in the prologue of the second book. The author bases the choice of his title on the fact that his poem is a lamentation for the present time:
> Vox clamantis erit nomenque voluminis huius,
> Quod sibi scripta noui verba doloris habet.
> 2.Prol.83 f.
> [And the name of this volume shall be The Voice of One Crying, because the work contains a message of sorrow of today.]

The Latin prose summary of the prologue expands the explanation, stating that the two significant components of the formula vox clamantis derive from the concepts vox omnium and clamor omnium:

. . . e't vocat libellum istum Vox Clamantis,
quia de voce et clamore quasi omnium conceptus
est [And he calls this book The Voice of One
Crying, since it was conceived, as it were,
by a voice crying over all things].
While the distich thus links the title to the elegiac
character of the work, the prose summary presents the
author as spokesman of the public opinion. Both sig-
nifications unite in the prologue of the third book,
that is, at the start of the class critique proper,
where the author stresses in ever-varying expressions
that he writes down his lament over the moral decay
of the present not in his own person, but in a
faithful reproduction of the voice of the people:
A me non ipso loquor hec, set que michi plebis
Vox dedit, et sortem plangit vbique malam:
Vt loquitur vulgus loquor, et scribendo loquelam
Plango, quod est sanctus nullus vt ante status.
. . . . .
Nescio quis purum se dicet, plebs quia tota
Clamat iam lesum quemlibet esse statum.
                              3.Prol.11-14, 17-18
[I am not speaking of these things on my own
part; rather, the voice of the people has reported them to me, and it complains of their
adverse fate at every hand. I speak as the
masses speak, and even as I write I lament
over what I say, namely, that no estate is
pious as in days gone by . . . No matter who
he is, a man will say he is innocent, for the
whole population now cries out that every
estate is the injured party.]
Here the voice of the people is used in the sense of
consensus omnium or communis opinio. Its value for
Gower is that it serves him as an unimpeachable witness for the justification of a radical class critique. Through an accord with the public opinion he
gains simultaneously support for his person and
weight for his cause. He was already aware of its
value as a witness in the MIROUR, where the frequent recourse to public opinion nearly resembles
a stylistic cliche or a convenient verse filler.
However, it is more than that, and in certain passages shows itself to be related to the idea of
vox clamantis. When, for example, Gower introduces
the class critique of the MIROUR (18421-26604) with

an appeal to the consensus omnium, employing the dual
concept vois et cry, the manner of the expression
recalls the statement in the prologue of the VOX
CLAMANTIS' second book (de voce et clamore quasi
omnium conceptus) and the content recalls the above-
cited prologue of the third book:
>Ce que je pense escrire yci
>N'est pas par moy, ainz est ensi
>Du toute cristiene gent
>Murmur, compleinte, vois et cry;
>Que tous diont je ne desdi.   MIROUR 18445-49
>[What I intend to write here
>Is not by me, but is
>Of all Christian people
>The murmur, complaint, voice and cry;
>I don't contradict what all say.]

Later, in the prologue of the CONFESSIO AMANTIS, the
allusion to the voice of the people will confirm the
author's objectivity and credibility:
>The world is changed overal,
>And thereof most in special
>That love is falle into discord.
>And that I take to record
>Of every lond for his partie
>The comun vois, which may noght lie.
>>CONFESSIO, Prol.119-24

Most instances in which Gower identifies himself with
the public opinion or the voice of the people occur,
naturally enough, in the VOX CLAMANTIS. Without
claiming to have located all, I would like to cite
the following examples:
>Non ego sidereas affecto tangere sedes,
>Scribere nec summi mistica quero poli;
>Set magis, humana que vox communis ad extra
>Plangit in hac terra, scribo moderna mala.
>>3.Prol.53-56
>[I do not aspire to reach the thrones of
>heaven, or seek to describe the mysteries
>of the lofty skies. Rather, I write of
>present-day evils which the common voice
>of mankind outwardly complains of in this
>country.]
>Non erit in dubio mea vox clamans, erit omnis
>Namque fides huius maxima vocis homo. 3.Prol.79-80
>[My crying voice will not hesitate, for every
>man will be a great warrant for its utterance.]

Hec ego que dicam dictum commune docebat,
Nec mea verba sibi quid nouitatis habent. 3.1269-70
[Common talk has taught me what I shall
say, and my words contain nothing new.]
Est nichil ex sensu proprio quod scribo, set ora
Que michi vox populi contulit, illa loquar. 4.19-20
[Nothing that I write is my own opinion;
rather, I shall speak what the voice of the
people has reported to me.]
Talibus iste liber profert sua verba modernis,
Vt sibi vox populi contulit illa loqui. 4.709-10
[. . . to such men of the present this book
offers its message, since the voice of the
people furnished the things for it to say.]
Hoc ego quod plebis vox clamat clamo, nec vllos,
Sint nisi quos crimen denotat, ipse noto. 6.15-16
[I cry out what the voice of the people cries
out, and I take note of none except those
whom wickedness stigmatizes.]

The first passage mentions the vox communis in the
context of exposition, the second refers to the public opinion (omnis homo="everyman") as witness to
the veracity of the class critique; the rest are designed to defend the author against the charge of
selfish intention or personal animosity.

The voice of the people has a more political
sound and a more direct relevance to the present
in the frame of the Mirror for a Prince in Book VI,
in which instance the A- and B-Texts differ. The
introduction in the B-Text has both vox populi and
vox plebis:
Nunc magis in specie vox plebis clamat vbique
Pectore sub timido que metuenda fero.
6.545-46, B-Text
[Now in particular does the voice of the
people cry out, and I have fears within my
trembling breast.]
Talia vox populi conclamat vbique moderni
In dubio positi pre grauitate mali:
Sic ego condoleo super hiis que tedia cerno,
Quo Regi puero scripta sequenda fero.
6.577-80, B-Text
[Everywhere the voice of the people of today,
who are placed in doubt in the face of the

enormity of evil, cries out about such things.
I accordingly grieve even more than they over
the disgusting things which I see, for which
reason I offer the following writings for the
boy king.]
The B-Text also appeals to the vox plebis at the end
of the open letter to the king:
Nunc tamen in plebe vox est, quod deficiente
Lego dolus iura vendicat esse sua. 6.1179-80, B-Text
[Nevertheless, there is a cry nowadays among
the people that because the law is failing,
wrongdoing claims to be its own justification.]
The earlier redaction, the A-Text, has only one passage to set against these three and it speaks not
of the vox plebis or populi, but of the vox clamantis:
Nunc magis ecce refert verbi clamantis ad aures
Vox, et in hoc dicit tempore plura grauant.
6.545-46, A-Text
[Behold, a voice of doleful expression now
speaks to the ears, and it says that there
are many burdens in these days.]
The interpretation of the original version is unsure
because the grammatical referent of the two geni-
tives verbi and clamantis cannot be clearly determined. Nevertheless, one thing is certain: however
the author may originally have intended the lines,
the possible biblical assoication vanishes before
the emphatic repetition of the voice of the people
in the later B-Text revision. Does that indicate
a change in Gower's attitude toward his theme? And
if such should be the case, how is it to be explained?

      It is not our task here to show how the four-
teenth-century English commoner gradually developed
and constantly increased in importance as a political and social factor. Also, we must expediently
relinquish to the historian the question of the
influence which the public opinion--or, to remain
in the usage of the time, the voice of the people--
exerted on contemporary politics. That Gower con-
tinually worked with concepts such as vox populi,
clamor populi (in the VOX CLAMANTIS), commun vois,
commun clamour (in the CONFESSIO AMANTIS) and
commune voys, commune tesmoygnance du poeple (in
the MIROUR DE L'OMME) demonstrates to us that a

political slogan of this kind was readily available.
In every passage where Gower employs the vox populi,
it acts as a lament or grievance, that is, as a
negative critique of existing conditions. The necessity and urgency of reform are confirmed through the
witness of the people's voice; however, a positive
program of reform is never drafted in its name. Nor
is the possibility of self-help for the oppressed,
if the voice of the people should remain unheard,
a part of Gower's conception of the divine ordo.
Thus, as political factors, the vox communis and
clamor populi are considerably limited in their
direct efficacy. Nevertheless, we must not under-
estimate the significance of the triple appeal to
the people's voice in the later version of the
Mirror for a Prince. The latent threat expressed
in the clamor populi is not, to be sure, directly
political in nature, but metaphysically anchored
and thereby doubly important. This threat arises
from the correspondence of the voice of the people
with the voice of God. The lament of the common
people is heard by God, and God, not the people,
threatens the ruler if he refuses to listen:
        Vox populi cum voce dei concordat, vt ipsa
        In rebus dubiis sit metuenda magis. 3.1267-68
        [The voice of the people agrees with the
        voice of God, so that in critical times it
        ought to be held in greater awe.]
Thus Gower moves completely along biblical paths of
thought. The Psalter above all is rich in allusions
to God as the protector of the poor against the
arrogance of the mighty. The Ninth Psalm [9.10, 13]
says of the clamor pauperum:
        Et factus est Dominus refugium pauperum,
        adjutor in opportunitatibus et in tribula-
        tiones . . . non est oblitus clamorem pauperum
        [And the Lord is become a refuge for the poor:
        a helper in due time in tribulation . . . he
        hath not forgotten the cry of the poor].
In 9.17-19 the connection between the clamor populum
and God's justice is disclosed:
        Cognoscetur Dominus judicia faciens: in
        operibus manum suarum comprehensus est
        peccator. Convertantur peccatores in infer-
        num, omnes gentes, quae obliviscuntur Deum.

Quoniam non in finem oblivio erit pauperis:
patientia pauperis non peribit in finem.
[The Lord shall be known when he executeth
judgments: the sinner hath been caught in
the works of his own hands. The wicked
shall be turned into hell, all the nations
that forget God. For the poor man shall not
be forgotten to the end: the patience of
the poor shall not perish for ever.]
Yet, not only biblical trains of thought are present,
but also concrete historical allusions, appropriate
because they give emphasis to the vox populi in the
crisis years of Richard II's reign.

The formula vox populi, vox dei already had a
political past at the time. It had played a role
in the history of England for the first time in
the events of 1327, at which time a legitimate English king was deposed in a kind of civil proceeding
and his son chosen as his successor. We know little
of the constitutional basis of the event. However,
Walsingham, who is a reliable source, reports that
the Archbishop of Canterbury, after consenting to
the choice with the rest of the prelates, sought to
win the concurrence of the people to the accession
of Edward III through a public sermon on the theme
vox populi, vox dei.[20] As a sermon theme it is unusual, for according to ecclesiastical practice the
theme of a sermon was always to be taken from the
Bible. The unusual situation obviously caused the
unusual choice of text.[21] To reason a posteriori
about the political significance which the archbishop attributed to the theme is, moreover, possible.
The parallels between Edward II and Richard II, as
far as character and fate are concerned, lie ready
to hand, and may already have been noted in Richard's
lifetime. In this connection it is perhaps no accident that Gower placed the greatest stress on the
importance of the people's voice in his poem "O Deus
Immense,"[22] which according to the witness of three
manuscripts is his last poem under the rule of
Richard II. It gives, in one hundred four wretched
leonines, the skeleton of a speculum principis that
agrees essentially in all important respects with
that of the VOX CLAMANTIS, although in tone far
more impersonal and importunately schoolmarmish.

81

The poem distinguishes itself from the analogous
section of the VOX CLAMANTIS in distribution of
emphasis by extolling the significance of the people's
voice more conspicuously:

Consilio tali regnum magis in speciali
Vndique turbatur, quo Regis honor variatur:
Nunc ita sicut heri poterit res ista videri,
Vnde magis plangit populus, quem lesio tangit.
. . . .
Set qui prescire vult causas, expedit ire,
Plebis et audire voces per easque redire:
Si sit in errore Regis vel in eius honore,
Hoc de clamore populi prefertur ab ore.
. . . .
Nomen regale populi vox dat tibi, quale
Sit, bene siue male, deus illud habet speciale.
Rex qui tutus eris, si temet noscere queris,
Ad vocem plebis aures sapienter habebis.
                    O Deus Immense, 43-46; 53-56; 61-64
[By such counsel, especially, is the kingdom
Disturbed on every side, and the honor of the
                              king marred:
The same thing can be seen today,
For which reason the people, whom the injury
                         touches, complain more.
. . . .
But he who wishes to discover the causes
                    hastens to go
And hear the voices of the people, and returns
                              to them:
Whether it concern the error of the king, or
                              his honor,
This clamor of the people should be voiced.
. . . .
The voice of the people gives you the royal name,
Such as it is, whether good or bad, and God pays
                         special attention to it.
You who would be secure as a king, if you wish
                    to know yourself,
You will wisely have ears for the voice of the
                              people.]

This glorification of the people's voice sounds,
in the last years of Richard II, especially relevant
and critical. That is not only because Gower con-

fers a somewhat prophetic nature upon it (53 f.: Set
que prescire vult causas . . .), or because he recommends it to the king as the surest source of self-
knowledge, but because he links it in a politically
taut situation with the voice of God (61 f.) so that
at least in retrospect it operates as a warning
against a repetition of the events of 1327. Gower
himself may hardly have been aware of the immediate
relevance of his precept of the vox populi. He often
appeals to the public opinion only in an attempt to
protect himself from the charge of personal malice.
When, however, in the late version of the Vox
Clamantis and in the last poem to Richard II he
reaches the point at which he sees the manifestation of a divine judgment in the witness of the
people's voice, he thus unites the two apparently
so different meanings of vox clamantis. Whether the
poet steps forward as spokesman of God or as representative of the public opinion, his words are up-
held in either case by the weight of a divine warning to reverse course.

We have seen which function the title **VOX
CLAMANTIS** assigned the author, both with reference
to the medieval sermon and to Gower's own conception.
The accompanying verses that precede the text in
three manuscripts of the **VOX CLAMANTIS** show him in
another role. These verses were probably located
between the summary of contents and the headnote of
Book I[23] in all the B-Text MSS, whereas neither
summary nor accompanying verses survived in the
two A-Text MSS.[24] The contaminated MS L has them,
surprisingly, in another place, namely at the beginning of the third book. They read the same in
all four MSS:
     Ad mundum mitto mea iacula, dumque sagitto;
     At vbi iustus erit, nulla sagitta ferit.
     Sed male viuentes hos vulnero transgredientes;
     Conscius ergo sibi se speculetur ibi.
     [I hurl my darts at the world and I shoot my
                                             arrows;
     Yet where there is a just man, no arrow strikes.
     But I wound those transgressors who live evilly;
     Therefore, let him who is conscious of being in
                                          the wrong
     Look to himself in that respect.]

83

The verses are accompanied by a miniature that shows
an archer, possibly representing the author himself,
taking aim at a mappa mundi which, according to the
customary scheme, appears in three parts.[25] This
geographical division into thirds accords with familiar medieval notions about the division of society
into three classes. If L should actually have preserved the original arrangement, the verses are ad-
mirably suited to the beginning of the third book,
at which point the class critique begins with the
old tripartite division of clericus, miles, cultor.
The prologue of Book III also agrees with the motto,
placing great emphasis upon the assurance that the
author will attack no class as such, but only the
evil-doers within a class.[26] Unfortunately, L is
not to be trusted. Nevertheless, it is clear by
the contents that the verses belong to the VC: their
theme is so unlike that of the Visio that they cannot have been generated by the enlargement of the
VC through the Visio. It is more comprehensible
that a motto be shifted to the new beginning of a
work upon a rewriting of its opening than that it
should be shifted from the beginning to the third
book without a cogent reason. The absence of the
lines from the A-Text in no way proves that they
were first written for the B-Text. Indeed, the
B-Text is aligned with the political tendency of
the **CRONICA TRIPERTITA** and is no longer as strongly
interested in the class critique. Their absence in
the A-Text is connected rather with the omission of
the summary that precedes the motto. However, because the summary of the B-Text is clearly taken
over from the A-Redaction--although in no preserved
MS of the A-Redaction does a summary of contents
exist--[27]it is likely that the accompanying verses
which followed the summary also had their origin
there, although they disappeared along with the
summary from TH$_2$.

Whatever the fate of the accompanying verses
in the successive development of the VOX CLAMANTIS,
this much is certain: according to their contents,
and probably also according to manuscript evidence,
they belonged to the VC. One must not overlook
them when one seeks an explanation of the work's
objective.

Two images underlie the verses: the archer
(1-3) and the mirror (implicit in 4). The mirror
metaphor is more hinted at than realized, but in-
telligible without more ado since it is in accordance with the taste of the times[28] and is used by
Gower in his three major works.[29] The archer, however, does not appear elsewhere in his writing. In
this passage he appears to be more important than
the mirror, for three lines as well as the miniature
are allotted to him. It must be asked what led
Gower to the choice of precisely this role and how
it is compatible with the concept vox clamantis.

At first glance the archer has two associations that have little enough to do with the voice
of one crying in the wilderness. The archer is the
embodiment of English national military strength
around the turn of the 14th century, to whom the
great victories in France were owed. Could Gower
have chosen this emblem in order to emphasize the
national character of his class critique? The
likelihood is slim, since ad mundum mitto does not
permit of a unilateral national interpretation.
Besides, neither class critique nor speculum
principis is nationally restricted in the late
Middle Ages.[30] Nor is the archer's other association, which is based on the form of the statement,
much more helpful. Did the author wish to emphasize that his critique would rain down upon its
victim like a shower of arrows? Certainly he had
something of that sort in mind; however, the core
of the idea is derived from elsewhere.

The life of man is, according to good biblical
tradition, a constant war against the world, the
flesh, and the devil; psychomachia is therefore
one of the chief forms of religious allegory from
Prudentius to Bunyan. Mankind must be armed for
this war, and again it is the Bible that describes
the symbolic armor, most fully in the Epistle to
the Ephesians (6.11-17). Although Paul has in
mind the heavily armed Roman legionaire rather than
an archer, here nevertheless lies the point of departure from which the medieval fancy could develop
unhindered.

There is attributed to Bonaventura a work en-
titled PHARETRA,[31] the first book of which discusses
the classes and the second the virtues and vices,
which explains its title thus, that here as in a
quiver may be found the arrows of ecclesiastical
auctoritates (church fathers and biblical citations)
with which the reader can overcome the archenemy.[32]
The PHARETRA, therefore, provides an analogous view
of a subject closely related to that of the VC. One
difference, to be sure, must not be overlooked: the
book is considered an arsenal from which the warring
Christian--who is the warrior, not the object of
war--can withdraw for his own needs the iacula, the
missiles of patristic maxims. However, I wish to
emphasize the equation of iacula with auctoritates,
with biblical and patristic passages, since we
thereby enter into the broad tradition of ecclesiastical conceptions. The quiver, on the other hand,
may be the anonymous author's individual development upon the general conceptual basis.

The image of the word of God as a sword or
spear or arrow occurs in the Old as well as the New
Testament,[33] from whence it is transmitted to the
sermon. The preacher is thus assigned the role
of soldier when, for example, in the HOMILIES
Gregory the Great interprets the text (freely after
Habakkuk 3.11) In lumine jacula tua ibunt, in
splendore fulguris armorum tuorum [In the light of
your arrows they shall go, in the brightness of thy
glittering spear] in the following manner: Jacula
Domini sunt verba Sanctorum, quae corda peccantium
feriunt [the spears of the Lord are the words of the
saints, which strike the hearts of sinners];[34] or
when Honorius of Autun remarks: Verbum praedicationis
per simile dicitur gladius vel ensis, quia sicut
gladius animam a corpore separat [the word of a
sermon is said to be like a sword, because like a
sword it severs the soul from the body].[35] The object of the battle is the sinful man, or else the
sins or the devil himself; the weapons are the words
of God. Cardinal Humbert de Romanis depicts in his
manual the military service of the preacher as
follows:
Item praedicatores dicuntur milites Christi,
propter quod dicitur 2. Tim. 2 [2.3]: Labora

sicut bonus miles Christi: Glossa praedicando,
unde autem praedicando militare dicuntur?
Quia sic errores tam infidelitatis quam morum
regi suo contrarios, debellant.
[Thus preachers are said to be soldiers of
Christ, because it is said in 2 Timothy 2:
Conduct thyself in work as a good soldier of
Christ Jesus: Gloss for preaching; why, however, are they said to do battle by preaching?
Because thus they fight against the errors of
unfaithfulness, just as in the manner of kings
against their enemies.][36]
Bromyard writes (s.v. praedicator), concerning the
manner in which such a champion should use his weapons:
Sermo namque domini quandoque in sacra scriptura sagittae comparatur, Sap. 5 [5.22]. Sagitta
emissa in locum destinatum. Sagittam vero ad
hoc, quod feram occidat, sagittarius ita prope
ad cor dirigere nititur, sicut potest, quia hoc
est utilius pro eo: quia illo citius feram oc-
cidit. Sic volens vitam in peccatore destruere
bestialem, utilius sagittas verborum ad cor
quam ad aures dirigat . . . Patet ergo, quod
sermo efficaciter ad cor directus est utilior:
quia talia verba plures humiliant peccatores,
de quibus dicit Psal. 43. Sagittae tuae acutae,
populi sub te cadent, quia sc. diriguntur in
corda inimicorum regis. Quod autem tales sagittae spirituales plures a statu superbiae et
vacuitatis, quibus contra Deum eriguntur, ad
gradum humilitatis cadere et colla sub iugo
Christi humiliter submittere faciant, sequent-
ibus ostenditur exemplis. [For the word of
God in Sacred Scripture is occasionally likened
to an arrow, Wisdom 5 [5.22]. An arrow aimed
at a definite target. So that it kill the wild
beast, the bowman endeavors to guide the arrow
as near to the heart as he is able, since that
is more beneficial to him, because by that he
kills the beast more quickly. Thus wishing to
destroy the bestial life in the sinner, he directs the arrows of words more beneficially to
the heart than to the ears . . . It is obvious,
therefore, that words effectively directed to
the heart are more beneficial: because such
words humble more sinners, concerning whom

87

Psalm 43 [44.6] says, thy arrows are sharp,
under thee shall people fall, because of course
they are shot into the hearts of the king's
enemies. The following stories show, moreover, that such arrows strike down many souls
from a state of pride and emptiness, by which
they raise themselves against God, to a degree of humility, and make them humbly submit
their necks under the yoke of Christ.]

Six such exempla follow, to which Bromyard attaches the observation that simple sermons are most
useful for this purpose:
et . . . sic praedicantibus, sicut dicitur in
ps. 67 [67.12], Dominus dabit verbum evangel-
izantibus virtute multa, et . . . sub talibus
sagittis plures cadunt et humiliantur peccatores [and . . . thus to those preaching, just
as it is said in Psalm 67, the Lord shall give
the word to them that preach good tidings with
great power, and . . . many sinners shall be
felled and humbled under such arrows].
When Bromyard, the contemporary and countryman of
Gower, speaks of the homilist as an archer, one can
be certain that the image is common ecclesiastical
property. The great advantage of the Bromyardian
SUMMA for our purposes is that, by all standards of
vivacious expression and presentation, it is so completely unoriginal and mediocre. It thus makes possible a glance into the spiritual public property
of the time.

Gower's accompanying verses come remarkably
close to a passage from Thomas Waley's DE MODO COM-
PONENDI SERMONES. The English monk-preacher speaks
of the priests' charges and complaints that their
vices were ruthlessly denounced in public sermons
by the mendicant friars, and recommends a careful
choice of subject with regard to the composition
of the audience. It is the old principle of the
sermon ad status: one should preach about the transgressions of the clergy in the synod, about the sins
of the secular classes in the parish church. Difficulties arise only with a mixed audience. In this
case one should deal with those vices common to both
parties, that is, with the universal human vices.

Whoever should then feel attacked has only himself
to blame; no reproach can attach to the preacher.
For just as a soldier who practices archery in an
authorized place cannot be blamed if he should
wound someone who steps without authorization into
the target area, so likewise is the preacher not
to be blamed if he in a similarly appointed place
should shoot his arrows toward his target--sin or
the devil--and so wound someone who has toyed all
too closely with them:

> signum vero ad quod sagittat [sc. praedicator]
> est peccatum vel diabolus. Nullus igitur ibi
> aut prope stet, et nullus vulnerabitur aut
> laedetur [The target at which he shoots is sin
> or the devil. Therefore no one should stand
> there or close by and no one will be wounded
> or killed].[37]

Here the notion of the religious archer is already
formed even down to the particulars and, as in
Gower, combined with a protest against the charge
of character assassination.

The two conceptions of the preacher, as a vox
clamantis on the one hand and as a sagittarius on
the other, are therefore not only compatible with
one another: they interlock. If the title VOX
CLAMANTIS suggests John the Baptist, it is because
John is one of those of whom Gregory said:

> Jacula Domini sunt verba Sanctorum, quae
> corda peccantium feriunt [The spears of the
> Lord are the words of the saints, which
> strike the hearts of sinners].

A baptismal sermon of St. Martin relates the words
of Isaiah [49.12], Posuit me sicut sagittam electam
[he hath made me as a chosen arrow], to John the
Baptist: . . . non immerito etiam et Joannes sagitta electa est [. . . for I am unworthy and John
is the chosen arrow].[38] The transference of the
designation sagitta from the word of God to the
preaching of His word and, further, to the herald
of his word does not indicate a discrepancy between
Gregory and Martin. The allegorical interpretation
of the term vox, which points sometimes to the content of what has been said and sometimes to the
speaker, undergoes a similar metonymical shift.

The coexistence of several allegorical references disturbed no medieval reader.

The quotations cited do not have the purpose of suggesting Gower's dependence upon this or that author; they should convey only generally the conceptual milieu upon which he drew. He could, therefore, despite the brevity of reference, depend on his reader to understand the intention of his work; whereas the modern reader, not knowing the homiletic background, is apt to overlook the consciousness of and claim to divine mission upon which the seemingly secular lines are based. The vox clamantis and the sagittarius derive from the same tradition of the medieval sermon and testify to the poet's special task in this work.

B. The Topology of the Prologue

It is now time to return to a question which was left unanswered in the preceding section. We have seen that, with the formula vox clamantis and in the archer verses, Gower puts himself in the role of Christian homilist. Up to now we have not examined his qualifications for that role. The traditional places in which to obtain information about an author's own view of his function are prologue and epilogue. The VC contains two prologues, at the beginnings of Books II and III, and an epilogue, in Chapter 25 of Book VII.

An analysis of the prologues leads immediately to a dilemma. The late medieval reader looks for a work's four causae in a prologue, the modern reader for exordial topoi, both executed according to Mathew 7.7 [Ask, and it shall be given you; seek, and you shall find; knock, and it shall be opened to you]. There are, moreover, no certain criteria with which to distinguish topos from actual self-expression. Let us, to begin with, treat the prologue of the second book after the medieval method of interpretation.

The old quis, quid, cur, etc. formula of the rhetoricians appears to have found its way in the Middle Ages from the narratio to the prooemium. One required from a prologue information about the author, the subject, and the purpose of the work. The classical tradition--in this case the suasive-- is still clearly perceptible in the twelfth century in Honorius of Autun, who begins his commentary on the Song of Solomon:

, In principiis librorum tria requiruntur, sc. auctor, materia, intentio. Auctor, ut noveris nomen scriptoris, utrum ethnicus, an fidelis, utrum catholicus an haeriticus fuerit. Materia, ut scias utrum de bellis an de nuptiis vel de quibus rebus tractat. Intentio, ut cognoscas utrum rem de qua tractet suadeat vel dissuadeat, vel liber lectus quid utilitatis conferat. [Three things are required in the beginnings of books, namely author, subject, and purpose. The author, so that

91

you know whether he discusses war or marriage
or whatever. The purpose, so that you recognize whether he persuades or dissuades about
the subject, or, after the book is read, what
profit it has bestowed.][1]
Honorius employs no fixed terminology for these three
prologue requisites, whereas by the thirteenth century there are employed the designations causa efficiens, causa materialis, and causa finalis--to
which a fourth is added in case of need, the causa
formalis. Thus, for example, Robert de Basevorn
speaks of the four causae in his sermon manual as
of something universally known:
    . . . praesumpsi prosequi quod incepi, ab
    eadem [sc. re] nimirum judicans inchoandum,
    in qua quattuor hujus operis causae poterunt
    assignari quae in librorum principiis annotari
    solebant [I made bold to continue what I had
    begun, rightly judging that I must begin from
    the place in which could be assigned the four
    causes of this work, such as are usually noted
    in introductions].[2]
Honorius and Robert are ecclesiastical authors and
occupy themselves with ecclesiastical subjects: the
one with biblical exegesis, the other with sermon
composition. However, their model is also appropriate for works of a secular character, for example,
works of history. In an earlier chapter we had
occasion to concern ourselves with the John of
Bridlington prophesies.[3] These consist of an intentionally dark and oracular verse text from the
1370's accompanied by a prose commentary, both of
which probably stemmed from the same author. The
anonymous commentator occupies himself not only
with the contentual difficulties of his text, but
also enters with praiseworthy thoroughness upon
stylistic and compositional questions. Thus in
his first preamble he deals with the four causae
of the work, at first concisely, and then explains
them in his interpretation of the prooemium with
the help of the text. For example, he explains the
line Jussit de bellis me metrificare novellis [He
commanded me to make verses about new wars] in the
following manner:
    . . . notandum est quod in isto versu notantur
    tres causae hujus prophetiae. Primo, causa

efficiens, i. jussit me, i. Spiritus Sanctus
jussit me factorem esse hujus libri; secundo,
causa formalis, quando dicit metrificare, i.
scribere per metrum quia est forma hujus
libri; tertio, causa materialis, qui [sic]
dicit de bellis novellis, de quibus tanquam
de causa materiali in isto libro tractatur.
[. . . it must be observed that in these lines
are noted the three causes of this prophecy.
First, the efficient cause, that is, "he commanded me," that is, the Holy Spirit commanded
me to be the maker of this book; second, the
formal couse, when he said "to write verse,"
that is, to write in the meter which is the
form of this book; third, the material cause,
when he says "concerning new wars," with which
as it were concerning the material cause this
book deals.]4

In addition to the four causae, the commentator
also uses the opportunity to provide four regulae
according to which the text should be received and
understood by the reader. They are not unimportant
for an understanding of Gower's prologue, and generally for the evaluation of certain topoi, and
should therefore be quickly glanced at. They are
contained in the following grotesque lines:
    Si verum scribam, verum crede me fore scribam;
    Scripsero si vanum, caput est quia non mihi
                                                sanum.
    Non mihi detractes, sed falsa per omnia mactes.
    Nullus deliro credat pro carmine miro.
    [If I write the truth, believe me I write the
                                        truth by chance;
    If I shall have written something useless it
                            is because I am not well.
    You should not blame me, but destroy the false
                                            throughout.
    Let no man trust to a crazy man for a miraculous
                                                song.]5
The first line indicates that what is true in these
prophecies should be attributed to the Holy Ghost,
and not to the author: . . . et in hoc vitat arro-
gantiam, quod sibi non attribuit quod deo est at-
tribuendum [. . . and in this he avoids arrogance,
because he does not attribute to himself what must

93

be attributed to God]. The first rule is thus obvious: avoid false presumption. The second line
states that all falsehoods and errors are to be
charged to the author, who lies sick in bed:
> Et hic incurrit humilitatem, quia sibi
> assumit defectus eos a Deo removendo in
> quo nulla mala vel imperfecta inveniuntur
> [And here he practices humility, because
> he takes upon himself the defects, re-
> moving them from God, in whom nothing
> imperfect or incomplete is found].

The second rule is thus the counterpart of the first:
take responsibility for all errors. The third line
is directed against the detractores, the slanderers,
and solicits the correction of possible errors:
> Et ibi excludit praesumptiones auditorum,
> qui proniores sunt ad detrahendum quam ad
> laudandum facta aliorum vel corrigendum
> [And thus he prevents presumption in the
> listeners, who are more inclined to the
> slander of others than to their praise or
> correction].

The third rule is thus a rebuff of the slanderer
and a request for correction. The fourth rule is
especially tailored to the genre of the prophecy,
and is designed to protect the author against the
astutias sapientum mundi[6] [the foolish wisdom of
the worldly wise], who consider his story a delirium.
The four regulae thus concern the moral posture of
the author and his reader vis-a-vis the work.[7] The
author's choice is between arrogantia and humilitas;
the moral danger for the reader lies in praesumptio,
detractatio, and astutia. Here ideas are brought
together in a pattern which emerges again and again
in medieval prologues and which we shall also encounter forthwith in Gower.

If one wishes to consider Gower's prologue in
a contemporary sense, one must make clear its three
or four causae and look for its regulae. The term
causa occurs twice verbatim in the prologue of Book
II, once as causa materialis: Et visus varii sunt
michi causa libri (2.Prol.80) [And my several visions are the reason for the book], and again as
causa finalis:

Quicquid ad interius morum scriptura propinat,
Doctrine causa debet habere locum. 2.Prol.43-44
[Whatever morality a piece of writing supplies
for your inner being ought to have its place,
for the sake of its teachings.]8
If one wishes, one can analyze the entire prologue
according to these categories: 1) causa materialis
(1-2, 75-84), 2) causa efficiens (3-8, 65-74),
3) causa finalis (9-20,9 43-46), 4) causa formalis
(21-30). The four causae are treated successively.
Then follows a passage in which the rule concerning
the author's humilitas frames the rule contra detractores, in the midst of which are inserted in
their turn two distiches concerning the causa finalis.
A kind of chiasmus arrangement thus emerges: A (humilitas 31-32), B (contra detractores 35-41), C (causa
finalis 43-46), B (47-52), A (53-64). The causa
efficiens and causa materialis are defined once
again at the end, more fully than in the beginning.

When an author accommodates himself so completely to a traditional pattern as Gower has done
here, it is to be expected that he will also follow
traditional paths in the argument. Actually, the
prologue of Book II is so crammed with Curtius'
topoi that it creates the impression it is no more
than a motley heap of conventional banalities. A
quck survey reveals the following topoi:
1. Rejection of the appeal to the muses and
   invocatio of the Christian God: 3-10.
2. Modesty formulae:
   A. Res non persona: 11-14
   B. Precious vein in base mineral: 15-18
   C. Ignorance: 21-30
   D. Balaam's ass: 45 f.
3. Torpor: 31 f.
4. Contrast between age and youth: 33-40
5. Knowledge is an obligation: 53-60
   A. Sparks beneath the ashes: 55 f.
   B. The light under the bushel: 57 f.
6. The work as an offering: 61-66
7. Prayer for divine assistance: 67-74.

The prologue of Book III enters more vigorously
into the contents of the work and is thus less conventional. Its structure is based on a principle

of doubling. The first paragraph (1-22) contains
three themes:
    1. The division of society into three estates;
    2. The directing of the critique at issues,
       not people;
    3. The establishment of the poet as spokesman.
The second paragraph (23-36) then handles the same
themes in reverse order (3,2,1). After a connecting
link that expresses in a mildly allegorical tone the
poet's wish that God allow his seed to bear fruit
(37-42), there occurs another, final doubling in
the form of two prayers (49-70 and 83-104) that are
interrupted by an interpolated apostrophe to the
reader and a farewell to the book (71-82). Another
topos then forms the conclusion: the poet puts to
sea and begs the Holy Ghost to fill the sails.

    Because a work employs topoi does not necessarily
imply its inferiority. To be sure, they do have in
times of literary sterility a tendency to be transmitted like an endless disease and thus fall easily
into disrepute. However, it is only their misuse
which discredits them. The problem that must concern us here is: are Gower's topoi conventional forms
whose content has already become torpid, or are they
traditional means of expression whose vigor was preserved in or perhaps even sprang anew from areas
with which they historically had nothing in common?
Topoi, as Curtius has convincingly shown in the
example of the aged boy, originate in a certain
psychological situation.[10] Cannot a new psychology,
of an individual or general sort, avail itself of
an already rigidified topos and breathe new life
into it? It would be good if one could pursue the
inner history of a topos alongside of its outer.
One would at the same time have to feel its pulse
and observe how its life surges and ebbs as it
changes through the centuries. It may chance even
with literary figures of the second order, like
Gower, that traditional ballast is given a living
function. I would like to demonstrate this with
a few examples, especially of prayer and the modesty formula, from the VOX CLAMANTIS.

    The prayer and the modesty formula belong, ac-
cording to their origins, to two different categories:

the prayer, as a Christian variant of the appeal to
the muses, to the stilus grandis of the epic, the
modesty formula to the means of captatio benevolentiae
which Cicero recommends for the prooemium of an ora-
tion before a court of law. When Curtius warned,
in his controversy with Schwietering about protestations of humility, against making the Middle
Ages more Christian than they actually had been,
he doubtless was historically correct.[11] It remains
only to ask whether form and content are so inex-
tricably bound together that in the course of development a newer and, in this case, specifically
more Christian content could not have availed itself of the inherited form. For example, the wording of the first two regulae in John of Bridlington
establishes the literary humilitas of the author
in relation to God and not to the reader, thus in-
dicating that Christian and literary humility are
perhaps basically inseparable.

However, we shall begin with the beginning,
with the invocatio which introduces the prologue
of Book II of the **VOX CLAMANTIS**, that is, the prologue of the VC. It reads:
> Non tamen inceptis ego musas inuoco, nec diis
> Immolo, set solo sacrificabo deo.
> Spiritus alme deus, accendens pectore sensus,
> Intima tu serui pectoris vre tui:
> Inque tuo, Criste, laxabo nomine rethe,
> Vt mea mens capiat que sibi grata petit.
> Inceptum per te perfecto fine fruatur
> Hoc opus ad laudem nominis, oro, tui. 2.Prol.3-10
> [I do not invoke the muses for my undertaking,
> however, nor do I make offering to the gods.
> But I shall sacrifice to God alone. Merciful
> God of the spirit, fire the innermost depths
> of Thy servant's breast, kindling the feelings
> in his heart. In Thy name, O Christ, I shall
> spread my net, so that my mind may thankfully
> seize upon the things which it requires. I
> pray that this work, begun with Thy help for
> the praise of Thy name, may achieve a fitting
> conclusion.]
The situation is perfectly clear from the standpoint
of literary criticism. The rejection of the appeal
to the muses, together with the first distich's

application to God in its stead, is a topos. The
poet's enthousiasmos in the second distich is no
less so. The third distich is based on a New Testament metaphor (John 21.6 and Matthew 4.19 are obviously combined), and the fourth represents yet
another topos. Thus the invocatio is conventional,
patched together from four topoi. What could be
more devastating for the valuation of the author?
The impression that the invocatio is little more
than a cliche is reinforced by the recurrence of
two invocations at the end of Book III's prologue,
the specific value of which is hardly increased
by the verbatim borrowing of an entire distich
from Peter Riga's AURORA.[12]

   And yet these prayers are something other than
ornaments of an attempted high style. They also
go beyond the common Christian view that the aid of
God is necessary to the success of every human work.
Rather, they receive their import from the tradition
and the metaphysical mooring of the sermon.

   The structure of the contemporary sermon provides for, in addition to the traditional opening
and closing prayers, an invocatio at the end of the
prothema. After the reading of the sermon text
(the thema) follows a second, shorter Bible text
(the prothema), which is loosely bound to the thema
through the transference of a word or idea and whose
usually brief treatment has the purpose of leading
up to the prayer. The thema is repeated after the
prayer, and the sermon proper, with its divisiones
and subdivisiones, can then begin. In scope and
function the prothema and its execution perform the
part of a prologue.[13] The influence of the sermon
may be indicated when, in addition to an opening
and closing prayer, an invocatio appears at the
end rather than at the beginning of Book III's pro-
logue--where it can hardly be a substitute for an
appeal to the muses.[14]

   Now there would obviously be little gained if
one separated a topos such as the invocatio from
one tradition only to enclose it in another. What
is essential is the functional distinction between
the literary prayer and the sermon prayer. The

literary prayer became in the course of its development an arabesque affixed to a work, an embellishing ornament from which the existence of the poem is basically independent, that is, a topos in a mildly deprecative sense. The sermon prayer was spared such a degradation because it is not ornamentation, but prerequisite for and foundation of every sermon. An epic without an appeal to the muses is conceivable; a sermon without prayer loses its import. According to the Christian view, no man can convert another: the words are the preacher's, but the work of salvation God's alone. According to Matthew 10.20, God is the causa efficiens, the preacher the causa secundaria: Non enim vos estis, qui loquimini, sed spiritus patris vestri, qui loquitur in vobis [For it is not you who are speaking, but the Spirit of your Father who speaks through you].[15]

The sermon presupposes two divine graces that must be requested anew upon each occasion: the gratia sermonis for the preacher, the gratia auditus for the listener. It is not enough if, with the help of the gratia sermonis, the preacher speak well. Without the aid of the special gratia auditus the listener will be incapable of really absorbing what has been said. According to one of Gregory's remarks that was much quoted in the Middle Ages:

> formare vocem magistri exterius possunt, sed hanc imprimere interius non possunt. Nisi Spiritus Sanctus corda audientium repleat, ad aures corporum vox docentium incassum sonat [Teachers are able to form the outer voice, but they are not able to imprint the inner. Unless the Holy Spirit fills the hearts of the listeners, the voice of the teacher sounds in vain upon the ears of the body].[16]

When the gratia auditus is missing, the preacher finds himself in the position of the doctor who attains the object of his skill (finis essentialis) if he operates artfully. However, continues Alexander of Hales, from whom this simile derives, the healing of the patient (finis accidens) is in no way thus guaranteed. Likewise, the preacher attains the finis essentialis of his skill if he preaches well; however, the goal of salvation requires an additional divine action, the finis accidentalis.[17] The relationship of these two gratiae to one another occupies Scholastic debate; however, it need not concern us here.[18] It is important for our context to establish that the sermon prayer distinguishes itself from the literary prayer in two essential points: 1) In its function, because it constitutes the essential prerequisite for the preaching of the Gospel; 2) In its form, because it appears as a double prayer[19] or in the form of two prayers;[20] divine assistance must be solicited for the preacher as well as for his public, and that is a notion far removed from the classical appeal to the muses. Gower is soliciting the gratia sermonis in the first distich, the gratia auditus in the second, and is thus in the ecclesiastical tradition of the sermon, not in the literary tradition of the conventional appeal to the muses when he writes in the prologue of Book III:

Si qua boni scriptura tenet, hoc fons bonitatis
Stillet detque deus que bona scribat homo:
Fructificet deus in famulo que scripta iuuabunt,
Digna ministret homo semina, grana deus.
3.Prol.39-42
[If a piece of writing contains something
good, may the fountain of goodness distil it
and may God grant that a man write good things.
May God make fruitful in his servant those
writings which will be of use. Let man provide the proper seeds and God the grain.]

Thus the beginning of Book II's prologue is in the tradition of the sermon, and the prayer which replaces the appeal to the muses must be interpreted out of the spirit of the sermon. We must return now to the two distiches which follow the thwarted appeal to the muses.[21] The first places the author in the role of Old Testament prophet, with echoes of Isaiah and the Psalms,[22] the second in the role of New Testament apostle, with an allusion to the selection of the apostles.[23] Both notions are in harmony with Gower's claim to be the vox clamantis, the voice of one crying in the wilderness, and lead us anew to the question of the terms according to which a layman could consider himself a homilist.

The sermon had the three-fold task of fortifying the faith, teaching dogma, and encouraging moral conduct. The chief emphasis in the late Middle Ages was on its third function, that is, on the moral domain.[24] In this characteristic it turned into a correctio.

The praedicatio in the sense of a correctio is a precept of Christian charity and was never confined by orthodox medieval theologians to a professionally obligated priesthood. Gower speaks of the universal duty of correctio fraterna in the third book of the VOX CLAMANTIS:

Ecclesie fratres in Cristo nos sumus omnes,
Semper et alterius indiget alter ope:
Lex tamen hoc dicit, frater quod si tuus erret,
Corripe, sic et et eum fac reuenire deo. 3.1707-10
[We are all brothers of the Church in Christ,
and one always stands in need of another's
help. But the law says this, that if thy
brother trespass, rebuke him, and thereby
make him return unto God.]

He is thus within a tradition that leads from the Bible through Augustine and Gregory to the vernacular devotional literature of the late 14th century. A passage in Gregory relates Gower's vox and vocare theme to this point of view:

Cui enim jam vox vocantis Dei efficitur in
corde, necesse est ut proximis per praedicationis officium erumpat in voce; et idcirco
alium vocet, quia jam ipse vocatus est [Now
when the voice of God is effected in the
heart of the caller, it is inevitable that
it should break forth in the voice of our
fellow man through the efficacy of the sermon; and for that reason he calls another
because now he has himself been called].[25]

A passage which attempts to bring the duty of clamare home to the reader occurs in the SPECULUM CHRISTIANI, a compilation from around the turn of the fourteenth century:

Informare autem et docere potest vnusquisque
fratrem suum in omni loco et tempore opportuno,
si uideatur sibi expedire, quia hoc est
elemosina, ad quam quilibet tenetur. Domino
dicente: Quod gratis accepistis, gratis date.

Unde Petrus Apostolus: Unusquisque sicut ac-
cipit graciam, illam administrare debet in al-
terutrum. Quomodo potest quis ueraciter di-
cere se deum diligere et eius amorem appetere,
si eius ymaginem uideat denigrari et in ster-
quilinio peccatorum iacere, preciosissimum
sanguinem Christi sub pedibus conculcari,
spiritus sancti habitaculum pollui, sponsam
Christi prostitui, fidem catholicam deici,
preceptum dominicum et totam eius beatitudinem
pro uilibus uoluptatibus et uiciis contempni,
et ipse non curat, nec clamat, sed dissimulans
solum suam quietem requirit? [Everybody may
inform and teach his brother in every place
and fit time if it is seen to be profitable to
him, for this is charity, to which all are
bound. The Lord says: give freely what you
have freely taken. Whence the apostle Peter:
Just as every man takes grace, he ought to
give grace to another. How may any man say
truly that he loves God and hungers after His
love if he see His image thrown down and tossed
onto the dung heap of sins, the most precious
blood of Christ trodden under foot, the dwel-
ling place of the Holy Ghost defouled, Christ's
spouse a whore, the Christian faith cast down,
the Lord's commandment and all his beatitude
despised for vile lusts and vices, and not concern himself, nor cry out, but dissembling
seek only his own quiet?][26]

The BOOK OF VICES AND VIRTUES, the English ad-
aptation of the MIROUR DES PECHIEZ, likewise views
the correction of sinners as a duty of Christian men
that is restricted to no single class:
The Braunches of Mercye. The first is to jeue
good counseil to hem that han nede . . . But
thilke that han God to-fore here eijen and
reden the synful to leue synne, or thilke that
ben out of synne and teche hem to kepe hem
al-wey clene, as schrifte-fadres schulde do
and prelates of holi chirche and also othere
good men, of what staat thei ben, thes don the
first dede of mercye gostliche.[27]
In neither case are the words from a sermon. Formally there is a distinction between praedicatio and

doctrina;[28] Gower's VOX CLAMANTIS formally belongs
to doctrina. However, the distinction is actually
only of a technical-terminological kind. Doctrina
and praedicatio both belong to the ordo caritatis.
Both have the same goal: the glory of God and the
betterment of man.[29] Both originate in the same
moral duty and both have the same object: the correctio of sinful men. They approach each other
even in form in the fourteenth century. Versified
sermons were the order of the day and, according to
Owst,[30] were appointed not only for private reading
but for the pulpit. Thus the boundary between sermon and didactic literature of the kind of the VOX
CLAMANTIS was highly unstable. In service to the
same cause, the preacher became poet, and the poet,
preacher.

But now I would like to return once more to
Guibert. He states his own thoughts on the problem in that passage from his preaching manual in
which he renders Augustine's conception of the universal Christian duty of correctio:

. . . sunt qui bene ac continenter vivunt,
set quia pastoralem non habent in ecclesia
locum, aestimant se non debere fratribus
sanctae praedicationis verbum; quod valde
absurdum est: si enim per subjugale mutum,
id est per asinam, iuxta illud beati Petri
[2 Peter 2.16] Deus corripi voluit prophetae
insipientiam, quam multum et paene absque
comparatione dignior est humana natura ad
docendum et dandum coaequalibus disciplinam?
[There are those who live well and conti-
nently, but because they do not have a
pastoral place in the church they think
that they do not owe their brothers the
word of sacred preachment; such a thought
is very absurd: for if God, as St. Peter
tells us, desired that a prophet should rebuke a fool through a yoked mute, that is,
through an ass, then how much more greatly
and almost without comparison is human nature worthy of teaching and thence of e-
qual discipline?][31]

Here Balaam's Ass[32] appears as a significant

part in the discussion of the duty of brotherly admonition. When God chooses even the dumb animal to
bring human mistakes to light, to what greater extent does this duty belong to men? Thus, when one
reads in Gower: Verba per os asini qui protulit, hic
mea spes est,/Eius vt ad laudem cercius ore loquar
(2.Prol.45-46) [He who brought forth words through
the mouth of an ass is my hope that my lips may
speak resolutely in praise of him], one dare not see
the lines only as a curious specimen of the self-
disparagement topos, but must endeavor to understand them, within the context of ecclesiastical
trains of thought, as a legitimate expression of
a divineᴵ duty.

    Recent research has forcefully indicated how,
since the middle of the thirteenth century, the
moral problems and implications of preaching have
won out over the formal-technical in interest.
Gilson, in his investigation of the structure of
the sermon, came to the conclusion that "we are not
in the presence of a literary work to be composed,
but of a religious function to be fulfilled."[33]
Leclerq demonstrated in a lengthy series of quodlibets that the person of the preacher withdrew
more and more behind his function and the moral
problems connected with it.[34] The relatively large
number of medieval artes praedicandi that seek to
apply the formulae of rhetoric to the sermon
should not obscure the fact that preaching never
sank to "techne." Cardinal Humbert de Romanis, for
example, writes that the difficulty of preaching is
that one could learn all other arts through persis-
tent practice and many good teachers, while preaching is a special gift of God and its only teacher
the Holy Ghost.[35] Of the two chief requisites of
the preacher (recta intentio and scientia), intentio,
according to this supposition, must be allotted by
far the higher significance; that is, the ethical
problem dominates the technical.[36]

    According to Higden, the rectitudo intentionis
is guaranteed if the sermon is preached for the
glory of God, the edification of one's fellow man,
and the manifestation of truth:
        . . . quod tunc fit, quando praedicator ad

Dei glorificationem, ad proximi aedificationem et ad veritatis insinuationem, non ad
favorum aucupationem sicut faciunt adulatores
. . . praedicat [. . . it will be when the
preacher preaches for the glorification of
God, the edification of his fellow man, and
the insinuation of truth, not for the pro-
curement of favors such as flatterers do].[37]
Gower employs the same three points in his prayer to
Christ at the end of Book III's prologue:
In te qui es verus mea sit sentencia vera,
Non ibi figmentum cernere possit homo.
3.Prol.93-4
[Let my intent be true to Thee Who art true;
let no man succeed in discerning any fabri-
cation in it.]
Absit adulari, nec sit michi fabula blesa,
Nec michi laus meriti sit sine laude tua.
Da loquar vt vicium minuatur et ammodo virtus
Crescat, vt in mundo mundior extet homo.
3.Prol.97-100
[Let there be no flattery in my account, and
let it not be hesitant. Let there be no
praise for my accomplishment except Thine.
Let me speak out so that henceforth vice
will diminish and virtue flourish, in order
that mankind may become purer in this world.]
The order of appearance is altered, but they are
clearly recognizable, one distcih allotted to each.
Even the protest against the charge of flattery is
not forgotten. Now attacks against flatterers and
protestations that flattery is far from the author's
thoughts are so frequent in medieval literature that
they have a topos-like character. They occur in
great detail in John of Salisbury, and the article
on "adulator" is one of the longest in Bromyard's
compilation. They may be occasioned by the social
structure of the time. The socially dependent position of the man of letters may have caused him
to be bitter against more successful competitors.
However, this aspect is only of secondary importance
for the sermon and for sermon-literature. And since
Gower wrote here out of the ethos of the preacher,
the topos has a specifically Christian coloring.
In Gower, as in the medieval discussion of proper
preaching, adulatio is contrary to that praise of

God which is the sermon's goal, for it serves either
the advancement of the author's material interests
or the increase of his vainglory. Adulatio and inanis gloria are the two chief sins to which the
preacher is exposed and which threaten the redemp-
tive goal of his work. Here are a few examples
from church fathers, sermon manuals, and summae:

1. Raymond of Pennaforte; Non debet quoque
praedicator adulationibus quaerere ben-
evolentiam atque munuscula, set arguere
peccata [The preacher ought also not
seek good-will and favors from flatterers,
but censure sins].[38]

2. Gerard d'Abbeville; . . . tripliciter
potest esse malum praedicare placentia:
primo ex intentione adulandi principaliter . . ., secundo intentione seducendi
sicut haeretici . . . , tertio intentione
vanam gloriam extorquendi . . . Fraudu-
lenter opus Dei agunt qui favorem humanum
expectant, tales mundi favorem quaerunt
et gloriam suam, non gloriam Dei, unde
Glossa super illus: Si hominibus placerem
[sc. Christi servus non essem. Gal. 1.10]:
cum hominibus, inquit, placere volumus,
gloriam nostram quaerere non debemus sed
illorum salutem, ut bene ambulantes im-
itando non errent et inde non nos sed
Deum laudent qui tales nos fecit [Ordin.
7.79], ut non appetatur favor humanus tam-
quam merces recte sanctorum. [. . . there
are three conditions which make it an evil
to preach pleasingly: first, with the intention of flattering the mighty . . . ,
second, with the intention of deceiving
as it were into heresy . . . , third, with
the intention of deriving vainglory . . .
They do the work of God fraudulently who
expect human rewards; such seek the rewards of the world and their own glory,
not the glory of God, whence the Gloss
upon "If I would please men" [sc. "I would
not be the servant of Christ." Gal. 1.10]:
when we wish, it says, to please men we
ought not to seek our glory but their well-
being, so that following in imitation they

they do not err and thence they praise not
us but God who made us [Ordin. 7.79], so
that human recompense is not regarded as
the just reward of the holy.]39
3. Nicolas Byard; . . . non debet praedicator
aliud intendere nisi salutem audientium,
non gloriam, non commodum terrenum [. . .
the preacher ought not consider anything
but the well-being of the hearer, not glory,
not material goods].40
4. Thomas Waleys; . . . statuat sibi rectum
finem sermonis, ne videlicet ad sui os-
tentationem praedicet sed ad Dei laudem
et proximi aedificationem. Declinet in-
anem gloriam, quae ex bonis operibus solet nasci, et maxime se ingerat importune
hiis quae fiunt in publico in praesentia
multorum. Propter quod praedicator contra
motus inanis gloriae specialiter instat
bellum. [. . . he determines himself the
proper end of the sermon; he should not,
of course, preach for his own display but
for the glory of God and the edification
of his neighbor. He should avoid vainglory, which often arises out of good works,
and in the presence of the many he should
rudely expose those who are in public life.
Because the preacher should wage war especially against vainglory.]41

Wyclif expresses his opinion on this question
very forcefully in a sermon from his orthodox period. His theme is semen est verbum Dei (Luke 8.11),
and what he says applies especially to the preacher:
. . . Quam fatua ergo est intencio aptare
labores bonos de genere ut vel principaliter
vel mixtim captetur applausus populi. Idem
est enim sic facere et commutare amiciciam
Dei pro ficta et adulatoria fama mundi et per
consequens bonum eterni gaudii perdere pro
gaudio ypocrite quod est instar puncti breve,
ymmo constituere unum talem vilem peccatorem
Deum suum et sic (quantum in se est) perver-
tendo ordinem universi dum eius laudem pre-
fert laudi Dei. [. . . how foolish therefore
is the attempt to do a good work of a kind

107

that either principally or in part seeks the
approval of the people. For that is the same
as to make and to barter the friendship of God
for a counterfeit and the flattering fame of
the world, and as a consequence to lose the
joy of eternity for a gaudy hypocrisy that is
the very image of brevity, yea, to set up such
a vileness of sinners against God and thus
(how powerful the preacher is) to pervert the
order of the universe in preferring their
praise to that of God.][42]

The earnestness and vigor with which the sermon's
moral prerequisites were pursued in the thirteenth
and fourteenth centuries is shown by the constantly
debated question of whether adulatio and inanis
gloria are mortal or venial sins for the preacher.
Robert de Basevorn is convinced that they are mortal.[43] An anonymous quodlibet distinguishes between the sermon which is preached with the intention of seeking vainglory and is therefore a mortal sin, and the sermon which is only the occasion
of vainglory and therefore more gently judged.[44]

Seen against this background, Gower's plea of
absit adulare is far more than a literary convention. Indeed, in many of the texts mentioned there
appears alongside adulatio, when it is understood
in the sense of illicit concession to the audience,
a second item that is incompatible with recta intentio and that also occurs in Gower: the gratifi-
cation of curiositas. When he writes in the prologue of Book III,

Non ego sidereas affecto tangere sedes,
Scribere nec summi mistica quero poli;
Set magis, humana que vox communis ad extra
Plangit in hac terra, scribo moderna mala
[I do not aspire to reach the thrones of
heaven, or seek to describe the mysteries
of the lofty skies. Rather, I write of
present-day evils which the common voice
of mankind outwardly complains of in this
country (3.Prol.53-56)],

he calls to mind in a purely superficial way Curtius'
topos of the rejection of trite material, by which
the passage may have been formally influenced. The
content, however, is a protest against the charge

of vana curiositas. Thomas Waleys warns the preacher
aginst admitting vana, curiosa, and frivola into the
sermon in order to please the congregation. He
should be intent upon the profit, not the praise
or censure, of the listener. Otherwise it might
begall him according to the words of the Psalm:
Deus dissipavit ossa eorum qui hominibus
placent. Confusi sunt quia Dominus sprevit
eos. [For God hath scattered the bones of
them that please men. They have been con-
founded, because God hath despised them.
Psalms 52.6][45]
That is the same divine judgement that threatens
the adulator: Si adhuc hominibus placerem, Christi
servus non essem [If I were still trying to please
men, I should not be a servant of Christ (Gal.1.10)].

As Raymund explains in his SUMMA,[46] vana, curiosa, and frivola are theological sophistries, aston-
omy, secular poetry, and idle tales. That it is not
a question of clerical bias against secular literature is shown by the coexistence of fictiones
poetorum and fabulae inutiles on the one hand and
subtiles quaestiones theologiae and discursus
astrorum on the other, all of which are rejected.
The cause is, rather, the sermon's consciousness of
moral responsibility according to Ecclesiastes 7.1:
Quid necesse est homini maiora se quaerere, cum
ignoret, quid conducat sibi in vita sua numero
dierum peregrinationis suae? [What needeth a man
to seek things that are above him, whereas he
knoweth not what is profitable for him in his life,
in all the days of his pilgrimage?] The Dominican
Cardinal Hugo writes of the priority of morality
above all other sermon themes:
. . . Et sic iustum et honestum esset praedicatoribus supradicta [sc. de peccatis,
poenitentia, et bonis operibus] et similia,
in quibus homines quotidie cadimus, praedicare et alia alta et subtilia et curiosa
dimittere [And thus it would be right and
honest for preachers to preach the aforesaid things [about sin, penitence, good
works] and things of this sort into which
we, as men, fall every day; and to leave
aside anything else which is lofty, subtle,

109

or quaint].[47]
And a gloss in the manuscript of the SUMMA THEOLOGIAE
MORALIS that I used remarks:

Non dicant, quid tamen praedicare: Scio quid
dicturus est praedicator: Omnis enim sermo
in hoc concluditur: Declina a malo et fac
bonum. [Do they not say what preaching is?
I know what the preacher's maxim is: all sermons should end in this--shun evil and do good].[48]

The betterment of his fellow man also causes Gower
to renounce alta and curiosa, as he does when he
follows the cited lines with this statement:

Vtilis aduerso quia confert tempore sermo,
Promere tendo mala iam bona verba die.
                              3.Prol.57-58

[Since a useful discussion contributes something even though the times are hostile, I
intend for my words of good to bring evil to
light.]

The antithesis of astronomy and utile shows that the
author was not orienting himself towards a didactic
literary tradition, which would hardly have contrasted
the two, but towards the moral problem of establishing
the preacher's rectitudo intentionis.

Earlier we alluded to the two prerequisites of
proper preaching, recta intentio and recta scientia.
Most ecclesiastical authors discuss utilitas in the
context of recta intentio, and some few consider it
part of the integritas sermonis, that is, of the
second prerequisite. In either case it is closely
connected with veritas or insinuatio veritatis. For
example, the SUMMA THEOLOGIAE MORALIS defines the
integritas sermonis thus: quod fiet [?], si in eo
[sc. sermone] fuerint veritas, utilitas, claritas
[what will be, if in the sermon there will be truth,
profit, clarity].[49] Now as we saw, Gower's prayer
in Book III's prologue includes--beyond the rejection of adulatio and the double purpose of laus dei
(in this case Christi) and utilitas proximi--above
all the insinuatio veritatis. When the Christian
invocatio assumed the heritage of the classical
appeal to the muses, it usually directed itself,
as Curtius noted,[50] to the Holy Ghost or to Christ
as the word-become-flesh. The Christus-veritas
theme, on the other hand, points--probably in it-

self and certainly by its proximity to the train of
thought concerning the recta intentio--to the tradition of the sermon rather than to a literary cliche.

I wish now to quote in its entirety a passage
that was only abstracted above:
O sapiens, sine quo nichil est sapiencia mundi,
Cuius in obsequium me mea vota ferunt,
Te precor instanti da tempore, Criste, misertus,
Vt metra que pecii prompta parare queam;
Turgida deuitet, falsum mea penna recuset
Scribere, set scribat que modo vera videt.
In primis caueat ne fluctuet, immo decenter
Quod primo ponit carmine seruet opus:
Hic nichil offendat lectorem, sit nisi verum
Aut veri simile, quod mea scripta dabunt.
In te qui es verus mea sit sentencia vera,
Non ibi figmentum cernere possit homo. 3.Prol.83-94
[O Wise One, without Whom the wisdom of the
world is as nothing, Thou into Whose service
my devotions bring me, I pray Thee at this
time, O merciful Christ, to grant that I can
readily compose the verses I have striven for.
Let my pen avoid what is turgid, let it refuse
to write what is false; rather, let it now
write what it sees to be true. Let it take
care not to falter at the outset; instead,
let what it puts in the very first line
serve the whole work appropriately. Let
nothing that my writings are to offer offend
the reader, unless it is the truth or very
like the truth. Let my intent be true to
Thee Who art true; let no man succeed in
discerning any fabrication in it.]
The passage closely interweaves three themes: Christus
sapiens, Christ as helper in the poem's composition,
and Christus-veritas. The direct invocation of
Christus sapiens accords with sermon tradition.
Thomas Waleys provides the reason:
Tertium documentum est ut praedicaturus
verbum Dei consideret quod omnis sapientia
a Domino Deo est. Et ideo cum in sermone
specialiter requiritur donum sapientiae,
convertat se per devotam orationem ad
fontem Sapientiae, juxta illud Jacobi 1$^\theta$:
Si quis indiget sapientia, postulet a Deo,

qui dat omnibus affluenter, et non improperat
. . . Ita et praedicator sapientiam postulet
qua possit populum recte instruere. [The
third lesson is that a man about to preach
God's word should consider that all wisdom
is from God. And therefore when a special
gift of wisdom is required in a sermon, he
should apply through devout prayer to the
Fount of Wisdom, as in James 1 [James 1.5]:
If any of you is wanting in wisdom, let him
ask it of God, who gives abundantly to all
men, and does not reproach . . . And thus
the preacher should ask for wisdom so that
he may teach.]51

Thomas goes on to Gower's second point, Christ's
help in the composition of the poem, when he continues:
. . . omnino expedit ut precetur ad auxilium
divinitatis, plus confidens in divino auxilio
quam in proprio ingenio, ne forte Deus subtra-
hat seu potius non tribuat sibi verbum. [It
is altogether profitable that he should pray
for God's assistance, confiding more in divine aid than in his own skill, lest perhaps
God take away his power if he does not attribute the word to Him.]

The artes praedicandi also contain information about
divine assistance in the concrete difficulties of
composition. Robert de Basevorn interprets 2 Tim.
4.17 (Dominus mihi astitit et confortavit me, ut
per me praedicatio impleatur [But the Lord stood
by me and strengthened me, that through me the
preaching of the gospel might be completed]) in
the following manner:
Tunc enim aliquid formaliter traditur et
docetur quando ordinate quod principium
operis promittit vel inquirendum praetendit
continuatio prosequitur et finis concludit.
. . . Unde, Eccli. 24, de Deo qui istam
impletionem formalem facit et a quo est
principaliter quidquid a nobis fieri videtur,
dicetur quod adimplet quasi Phison sapientiam,
. . . et iterum quod adimplet quasi Euphrates
sensum, 1. sicut illa duo flumina Phison et
Tigris [sic] ordinate implent alveos suos,
ita Deus in tractatoribus sapientiae suae

facit, gratiam et sapientiam vel scientiam
eis infundens ordinate et formaliter pro-
cedendi, ut sic aperiente eo manum suam
omnia impleantur congrua bonitate. [A thing
is formally transmitted and taught when a continuation carries through in an orderly way
what the beginning of the work promises or
proffers for investigation . . . Whence the
saying, in Ecclus. 24, about God who brings
about this formal filling and from whom primarily comes that which seems to come from
us. It is said that He filleth up wisdom as
the Phison and, again, that He maketh understanding to abound as the Euphrates. In
other words, just as those two rivers, Phison
and Tigris, fill their beds in an orderly way,
so does God do in the case of those who deal
with His wisdom, pouring into them the grace
and wisdom, or the knowledge of proceeding
in an orderly and formal way, that thus by
the opening of His hand all things may be
filled with an agreeable goodness.]52
That calls to mind Gower's
    Inceptum per te perfecto fine fruatur
    Hoc opus . . . (2.Prol.9-10)
    [I pray that this work, begun with Thy help
    . . . may achieve a fitting conclusion]
and apparently also has a bearing upon another distich:
    Et si metra meis incongrua versibus errent,
    Que sibi vult animus congrua vota cape.
                                2.Prol.25-26
    [And if the inharmonious metres in my verses
    go astray, receive the harmonious offerings
    my soul intends for you.]
This view that divine assistance is more important
than human artistry can lead to the depreciation
of rhetoric, and I believe that herein lies the
source of many topoi of self-deprecation which appear at first glance to fall under the rubric of
"affected modesty." Thomas Waleys stresses in the
prologue of his manual that the rules of rhetoric
should not be unconditionally binding upon the
preacher and supports the argument with a verse
from the second letter to Timothy (verbum Dei non
est alligatum [the word of God is not bound],

2 Tim. 2.9).[53] William of Auvergne advises:
  Si vis habere modum praedicandi et copiam
  loquendi efficaciter et artificiose, . . .
  curiosum sermonem et politum devita et, ne
  simplex et nuda veritas verborum fusco
  corrumpatur, in exordio sermonis auxilium
  Dei invocare debes et ad orandum pro te
  inducere auditores, ne prudentie tue, contra
  consilium Salomonis, inniti videaris. [If
  you wish to possess the art of preaching and
  the power of speaking efficaciously and
  skillfully . . . avoid the ornate and em-
  bellished sermon and, lest the simple and
  naked truth of words be darkly corrupted,
  you ought to invoke the aid of God in the
  introduction of the sermon and persuade
  the audience to prayer for you, lest against
  the counsel of Salomon you be seen to depend
  on your knowledge.][54]
Could Gower's emphasis on simplicitas and ruditas
in the sense of deficient rhetorical schooling be
superficially attuned to the tradition of affected
modesty and yet at the same time reveal something
of the Pauline self-esteem of the man who knows
himself, as the instrument of God, to be above the
tricks of rhetoric? His definite lack of embarrassment shows that Gower, rather than being seriously distressed by simplicitas, perceived it to
be analogous with William of Auvergne's simplex
veritas:[55]
              . . . absque rubore
  Que mea simplicitas sufficit illa dabo.
                        2.Prol.31-32
  [. . . I shall nevertheless render without
  any embarrassment the things for which my
  ingenuousness is adequate];
  Ergo recede mee detractor simplicitati.
                        2.Prol.47
  [Therefore, let my detractor yield to my
  ingenuousness.]
The word "rudis," which surfaces three times--
  Et rudis ipse rude si quid tractauero . . .
  parce . . . (2.Prol.23-24) [And if I who am
  unskillful treat of something unskillfully
  . . . take pity]; Deque rudi dociles carmine
  sume notas (2.prol.42) [And single out the

114

                    sweet notes from my harsh song]--
is in a literary sense somewhat like the term rusticus,[56] and although the author here begs our indul-
gence, he may have done so conscious of the words
of Jerome:
    Multo quidem melius est ex duobus imperfectis
    rusticitatem habere sanctam quam eloquentiam
    peccatricem [Of the two, it is by far better
    to possess the simplicity of the imperfect
    man than the eloquence of a sinner].[57]

Notes to Chapter 3 Part A
    [1] Samuel M. Tucker, VERSE SATIRE IN ENGLAND
BEFORE THE RENAISSANCE (New York, 1908), denies the
existence of satire as a literary genre in England
before 1540. His reasons seem valid to me.
    [2] Isaiah 40.3.
    [3] Bromyard, SUMMA PRAEDICANTIUM, s.v. praedi-
cator, art. 1: Officium praedicationis assimilari
debet officio praeconis . . . qui iussa, et ordina-
tiones clamat regia . . . Primo quantum ad materiam
quam clamat: quia sicut praeco illorum materiam et
verba, quae ponuntur in ore suo: quantocumque sint
aliquibus terribilia, et grauia, atque displicentia:
illa nihilominus aperte clamat, nihil dimittens de
hoc, quod ponitur in ore suo? Ita praedicator uerba
. . . et iussa Dei, quae ei . . . praecipit. [The
office of the preacher ought to be compared to the
office of the herald . . . first, concerning the
matter that he proclaims: just like the herald,
the matter and words he announces are not his own
but another's. And as for the frightening, important, and displeasing messages which come from
others--should not the herald proclaim even these,
clearly, omitting nothing? Thus it is with the
words of the preacher . . . and the divine commandments which God has taught him.]
    [4] John Waldeby, SERMONES, MS. Bodl. 687, fol.
84 f. on the text : Ego vox clamantis in deserto
(John 1.23); see also Alanus de Insulis, DE SANCTO
JOANNE BAPTISTA: . . . Et sicut verbum Dei dicitur
interior mentis conceptus, sic vox verbi dicitur
exterior sonus. Unde, sicut Christus dicitur Verbum,
sic vox verbi aliquis praedicans verbum. Sicut quilibet etiam propheta posset dici vox verbi, quasi
verbum praedicans, tamen antonomastice Joannes

                          115

Baptista dicitur vox verbi. [And just as the word
of God is said to be a conception within the mind,
thus the voice of the word is said to be an external sound. Whence, just as Christ is said to be
the word, thus the voice of the word is the word
of anyone preaching. For anyone who will can be
called, just like the prophet, the voice of the
word, as it were, the word of preaching; nevertheless, as a title is John the Baptist called the
voice of the word.] LIBER SENTENTIARUM AC DICTORUM
MEMORABILIUM, Migne, PL 210:243.

5 Cf. below, pp. 100 ff.

6 St. Bonaventura, COMMENTARIUM IN EVANGELIUM
LUCAE (Quaracchi edition, 1895), Vol. 7.

7 On the technique of the late medieval ser-
mon, cf. Etienne Gilson, LES IDEES ET LES LETTRES
(Paris, 1932), pp. 93-154; G. R. Owst, PREACHING
IN MEDIEVAL ENGLAND (London, 1926), passim.

8 Loc. cit., p. 73.

9 Ibid.: Et quia severitati debet adiungi
pietas, ideo praemittitur increpatio; secundo vero
adiungitur exhortatio, ibi: Facite ergo dignos
fructus poenitentiae; tertio vero subinfertur comminatio, ibi: Jam enim securis ad radicem etc. Increpatio est culpae, admonitio poenitentiae, sed
comminatio poenalis vindictae. [And because piety
ought to be yoked to severity, therefore invective
is allowed; secondly, exhortation ought also to be
joined to severity; therefore, gather the worthy
fruits of penitence; thirdly, threatening should
be brought in: for the axe is to the root, etc.
Invective pertains to blame, admonition to penitence, but threatening to the pain of vengeance.]

10 The term "status" is not defined very clearly
in the medieval sermon manuals. It designates the
three estates which comprise the body politic, the
different walks of life, and also other categories
such as the married, widows, virgins, and the like.
Thus Alanus de Insulis, in his SUMMA DE ARTE PRAE-
DICATORIA (Migne, PL 210), places side by side the
following examples for the sermon ad status: Ad
Milites (Chpt. 40), Ad Advocatos (Chpt. 41), Ad
Principes et Judices (Chpt. 42), Ad Claustrales
(Chpt. 43), Ad Sacerdotes (Chpt. 44), Ad Conjugatos
(Chpt. 45), De Viduis (Chpt. 46), Ad Virgines (Chpt.
47), and, especially charming, Ad Somnolentos (Chpt. 48).

¹¹ Loc. cit., p. 75.

11 Loc. cit., p. 75.
12 Books 3-6.
13 Cf. especially 2.17-36:
Si tamen esse potest quod felix esset in orbe,
Dudum felices nos dedit esse deus:
Quicquid summa manus potuit conferre creatis,
Contulit hoc nobis prosperitatis opus.
Huius erat vite, si que sit, gloria summe,
Nobis pre reliquis amplificata magis.
Tuncque fuisse deum nobis specialius omni
Conuersum plebe clamor vbique fuit:
Famaque sic mundi, nobisque beacius omni
Tempus erat populo nuper . . .
[Long ago, God granted that we be happy, if
it is possible that one may be happy on earth.
Whatever the hand of the Most High could be-
stow upon His creatures, it bestowed this
piece of good fortune upon us: the glory, if
such it is, of the highest kind of life was
extended to us above all others. And then
there was shouting everywhere that God had
turned against us in particular, rather than
against all people. So ran the common talk
of the world, yet times were once happier
for us than any people.]
14 2.26-36.
15 2.37-50. So much for the first chapter of
Book II; for the following chapters cf. below, pp.
171 ff.
16 7.1289-1302:
Singula que dominus statuit sibi regna per orbem,
Que magis in Cristi nomine signa gerunt,
Diligo, set propriam super omnia diligo terram,
In qua principium duxit origo meum.
Quicquid agant alie terre, non subruor inde,
Dum tamen ipse foris sisto remotus eis;
Patria set iuuenem que me suscepit alumpnum,
Partibus in cuius semper adhero manens,
Hec si quid patitur, mea viscera compaciuntur,
Nec sine me dampna ferre valebit ea:
Eius in aduersis de pondere sum quasi versus;
Si perstet, persto, si cadat illa, cado.
Que magis ergo grauant presenti tempore, saltem
Vt dicunt alii, scismata plango michi.
[I love all the kingdoms which the Lord has
established for Himself throughout the world

117

and which bear standards in Christ's name.
But above all I love my own land, in which my
family took its origin. Whatever other lands
may do, I am not shaken by it, as long as I
stand apart at a distance from them. But if
the native land which bore me as a young child,
and within whose realms I always remain fixed--
if she suffers anything, my innermost feelings
suffer with her, and she shall not be able to
suffer her misfortunes apart from me. I am almost overwhelmed by the weight of her adversities. If she stands firm, I stand firm, if
she falls, I fall. Therefore, I bewail the
schisms which, at least so others say, are so
oppressive at this present time.]
[17] 7.1328-38.
[18] C. S. Lewis, THE ALLEGORY OF LOVE (Oxford,
1936), pp. 198 f.
[19] This is important not only for Latin, but
above all for vernacular literature also. The
history of the adaptations and alterations of the
SOMME LE ROI of the 13th century Dominican Lorens
d'Orleans provides an instructive example; cf. EETS
OS 217 (THE BOOK OF VICES AND VIRTUES), Introduction.
[20] Archiepiscopus vero Cantuariensis praesenti
consentit electioni, ut omnes praelati; et Archiepiscopus quidem, assumpto themate, "Voc populi,
vox Dei," sermonem fecit populo, exhortans omnes
ut apud Regem Regum intercederent pro electo.
[The Archbishop of Canterbury agreed to the present
election, as well as all the prelates; and the Archbishop, having taken up the subject "The voice of
the people is the voice of God," delivered a sermon to the people, exhorting all that they inter-
cede with the king on behalf of an election for
king.] HISTORIA ANGLICANA, ed. H. T. Riley, Rolls
Series (London, 1863), I, 186.
[21] The rule first emerges, to my knowledge,
in a letter of Alcuin to Charlemagne; there, however it appears to be already proverbial. Moreover, Alcuin warns against it. Epistola CXXXII
seu Capitulare Admonitionis ad eundum Carolum, cap.
9, Epistolae Karolini Aevi, in MGH EPISTOLAE, ed.
E. L. Dummler (Berlin, 1895), II, 199.
[22] Macaulay, IV, 362.
[23] The two distiches occur in CEG in the above-

.nentioned place. In S and H, which likewise belong
to the B-Text, they are missing: in S because two
leaves with the end of the summary have disappeared
after fol. 5, in H because the MS is defective in
the beginning, first starting with Book I, 502.
   24 T and H2.
   25 Macaulay gives the drawing opposite the
title page of Vol. 4 of his edition.
   26 Cf. Book III, prologue, esp. 23 ff.:
   Nouimus esse status tres, sub quibus omnis in orbe
   More suo viuit atque ministrat eis.
   Non status in culpa reus est, set transgredientes
   A virtute status, culpa repugnat eis.
   [We recognize that there are three estates.
   In his own way, everyone in the world lives
   under them and serves them. No estate is
   accused as being at fault, but when estates
   transgress against virtue, their fault declares against them.]
   27 Such a statement can be confidently maintained due to the wording of the summaries of Book
III, Chapter 1 and Book VI, Chapters 7 and 18, which
accord with the chapter headings of the A-Text and
have been left untouched by the alterations of the
B-Text.
   28 Cf. such titles as SPECULUM LAICI (anonymous); SPECULUM CHRISTIANI (anonymous); SPECULUM
MORALE, SPECULUM HISTORIALE (Vincent of Beauvais);
SPECULUM ECCLESIAE (the Dominican Cardinal Hugo);
SPECULUM HUMANAE VITAE (Roderigo of Cagliari). A
short study of the title Speculum occurs in EETS
ES 75, pp. xxii ff.
   29 The MIROUR DE L'OMME or SPECULUM MEDITANTIS
has the mirror already in the title. In the VOX
CLAMANTIS it appears once again in the Mirror for
a Prince:
   O bene si speculo, rex, te speculeris in isto,
   Quid magis expediens sit tibi scire potes.
                                          6.1051 f.
   [O King, if you were to look at yourself well
   in this mirror, you could learn how very help-
   ful it is to you.]
   30 W. Kleineke, "Englische Fürstenspiegel vom
POLICRATICUS Johanns von Salisbury bis zum BASILIKON
DORON König Jakobs I," STUDIEN ZUR ENGLISCHEN PHILO-
LOGIE, 90 (1937), 10.

[31] LIBER SALUTARIS BEATI BONAVENTURE CARDINALIS ORDINIS MINORUM PHARETRA VOCATUS (Paris: Berthold Rembolt, 1518).

[32] Loc. cit., prologue: Opulculum autem istud Pharetram appelavi, quia sicut in pharetra iacula reponuntur, quibus hostem hostis ferit, vulnerat, et deiicit, sic et hic varie auctoritates fidedignorum quas si manu operationis tenemus, hostem antiquum deiiciemus. [This little book has been named THE QUIVER, because just as we keep in a quiver darts to attack, wound, and kill the enemy host, so if we grasp with the hand these various authorities worthy of the faith we shall overcome the ancient enemy.]

[33] For example, Hebrews 4.12: Vivus est sermo Dei, et efficax et penetrabilior omni gladio ancipiti [For the word of God is living and efficient and keener than any two-edged sword]. In a similar manner are understood Psalms 44.6: Sagittae tuae acutae, populi sub te cadent, in corda inimicorum regis [Thy arrows are sharp, under Thee shall people fall, into the hearts of the king's enemies] and Psalms 119.4: Sagittae potentis acutae cum carbonibus desolatoriis [The sharp arrows of the mighty, with coals that lay waste].

[34] HOMILY ON EZECHIEL, lib. I, hom. 5; Migne, PL 76:827.

[35] EXPOSITION OF THE SONG OF SOLOMON, Chpt. 3, on the text: Uniuscuiusque ensis super femur suum [every man's sword upon his thigh] (Canticles 3.8). Migne, PL 172:405.

[36] DE ERUDITIONE PRAEDICATORUM. OPERA OMNI (Quaracchi edition), II, 401.

[37] DE MODO COMPONENDI SERMONES, ed. Thomas M. Charland (Paris, 1936), p. 338.

[38] Sancti Martini Legionensis Sermo II Sancto Joanne Baptista. Migne, PL 209:18.

Notes to Chapter Three Part B

[1] EXPOSITIO IN CANTICA CANTICORUM, Migne, PL 172:347.

[2] Robert de Basevorn, FORMA PRAEDICANDI, ed. Thomas M. Charland, ARTES PRAEDICANDI (Paris, 1936), p. 234. They are the causae finalis, efficiens, materialis, and formalis, as subsequent statements

indicate. [The translation is that of Leopold Krul, in THREE MEDIEVAL RHETORICAL ARTS, ed. James J. Murphy (Berkeley, 1971), pp. 109-215.]

3 Cf. above, pp. 32 f.

4 Loc. cit., p. 130.

5 Loc. cit., p. 129, commentary p. 131.

6 . . . ubi sapientum mundi excludit astutias, qui capiunt verba sicut sonant secundum communem expositionem, et sic in proposito non sunt accippenda. [Wherefore he shuts out the foolish wisdom of the worldly wise, who understand words just as they sound, according to common exposition, and thus they are not acceptable in a proposition.] Loc. cit., p. 131.

7 In Bonaventura there are, alongside the traditional four causae (which he always combines under the two headings of causae extrinsecae—efficiens and finalis—and intrinsecae—materialis and formalis), two more that he designates insinuativum duplicis personae ad opus necessariae, scil. doctoris et auditoris [the penetration of the two-fold persona necessary to the work, namely of the teacher and the listener], upon which he enlarges: Primo igitur propositum verbum [that is, the first clause of his Bible text] secundum intellectum generalem indicat nobis, quis et qualis debeat esse doctor huius Scripturae evangelicae, adiungens nihilominus, qualem debeat habere auditorem [Firstly, therefore, the words that are the subject . . . disclose to us, according to general understanding, what sort of man ought to be the teacher of this Gospel, and no less the related issue, what sort ought to be the listener]. PROOEMIUM COMMENTARII IN LUCAM, loc. cit., p. 3.

8 In this line causa is, of course, hackneyed.

9 Lines 11-20 revolve, for no apparent reason, around the idea of honestum. However, the situation becomes more comprehensible if one refers to John of Bridlington. There the commentator distinguishes three causae finalis: utile, delectabile, and honestum. The first two conform to the traditional aut prodesse volunt aut delectare poetae [poets wish either to be useful or to delight]. I cannot account for the separation of honestum from the stoic ethic (de utile et honesto).

10 Loc. cit., pp. 106 f.

[11] Loc. cit., p. 415: "The foregoing remarks can supply a few guiding principles and furnish a warning against making the Middle Ages more Christian or more pious than it was. A constant literary formula must not be regarded as the expression of spontaneous sentiment." Trans. Willard Trask.

[12] 3.Prol.101 f. and AURORA, Prologue, MS Bodl. 822, fol. 4b. Macaulay overlooked the parallel.

[13] On the structure of the sermon in the 13th and 14th centuries, see E. Gilson, LES IDEES ET LES LETTRES, pp. 93-154; Charland, ARTES PRAEDICANDI, pp. 107-36; Owst, PREACHING IN MEDIEVAL ENGLAND, passim.

[14] It is all the same in this case whether one considers Book II as prologue to the class critique of Books III-VI, or reckons with the possibility that it was belatedly placed before the class critique.

[15] Resembling 2 Corinthians 2.17 and I Peter 4.10 f. See also Robert de Basevorn's interpretation of 2 Timothy 4.17 (Dominus autem mihi astitit, et confortavit me, ut per me praedicatio impleatur [But the Lord stood by me and strengthened me that through me the preaching of the Gospel might be completed]) in the prologue of his FORMA PRAEDICANDI. The author explains in respect to the phrase "per me" the sense in which God and the sense in which the preacher are the sermon's causa efficiens: Licet enim Deus, qui et finis, sit causa principaliter efficiens tanquam universale influens . . . ego tamen instrumentum immediatius sum, istud executioni demandans. Quia tamen prima causa plus influit, non audeo mihi aliquid tanquam ex me attribuere. [May God, who is also the end, be primarily the efficient cause, influencing the whole . . . whereas I am more immediately the instrument putting the task into execution. However, because the primary cause has more influence, I do not dare to attribute anything to myself as proceeding from me. Trans. Leopuld Krul.] Loc. cit., p. 234.

[16] Loosely after MORALIA IN JOB, lib. 27, cap. 38: Migne, PL 76:437.

[17] SUMMA THEOLOGICA (Quaracchi Edition, 1948), III, 1060.

[18] See J. Leclercq, LE MAGISTERE DU PREDICATEUR AU XIIIe SIECLE, ARCH. D'HISTOIRE DOCTR. ET LITT. DU

MOYEN AGE, 15 (1946), passim; and Alexander of Hales,
loc. cit., p. 1060, especially the treatment of the
question utrum ad aedificationem auditorum sufficiat
gratia sermonis [whether the grace of the sermon
is sufficient to the edification of the audience].
[19] Guibert de Nogent, LIBER QUO ORDINE SERMO
FIERI DEBEAT: . . . sermonem praecedat oratio, ut
animus fervens amore divino ardenter, quae de Deo
sentit, enuntiet, et sicut apud se intrinsecus ardet,
sic auditorum corda inflammet [prayer should precede the sermon, so that the soul hotly glowing
with divine love may set forth what it knows about
God, and just as it burns within itself, so will
it inflame the hearts of the listeners]. Migne, PL
156:24.
[20] Bromyard, loc. cit., s.v. praedicator: . . .
sed quia nec tam excellentis praedicationis operatio,
nec tam purae mentis intentio sine Dei possunt haberi
adiutorio, praedicator ante omnem praedicationis
actum, vel studium, orare habet ad impetrandum
gratiam bene, et bona intentione verbum Dei semi-
nandum, sicut agricola orat bonum tempus, et aeris
amoenitatem seminandi terram suam, quod seminatum
multipliciter. Sicut ergo agricola duo desiderat:
vnum, quod tempus aptum habeat seminandi: Aliud,
quod seminatum semen bene cooperiatur et crescat:
ita praedicator ante praedicationem, immo ante
omne praedicationis studium orare debet, vt verbum
Dei apte primo concipiatur, et postea bene seminetur.
Post praedicationem vt bene crescat et fructificet,
. . . [he quotes from Chrysostomus]. Orate ergo
ante omne studium et praedicationem et post ne sit
inanis praedicatio vestra. [But because neither
the effectiveness of the excellent sermon nor the
intention of a pure mind can be had without the
assistance of God, the preacher has to pray before
every presentation of or study for a sermon in
order to obtain the proper grace and plant the Word
of God with good intention, just as the farmer
prays for good weather and a pleasant air while
seeding his land, that the sowing multiply. Just
as, therefore, the farmer desires two things (the
one that the time should be appropriate for seeding,
the other that the sown seed be well covered and
grow) thus the preacher ought to pray before a
sermon, yea befoe all study for a sermon, that the

word of God be in the first place appropriately
understood and after that well planted. And after
the sermon so that it grow well and be fruitful . . .
Pray therefore before all study and preaching and
afterwards, lest your sermon be useless.] The lines
are reminiscent of I Cor. 15.14.

21 Spiritus alme deus, accendens pectore sensus,
   Intima tu serui pectoris vre tui:
   Inque tuo, Criste, laxabo nomine rethe,
   Vt mea mens capiat que sibi grata petit.
                                      2.Prol.5 ff.
   [Merciful God of the spirit, fire the
   innermost depths of thy servant's breast,
   kindling the feelings in his heart. In
   Thy name, O Christ, I shall spread my
   net, so that my mind may thankfully seize
   upon the things which it requires.]

22 Cf. Isaiah 6.5-7; Psalms 16.1-4; Psalms 25.2.

23 Cf. Matthew 4.19 (Venite post me, et faciam
vos piscatores hominum [Come, follow me, and I will
make you fishers of men]), combined with John 21.6.
On the subject of the preacher as fisher of men,
see Bromyard, loc. cit., s.v. praedicator, art. 1:
Tertio officium, et actus praedicatoris assimilari
debet actui piscatoris . . . [an allusion to
Matthew 4.19]. Executio vero eo modo fiere debet,
quo plures capere possunt peccatores, quod ita
fiere potest, si contra vicia praedicetur in
speciali . . . Nam praedicatio generalis est quasi
rete nimis latam [sic] habens foramina per quae
multi pisces euadunt: specialis, quae nititur omnes
tangere, est quasi rete arctum, quod omnes, quantum
omnes [sic], quantum in se est, capit: propter hoc
enim illi piscatores descendebant et reficiebant
retia sua, ne aliqui evaderent. Lucae 5. [Thirdly,
the office and performance of the preacher ought to
be compared to the performance of the fisherman
 . . executed in such a way that the most fish
 an be taken, which is possible if the sermon is
preached against a sin in particular . . . For
the general sermon is as it were a net with too
wide spaces through which many fish escape: the
particular, which endeavors to touch all men, is
as it were a tight net that seizes everything,
large or small, in it: because of this those
fishermen go down and repair their nets, lest any-

thing escape.]

24 Cf. Guibert, loc. cit., col. 27: Nulla enim praedicatio salubrior mihi videtur quam illa quae hominem sibimet ostendat, et foras extra se sparsum in interiori suo, hoc est in mente, restituat atque eum coarguens quodammodo depictum ante faciem suam statuat. [For no sermon seems to me more sound than that one which shows man to his senses, and brings him, formerly having been distracted outside himself, back inside himself, i.e. in his mind, and, proving him wrong in a certain way depicted before his face, restores him.] That is precisely Gower's method, and calls to mind the last line of the accompanying verses: Conscius ergo sibi se speculetur ibi [Therefore let him who is conscious of himself look to himself]. The sermon de vitiis et virtutibus attained such an eminent position partly because Lent was the principal sermon time of the year and partly for reasons discussed below, pp. 108 f.

25 HOM. IN EZECH., Migne, PL 76:950 f.

26 SPECULUM CHRISTIANI, Prologue, EETS OS 182, p. 3.

27 THE BOOK OF VICES AND VIRTUES, EETS OS 217, p. 199.

28 Alanus de Insulis distinguishes in his SUMMA DE ARTE PRAEDICATORIA among praedicatio, doctrina, prophetia, and concionatio, defining them in the following manner: Praedicatio enim est illa instructio quae pluribus fit, et in manifesto, et ad morum instructionem; doctrina vero est quae vel uni, vel pluribus fit, ad scientiae eruditionem; prophetia, est admonitio quae fit per revelationem futurorum; concionatio est civilis admonitio, quae fit ad reipublicae confirmationem. [Preaching is that instruction which should be for the many, and in public, and directed to the formation of morals; doctrine is that which should be either for the individual or the many, directed to the advancement of learning; prophecy is admonition that should be for the revelation of future things; oratory is civil admonition directed towards the strengthening of the commonwealth.] Migne, PL 210:112

29 Bromyard, s.v. praedicator, art. 5: Qui enim ad praedicandum mittitur duobus praeceptis geminae charitatis, sc., de dilectione Dei, et

proximi debet esse munitus. Et est hic argumentum,
quod nullus officium praedicandi debet assumere,
nisi prius labia cordis igne charitatis habeat
decocta, et post purgationem peccati. licite potest
aliquis assumere officium praedicandi. [He who
dedicates himself to preaching ought to be forti-
fied with the two precepts of twinned charity,
namely with the lover of God and neighbor. And the
argument here is that no one ought to assume the
office of preaching unless first he shall have
melted away the stains of the heart with the fire
of charity, and after he has been purged of sin let
anyone who is able assume the office of preaching.]
On the goal of knowledge in gloriam dei et utilitatem proximi [for the glory of God and the benefit of our neighbor], cf. below, pp. 104 f. The
expression survives until Francis Bacon, although
he already gives the second element a more mater-
ialistic meaning: "for the glory of the Creator
and the relief of man's estate."

[30] Loc. cit., pp. 90 f.
[31] Loc. cit., col. 22.
[32] The story occurs in Numbers 22.
[33] LES IDEES ET LES LETTRES, p. 98.
[34] LE MAGISTERE DU PREDICATEUR AU XIII[e] SIECLE,
loc. cit., pp. 108 f.: "Preaching appears here to
be a social function. The preacher only fulfilled
an intermediary or interpretive role. It was his
duty to assure the diffusion among men of the truth
which he had received from Christ through the
Apostles: he must therefore place himself in the
service of the message which he had to transmit,
and take a back seat to his duties."
[35] DE ERUDITIONE PRAEDICATORUM, cap. VI: . . .
Aliae enim artes acquiruntur per assuefactionem
ex frequenti agere . . . Gratia vero praedicandi
ex dono Dei speciali habetur. Unde Eccl. 10 In
manu Dei potestas hominis; id est, praedicatoris,
secundum Glossam. Quod ideo dicitur quia ex dono
Dei est quod homo habeat potestativam praedicationem: quae autem homo ex opere suo non potest,
sed aliunde oportet venire, difficilius est.
Porro causae quare difficile est hujusmodi officium
ad bene faciendum, sunt tres. Una est ex parte
magistri: aliarum enim artium plures inveniuntur
magistri, et qui facile possunt haberi: hujus vero

artis unicus est magister, cujus copiam pauci habent, sc. Spiritus Sanctus. [Other arts are acquired through practice from having to exercise them frequently . . . The grace of preaching is given by God as· a special gift. Whence Ecclesiasticus 10: the power over men--that is, according to the Gloss, over the sermon--is in the hand of God. That is said because it is by the gift of God that man has the preaching power; moreover, it is the more difficult because it is necessary that man, unable to preach by his own power, acquire this skill another way. There are three causes whereby it is difficult to perform this office well. One has to do with the teacher. For the other arts, which are easily mastered, there are many teachers to be found, but the master of this art which few have mastered, namely the Holy Ghost, is unique.] B. HUMBERTI DE ROMANIS OPERA, ed. J. Berthier (Paris, 1889), II, 393.

[36] Leclercq, loc. cit., p. 137: "Is it not admirable indeed that almost all the moral problems studied in the Quodlibets are problems of intention? We perceive here the extent to which spiritual preoccupations dominate the medieval clergy."

[37] DE FORMA PRAEDICANDI, MS. Bodl. 316, fol. 176[v].

[38] SUMMA THEOLOGIAE MORALIS, MS. Bodl., Canon. Misc. 522, fol. 18[v].

[39] Quodlibet X, q. 2; in Leclercq, loc. cit., p. 122.

[40] DISTINCTIONES; ibid., p. 109.

[41] DE MODO COMPONENDI SERMONES, cap. 1; ed. Charland loc. cit., p. 330.

[42] SERMONES QUADRAGINTA, Sermo XXXI, pp. 217 f.

[43] FORMA PRAEDICANDI, cap. 5, loc. cit., p. 242: Videat autem praedicator prae omnibus quod finem bonum sibi faciat sui sermonis, puta laudem Dei vel sanctorum suorum, vel aedificationem proximi, vel aliquod tale meritorium ad vitam aeternam. Si etiam alium finem secundario convolvat, ut vel reputetur, vel aliquod temporale lucretur vel aliquod tale, adulter est verbi Dei, quod reputatur mortale. [Let the preacher see to it above all that he have a good purpose for his sermon--such as the praise of God, or His saints, or the edification of his

neighbor, or some such object deserving eternal
life. If, secondarily, he also includes another
purpose--that he be famous, or that he gain something temporal, or the like--he is an adulterer of
the Word of God, and this is considered a mortal
sin. Trans. Leopold Krul.]

44 Si aliquis incipit praedicare bona voluntate et postea occasione praedicationis glorietur
de hoc quod bene praedicavit, talis gloria non
facit praedicationem peccatum, sive sit venialis
sive mortalis, sed si vana gloria moveat hominem
ad praedicandum, ut praedicatio referatur ad finem
inanis gloriae, tunc praedicatio illa est peccatum
mortale. [If anyone should begin to preach with a
good will and afterwards should pride himself on
the occasion of the sermon because he preached
well, such pride does not constitute a preaching
sin, neither venial nor mortal, but if vainglory
should move a man to preaching, so that the sermon is delivered to the end of vainglory, then
that sermon is a mortal sin.] Leclercq, loc.
cit., p. 118.

45 . . . praedicator non conetur sic hominibus in praedicando placere ut sequatur aliquorum
vanitatem qui frequentantes sermones ea quae sunt
curiositatis commendant. Multi enim praedicantes
talibus placere studuerunt, et ideo multa vana et
frivola, et quae plus obsunt quam prosunt, intro-
duxerunt; . . . Sed non expedit praedicatorem
talium auditorum laudibus aut vituperiis commoveri.
Quominus sic praedicet quo poterit auditoribus
bonis prodesse, consideret illud Ps. Deus dissipavit ossa eorum qui hominibus placent. [. . .
thus the preacher should not strive to please men
in preaching so that he aim at the vanity of those
who frequent sermons and praise those features
which are clever. For many such preachers take
pains to please, and thus they introduce many
empty and frivolous things which hinder more
than they help . . . But it is not advantageous
to the preacher to be affected by the praise or
criticism of such listeners. To convince himself that he should not preach thus in order to
be able to benefit good listeners, let him consider that Psalm: God hath scattered the bones
of them that please men.] Loc. cit., pp. 336 f.

[46] Non debet praedicare subtiles quaestiones theologiae, puta de esse et essentia, discursus astrorum, fictiones poetarum, fabulas inutiles, sed ea quae faciunt ad salutem. [He ought not to preach the subtle questions of theology, for instance, about being and essence, the motion of the stars, the fictions of the poets, idle tales, but those which lead to salvation.] Loc. cit., fol. 19.

[47] SPECULUM ECCLESIAE (Hispalis: J. Kronberger, 1512), unpaginated.

[48] Loc. cit., fol. 19ᵛ.

[49] MS. Bodl., Canon. Misc. 522, fol. 18ᵛ.

[50] Loc. cit., pp. 240 ff.

[51] DE MODO COMPONENDI SERMONES, loc. cit., pp. 330 ff.

[52] FORMA PRAEDICANDI, pp. 233 f. Trans. Leopold Krul.

[53] Obviously, he thinks he perceives in the Pauline verse the technical term "allegare," which means a certain way of linking two Bible passages in the sermon: Placeat autem diligenter advertere quod, sicut dicit Apostolus, ad Tim. 2: Verbum Dei non est alligatum. Ed idcirco nullatenus est credendum quod verbum Dei praedicationis officio fidelibus ministrandum alligetur consuetudine alicui humanitus introductae seu regulis humano ingenio adinventis quae in hoc opere inseruntur, quasi contra eas praedicatori agere non liceat, aut, si praedicando illas servare omiserit, reputari debeat huiusmodi omissio vitiosa. [However, he should resolve diligently to perceive that, just as the Apostle says in Timothy 2: the word of God is not bound. And for that reason it is altogether incredible that the word of God ministered to the faithful through the office of preaching should be bound by any custom introduced by man, whether in regards to rules--which are discussed in this work--introduced by human ingenuity as if it is not permissable to preach contrary to them, or as if the preacher who omits to keep them ought to be held culpably negligent.] Loc. cit., p. 329.

[54] ARS PRAEDICANDI, ed. Alphonse de Poorter (Bruges, 1927), p. 197.

[55] Cf. also Humbert de Romanis, DE ERUDITIONE PRAEDICATORUM, loc. cit., p. 403, in which the simplicitas sine curiositate ornatur rhetorici

[simplicity without the clever embellishment of rhetoric] is commended with reference to a passage from Seneca's letters: Oratio quae veritati dat operam, incomposita esse debet et simplex. Aliae artes ad ingenium pertinent: hic negotium animarum agitur. [The speech that gives a work truth ought to be irregular and simple. Other things attain through art to cleverness: this is done by working through the soul.]

56 Cf. Curtius, p. 415.

57 Known to me only indirectly from PHARETRA 1.15: De Praedicatoribus Malis.

Chapter Four
The Mirror for a Prince

It does not pay for the literary historian to
treat Gower's class critique in detail. The subject
resists artistic shaping except in the form of satire,
and satire in return resists the author's moral earnestness and edificational intention. The SPECULUM
STULTORUM of Nigellus Wireker and several branches
of the French Reynard tales show what could be artistically accomplished in this area. The class
critique of the VOX CLAMANTIS is not their equal.
Gower does not even achieve the vividness of a few
descriptions of situations in his MIROUR. One receives the impression that this man, whose power lies
in the unassuming simplicity and liquid clarity of
his English and, often, also his French style, was
possessed of the pernicious notion that solemnity
and abstraction are the only suitable means of expression in Latin. Some few passages do raise themselves above the bleak, never-ending sterility of
the elegiac distiches, and the reader breathes a
sigh of relief. One such example is the portrait
of the priest who forsakes his parish with the approval of his bishop in order to devote himself to
theological studies at the university. He is in-
spired by the commendable zeal to put what he learns
immediately into practice. Accordingly, his study
of Genesis goes as follows:
"Ve soli," legimus ex scripturis Salomonis,
Namque virum solum nemo requirit eum:
Qua racione scole mos est, quod quisque studere
Debet cum socia doctus in arte sua.
Ipse deus sociam fecit per secula primam,
Vt iuuet hec hominem, sicque creauit eam:
Masculus in primo factus fuit, atque secundo
Femina, sic vt in hiis det deus esse genus:
Istaque principia discretus rector agenda
Perstudet, et vota prebet in arte pia.
Quis laterisque sui costam quam sentit abesse
Non cuperet, per quam perficeretur homo?
Prima viri costa mulier fuit ipsa creata,
Vult igitur costam rector habere suam.
Nam deus humanam precepit crescere gentem,
Cuius precepto multiplicabit homo:

Sic sibi multiplicat rector, dum semen habundat,
Vt sit mandati non reus ipse dei.   3.1417-34
["Woe to him that is alone," we read in Solomon's
writings, for no one looks after the man who is
alone. For this reason it is the college's custom that everyone learned in his art ought to
study with a female companion. God Himself
made the first female companion in order that
she might help man forever, and so He created
her. Man was made first, and woman second, so
that God might bring the human race into being
through them. The discerning rector is very
eager to carry out these precepts, and offers
his devotions in a dutiful way. Who would not
want the rib he feels missing from his side,
the rib by which man is to be perfected? The
first woman was created out of man's rib, and
the rector accordingly wants to have his own
rib. For God commanded the human race to be
fruitful; by His command man is to multiply.
Thus, since his seed is so copious, the rector
does multiply, so that he will not be guilty
in the light of God's mandate.]
Such lumina are, however, so infrequent that one wonders whether this kind of sarcasm was really one of
Gower's intellectual characteristics.

From a sociological point of view, the statements
of the VOX CLAMANTIS are to be evaluated with great
caution. What Owst proved for PIERS PLOWMAN is certainly to a considerable extent also valid for Gower:
he employs cliches inherited from the class sermon
which in every single instance must be validated both
for England and for the second half of the fourteenth
century.[1]

I shall therefore not examine the class critique
as a whole. Nevertheless, I wish to go into a few
questions which result from its conclusion, the Mirror for a Prince. This speculum principis, an open
letter to the young Richard II, is by its position
alone elevated superficially above the frame of the
class critique. In the MIROUR Gower had followed
the traditional scheme of handling the religious and
secular classes by degrees downward from the top.

Thus he began the first section with the pope (or the curia),[2] the second with the emperor, followed by king, magnates, knights, lawyers, merchants, guildsmen, peasants, and serfs. In the VOX CLAMANTIS, on the other hand, he organizes the class critique around the principle of the three estates, which was already becoming antiquated.[3] They are discussed from Book III, Chapter 1 to Book V, Chapter 10. To the third estate is attached the urban populace, which occupies the rest of Book V. Emperor, king, and advocate of the law were not to be accommodated in this three-class frame. The emperor is not mentioned in the VOX CLAMANTIS, perhaps because a successor had not yet been crowned following the death of Charles IV, perhaps because the special character of the Mirror for a Prince left no room for him. The guardians of the law receive their own book, the sixth, and unlike the other classes are presented not in descending but in ascending order of rank, until one passes beyond the royal advisor to the king himself as the highest representative of justice. This sixth book is not mentioned in the plan of the class critique that Gower outlines in the prologue to Book III.[4] Its absence and the altered arrangement vis-a-vis Books III-V create the impression that either the Mirror for a Prince is a belated rounding off of the class critique, or the class critique is a kind of prelude to the Mirror for a Prince. In any case, Gower abandoned in the VOX CLAMANTIS the customary scheme that he had accepted without any modifications in the MIROUR. He isolated the section concerning the king and thus raised it to a special prominence.

In addition to the superficial factor of the arrangement, form and content determine the special character of the Mirror for a Prince within the class critique. According to its form, it is an open letter to the young king. Now personal address as a means of enlivening the subject matter occurs so frequently in the VOX CLAMANTIS that in itself it is not very noteworthy. The letter form also appears, at least in rudiment, in another place.[5] However, nowhere does there occur an open letter of the Mirror's extent, so entirely complete in itself

and so clearly detached from its context. Its beginning and end are carefully set off from the surrounding text. The introduction is a distich that
establishes motivation,

>Hinc est, quod normam scriptis de pluribus ortam
>Regis ego laudi scribere tendo mei (6.587-88)
>[Hence it is that for the honor of my king,
>I intend to set down a rule of conduct taken
>from many writings],

from which the direct address to the king follows.
The end, however, is marked differently in the two
redactions of the text. Only in the A-Text does
Chapter 18 have the character of an epilogue. It
contains a closing prayer, a benediction for the
young monarch, the presentation of the letter,[6] and
a formula of valediction. There is no transition
from the close of the letter to the following chapter. As to the development of the VOX CLAMANTIS,
one can hardly derive a reliable conclusion from
this state of affairs. Yet, one may with some certainty consider the later version an attempt to
bridge an old gap between sections.[7]

The special position which the Mirror for a
Prince occupies is due to the fundamentally dissimilar character, despite all their overlappings,
of class critique and speculum principis. The didactic interest of the latter is of a pedagogical
nature and posits not only an optimistic view of
human educational capacity and willingness, but
also a positive, or at least neutral, human educational substance. The class critique, on the other
hand, while it too cannot manage without the belief
that mankind is educable to a certain degree, proceeds from the negative assumption that human nature is powerfully corrupt and perverse. Gower sees
himself readily in the likeness of the doctor; one
[c]ould call his objective in the class critique
[th]erapy and his goal in the Mirror for a Prince
[pr]ophylaxis.

We come now to the Mirror for a Prince itself.
[I]t is no systematic treatise, but a random file of
[c]urrent themes, among which the first and most im-
[p]ortant is the theme of justice. Any attempt to

ascertain its precise sources would be a waste of time. Gower did not follow directly the two basic models for the medieval speculum principis, Deuteronomy 17.14-20 and the pseudo-Cyprian's DE XII ABUSIONIBUS SAECULI. His acquaintance with the pseudo-Aristotelean SECRETUM SECRETORUM has been proven for the CONFESSIO AMANTIS,[8] and may be considered equally certain for the VOX CLAMANTIS.[9] His ideas were in a general way influenced by the pseudo-Plutarch's INSTITUTIO TRAIANI and its interpretation of the state as an image of the human organismus; however, he did not, unlike the authors of many other medieval mirrors for princes, take it over in toto.[10] He nowhere refers directly to John of Salisbury and seems not to have known Giraldus Cambrensis. His field of vision does not extend to Thomas Aquinas and Albertus Magnus. Gower probably did not draw his knowledge at all from specialized studies. Every major summa transmitted knowledge of the pertinent passages from the church fathers. The convenient compilations of Vincent of Beauvais,[11] Roger of Waltenham,[12] and John Bromyard[13] provide the best insight into the sort and extent of the knowledge which in this province may be considered representative of the second half of the fourteenth century.

For Gower the central problem of the Mirror for a Prince, as well as of the entire sixth book, is the question of law and justice in the state. In the transition to the Mirror he defines the function of the laws in the following manner:
Pro transgressore fuerant leges situate,
Quilibet vt merita posset habere sua.   6.469-70
[Laws were established for the transgressor, so that each man might receive his due rewards.]
Here law is understood primarily as criminal law. It conforms to the usual medieval view of statute law as an arrangement of force which became necessary through man's moral degeneration in the Fall. One could interpret Gower through Wyclif, obviously without suggesting a dependency:
Jus autem civile est jus occasione peccati humanitus adinventum ad justificandam rempublicam coactive quoad bona corporis et

fortune. [Civil law is law made necessary by the
advent of human sin in order that legitimate public matters may be ordered to the benefit and
fortune of the state.]14

This introductory chapter of the Mirror for a
Prince also discusses justice as a constituent and
preserving principle of the state. Because it is
Gower's chief concern, he devotes to justice a lengthy
passage which, despite the fact that it lacks concep-
tual clarity and is to a considerable extent permea-
ted with biblical ideas, can be traced to Cicero's
definition of the state:
Gens sine lege quid est, aut lex sine iudice quid
nam,
Aut quid se iudex sit sine iusticia?
In patria nostra si quis circumspicit acta,
Hec tria cernet ibi sepe timenda michi.
Omnia dampna grauant, set nulla tamen grauiora,
Quam cum iusticiam iustus habere nequit.
Ex iniusticia discordia crescit, et inde
Cessat amor solitus, murmurat atque domus:
Murmur si veniat, venit et diuisio secum,
Terraque diuisa non bene stabit ea;
Et quodcumque sit hoc per se quod stare nequibit,
Ve sibi, nam subito corruet absque modo.
Testis enim deus est, dicens quod regna peribunt
In se diuisa, credoque dicta sua.   6.481-94
[What is a people without law, or what is law
without a judge, or what is a judge, if without
justice? If anyone looks at the doings in our
country, he will observe three things there which
are frightening to me. All misfortunes are bur-
densome, but none more so than when a just man
cannot get justice. Strife grows out of injustice,
and as a result one's customary affection leaves
off, and the household grumbles. And if grum-
bling comes, dividedness comes with it, and the
land divided does not stand firm. And woe to that
which cannot stand by itself, whatever it may be;
for it will suddenly fall to utter ruin. For God
is [my] witness, saying that kingdoms divided
against themselves shall not stand, and I place
trust in His pronouncements.]
Does Cicero's populus est coetus multitudinis iuris

consensu . . . sociatus [the people is . . . the
coming together of a considerable number of men who
are united by a common agreement about law and rights]*
in the DE REPUBLICA (1.25.39) become gens sine lege
quid est in Gower's uncertain terminology?[15] When
Gower maintains in imitation of the Bible that, ex
iniusticia discordia crescit . . . venit et diuisio
. . . regna peribunt in se diuisa [strife grows out
of injustice . . . dividedness comes with it . . .
kingdoms divided against themselves shall not stand],
he stands in a classical tradition, transmitted by
the church fathers, that regards the state above all
as an arrangement for the maintenance of justice
among men.[16] On this concept of the state depends
the statement about the ruler's function with which
Gower begins the Mirror for a Prince:
Regis et est proprium, commissam quod sibi plebem
Dirigat, et iusta lege gubernet eam.   6.585-86
[And it is proper for the king to guide the
people entrusted to him and govern it with just
law.]

The phrase "commissa plebs" implies the view that
kingship is a divine institution.[17] The phrase "iusta
lege gubernare" describes, in the metaphor customary
since antiquity, the king's function as executor of
the law. From this two-fold statement results the
necessity of a more precise definition of what should
be the king's relationship to God as the origin of
his kingship and to the law as its norm and means.
In the beginning of the Mirror for a Prince Gower
therefore furnishes guidelines that tell the king
how he should exercise his authority in harmony with
the demands of the law and of God:
O pie rex, audi que sit tua regula regni,
Concordans legi mixtaque iure dei.   6.589-90
[O pious king, hear what your kingdom's rule
should be, in harmony with the law and joined
with God's justice.]
The word "guidelines" is perhaps an unfortunate
choice, since no official authority stands behind
Gower's statements. And yet he claims for his Mirror
a degree of binding force that is not inherent in his
modest collection of advisements to the king. The
term "regula," with which he designates his compi-

lation in the lines cited,[18] must have expressed an
authoritative importance in an age that knew a "reg-
ulated" life not only in the ecclesiastical orders
but also in other religious and lay communities.[19]
It can be found applied to the prince in Bromyard,
whose article on "regimen" in the SUMMA PRAEDICANTIUM
begins in a manner similar to Gower's Mirror for a
Prince:
> Primo ostenditur regula per quam seipsos et
> alios regere deberent atque regularent [sc.
> regentes]. [First, there is presented a rule
> by which they [sc. rulers] ought to rule them-
> selves and govern others.]

For Bromyard this rule is of two-fold derivation: it
stems on the one hand directly from God, on the other
from Cyprian--a somewhat surprising combination.[20]
His regula is therefore a summary of Deuteronomy 17.
14-20 and the DE XII ABUSIONIBUS, that is, of the
Bible and the wisdom of the church fathers. Gower's
regula makes reference to a large number of unnamed
sources, that is, to the mass of auctores. However,
it derives its real claim to authority less from
these references than from its accord with the lex
and the ius dei. Of course, I am not taking dei in
connection with both lex and ius; rather, I am of
the opinion that Gower is talking about statute law
and God's commandments. It would certainly be rash
to infer from the joining of these two concepts that
the ruler should be subject to the law in the same
way as to God's commandments, perhaps in the manner
demanded by the most important English lawyer of the
thirteenth century: ipse autem rex . . . debet esse
. . . sub deo et sub lege [the king himself . . .
ought to be . . . subject to God and to the law].[21]
Gower makes several other complementary statements
about the relationship of the ruler to statute law,
but without being very systematic:
> 1. Tu super es iura, iustus set viue sub illis
>   (6.613)
>   [You are above the laws, but live as a just
>   man under them];
> 2. Legum frena tenens freno te forcius arce
>   (6.591)
>   [When I grasp the reins of the laws, I hold
>   you in check more strongly than a fortress];

3. Iuraque dans plebi, des ita iura tibi (6.604)
[You who subdue others, work to subdue yourself].
Naturally, Gower knew the Roman principle "princeps
legibus solutus," which was understood in the Middle
Ages to mean he was exempt from the law.[22] And, like
most medieval authors, he acknowledges it[23] although
it in no way accorded with the position of the English
king in the second half of the fourteenth century.
The acknowledgement is academic, however, not only
because of its practical meaninglessness, but above
all because of its incompatibility with the principle
that justice is the foundation of the state.

From this point the royal exemption from the law
experiences its first limitation, which is connected
with the ideal of the rex iustus. When Gower admon-
ishes the ruler, Tu super es iura, iustus set viue
sub illis (1), we are reminded of Isidore, who set
down in the SENTENCES the subordination of the ruler
to the law as a requisite for law and justice.[24]
Gower does not follow Isidore's argument in all the
details and is very frugal with his proofs. On the
most important point, however, he agrees vigorously
with the SENTENCES, namely that the ruler as rex
iustus is obligated by inner necessity, even though
not by external forces, to keep the lex iusta if he
does not wish to carry ad absurdum the principle
that he embodies iustitia. Isidore's thesis that
principes teneri legibus suis, neque in se posse
damnare iura quae in subiectis constituunt [princes
themselves should obey the laws, nor are they able
in themselves to denounce the law which they establish for their subjects], is reflected in Gower's
demand (3) that iuraque dans plebi, des ita iura
tibi.[25] Isidore expands on the term "licere" in
his proof; Gower discusses at length the relationship of licere and posse, of licitum and probum.[26]
Because he employs licere indiscriminately, now in
the sense of what is legally, now in the sense of
what is morally permissible, the clarity of his
presentation suffers.[27] However, the train of
thought, which was plainly influenced by a remem-
brance of Cassiodorus, can be supplemented with the
help of the VARIAE.[28] His regard for the welfare of
the state (611-14) and his own honor (617-20), which

is probably to be understood here as moral integrity, keep the king from exploiting that immunity which is his by law. The result is that the royal autonomy suffers its first limitation from honestum and utile.

There is also another and, for Gower, a more important limitation, which originates in the divine world order. With it we come to the second point, the relationship of the ruler to God, the source of his authority. The principle of the ordo manifests itself not only in the hierarchical gradation of created beings, but in a chain of dependent relationships which links the individual elements of the creation. Thus the ruler's obligation to obey God matches that of the subjects to obey him:
Est propter mundum tibi subdita sors aliorum,
Tu propter celum subditus esto deo.
Vt tibi deseruit populus de lege subactus,
Cristi seruiciis temet ad instar habe. 6.597-600
[For the sake of the world, the fate of others is subject to you; for the sake of heaven, be subject yourself to God. Since the people subjected to you by law serve you devotedly, conduct yourself like a Christ toward your servants.]

In both instances the relationship is characterized through subiectio and servitus.[29] Elsewhere in the VOX CLAMANTIS and the MIROUR, as well as in the CONFESSIO AMANTIS, the equation is of course not Subject:Ruler::Ruler:God, but Creature:Man::Man:God.[30] Since, according to Genesis 1.28 ff., all creatures are subject to man and obligated to obey him, so man is subject to God and placed at his service. Thus there is not only a parallelism, but a causal nexus between the two obedience equations. The revolt of man against God inevitably brings about the revolt of creation against man.[31] This general human situation becomes specifically political when the citizenry are substituted for the creation. The analogy between the political cosmos and the created cosmos is so far-reaching for Gower that elsewhere he allows it right up to the point of rebellion.[32] However, there is no trace in Gower of the finer distinctions of these two orders, such as occupy the church fathers when they perceive the political-social cosmos with

its authority of man over men as a consequence of
the Fall and contrast it to the original, God-
intended condition of equality for all men that
allowed only a mastery of men over the creation.[33]

We have spoken of justice as the foundation of
the state, of the duty of the king to realize justice
in the state, of his relationship to the law, and of
the duality of his place within the divine ordo.
But we have not yet inquired about Gower's definition
of the prince. The usual medieval attempts in this
direction are variations on the formula which Isidore
handed down in the ETYMOLOGIES. He derives rex from
recte facere:
> Reges a regendo vocati; . . . Non autem regit,
> qui non corrigit. Recte igitur faciendo regis
> nomen tenetur, peccando amittitur. Unde apud
> veteres tale erat proverbium: Rex eris si recte
> facies, si non facies, non eris. ["Royal" is
> said to be derived from "ruling"; . . . however,
> he will not rule who does not make amends. Through
> doing right, therefore, the name of king is held,
> through sinning it is lost. Whence among the
> ancients was the proverb: you will be king if
> you act justly; if you do not, you will not.][34]
This formula provides not a constitutional, but an
ethical definition of the ruler. If it is a flaw
that medieval mirrors for princes so frequently degenerate into catalogues of virtues, the source may
lie here. Certainly, this kind of definition is the
only one suitable within the compass of a view of
history that regarded the fate of individuals and
of peoples as the result of moral conduct. And there
is yet another factor. The notion that political
science is a branch of ethics quite naturally gained
force in a time that barely knew the abstract idea
of the state and that identified it largely with the
person of the ruler.

The formula rex a recte faciendo occurs in Gower
in the context of individual ethics as well as of political science. It appears in its general meaning
in the seventh book--Rex est quisque sui, bene qui
regit acta, beatus (7.927) [Every saintly man who
governs his actions well is king over himself]--and

141

is applied to the king in the Mirror for a Prince:
    Si rex esse velis, te rege, rex et eris.
    Qua fore se regem poterit racione fateri,
    Mentis qui proprie non regit acta sue? 6.606-8
    [If you wish to be a king, rule yourself and you
    will be one. By what right could a man who does
    not even reign over the workings of his own mind
    say he was a king?]
It is used yet again in a later part of the Mirror
to distinguish the king from the tyrant:
    Qui bene regis agit regimen, rex est, set inique
    Qui regit in viciis, ipse tirannus erit. 6.1003-4
    [He who wields a king's command well is king, but
    he who rules unjustly amidst corruption is a tyrant.]
Because Gower creates out of the common property of
his time, he does not require a systematic foundation.
The relationships between the general and political
aspects of the formula remain unexplained. If one
uses as an aid the article "regimen" from Bromyard's
approximately contemporary summa, then one obtains
detailed information on this question. Bromyard
divides ethics in the customary fashion into individual, social, and political ethics (monastica,
iconomica, and politica philosophia).[35] These are
not independent branches, but stages which are successively attained. It would be absurd if someone
who had not mastered the task of the most basic
stage would presume to advance to the following or
even to the ultimate stage. Whoever does not know
how to govern himself is unsuited to rule over a
larger community, be it of an ecclesiastical or
political kind: gradatim ascendendum est, quia absurdum est quod qui seipsum regere nescit, accipere
presumat regimen animarum vel cuiuscunque communitatis [the upward motion proceeds by degrees, for
it is absurd that he who knows not how to govern
himself should presume to accept the guidance of
sou s or of any community whatsoever].[36] That is
    tly what Gower expresses in the verses cited
  e (6.606-8) and what recurs with a slight shift
 f emphasis in the distich,
    Est tibi, rex, melius quod te de lege gubernes,
    Subdere quam mundi singula regna tibi. 6.595-96
    [It is better for you, O king, to govern yourself
    according to the law than to subjugate all the

142

kingdoms of the world to yourself.]
Here--depending, indeed, on two biblical passages--37
the Christian element is stressed more strongly than
in the other variants of the rex a recte faciendo
formula. Yet, one may in no way deduce from the lines
a renunciation of the world. They are part of the
context of the Stoic-Christian monarchic ideal. It
necessarily follows from them that instruction in the
virtues and vices is more important as royal propae-
deutic than any specific political, military, or
diplomatic schooling. A catalogue of virtues is
necessarily the central piece of any speculum principis, for all other things will of their own accord
fall to the lot of the virtuous ruler:
> Rex, ita si fugias viciorum pondera, mores
> Et teneas, poteris quicquid habere velis. 6.915-16
> [If you shun the influence of vice in'this
> way, O King, and keep your good morals, you can
> accomplish anything you wish.]

In this his characteristic feature, the rex iustus
gains simultaneously the earthly and the divine kingdoms, and need have no fears about the stability of
his kingship:
> Lucratur populum que deum rex iustus vtrumque,
> Statque per hoc regni firma corona sui. 6.1007-8
> [A just king wins both God and the people, and
> by this means the crown of his realm stands secure.]

    Perhaps it is permissible at this point to cast
a side glance at Langland and at the relationship of
the king to the law and justice in PIERS PLOWMAN.38
The question is treated in detail in B 19.462-73
(C 22.467-78):
> Then cam ther a kynge and by hus corone seide,
> "Ich am a kyng with corone the comune to reule,
> And holychurch and clergie fro corsede men to de-
>   fenden.
> And yf me lacketh to lyue by the lawe wol that ich
>   take
> Ther ich may haue hit hastelokest for ich am hefd
>   of lawe,
> And ye ben bote membrys and ich a-boue alle.
> Sitthen ich am youre alre hefd ich am youre alre
>   hele,
> And holychurches chef help and chefteyn of the
>   commune.

And what ich take of yow two ich take hit at
                                        techynge
Of spiritus iusticie for ich Iugge you alle;
So ich may baldely beo housled for ich borwe neuere,
Ne craue of my comune bote as my kynde asketh."
Langland proceeds more intensely than Gower from the
then acute problem of royal taxation, which he ties
to the king's threefold duty to be guardian of justice,
defender of the realm, and protector of the church.
In every other respect his formulations match those
of Gower. The king is the head (hefd, caput) and
the health (hele, salus) of the political organismus,
just as in the first chapter of Gower's Mirror for a
Prince. The monarch's designation of himself as the
"hefd of lawe" (C 22.471) is not entirely clear. It appears as if the king here claims for himself a position above the law like that expressed by Gower in
6.613 (Tu supra es leges).[39] However, Langland continues, "And ye ben bote membrys and ich a-boue alle."
In the following line, in the statement "Sitthen ich
am youre alre hefd," the matter is taken up again.
Obviously the discussion is not about the head and
members of the law but of the political community,
and "give" and "take" in the sense of taxation are
to be understood according to the analogy of the
story of Menenius Agrippa or the INSTITUTIO TRAIANI.
Accordingly, the genitive "of lawe" (in the half-
line "for ich am hefd of lawe") must be understood
adverbially ("by law, legally") which is grammatically
possible. Be that as it may, it clearly follows from
the subsequent lines that the king regards himself
only as a functionary of law and justice (l. 470:
"The lawe wol that ich take"; l. 476: "ich take hit
at techynge of spiritus iusticie") and that the
execution of justice does not cease before the person of the king:
    Spiritus iusticie spareth nat to spille
    Hem that beoth gulty and for to corecte
    Thy kyng, and the kyng falle in eny thynge gulty.[40]
If the relationship is reversed and justice bows to
royal caprice, then perversion sets in and the stability of the state founded in law is endangered:
    And spiritus iusticie shal Iugen, wol he, nul he,
    After the kynges counsaile and the comune lyke.[41]
Thus Langland's monarch ideal is also determined by

the concept of the rex iustus.

When Gower implores the young king to strive after virtue as the highest value, he distinguishes it from other, lesser values, raising the question of what role these other values play in his portrait of the ruler:

O bone rex iuuenis, fac quod bonitate iuuentus
Sit tua morigeris dedita rite modis.
Quid tibi forma iuuat vel nobile nomen Auorum,
Si viciis seruus factus es ipse tuis?   6.627-30
[O good young king, act so that through your
goodness your youth may be properly dedicated
to moral ways. What will your handsomeness
or the noble name of your ancestors avail you,
if you have become a slave to your own vices?]

Medieval doctrine about possessions distinguishes three dona: naturae, fortunae, gratiae. Of the dona naturae, Gower mentions in the lines cited the noble body ("forma"), of the dona fortunae, noble lineage ("nobilitas").[42] His attitude toward the beauty of the noble body is not at all original, but yet apparently not clear enough to preclude misunderstandings. Thus Kleineke writes in his short section on the VOX CLAMANTIS' Mirror for a Prince: "The eye for noble physical forms and the related demand that a beautiful soul and spirit should be harmoniously suited with a well-shaped body belong to a world newly discovered by chivalry."[43] Kleinike refers to 6.1081 ff.:

Nobile corpus habes et singula membra decora,
Sit virtus animi sic magis illa tibi:
Vt foris est forma tibi splendida, splendeat intra
Mens tua, quod tibi, rex, sit decor ille duplex.
[You have a noble body and comely limbs, so let
the virtue of your spirit be all the greater.
Just as your outer beauty is brilliant, let your
spirit within be bright, so that your comeliness
may be two-fold, O king.]

To begin with, the triad body, soul, and spirit in Kleineke's statement is not entirely correct. Gower sees mankind dualistically. The entire psychomachia of the MIROUR is based on the duality of "corps" and "alme," of "passiouns" and "raisoun," and the con-

145

ception is not altered in his later works. It is
expressed in the distiches cited by the word "duplex,"
which clearly shows that the second distich is to be
understood as a variation upon the first, and that
"mens" must be understood as a synonym for "animus,"
not as a third new quantity alongside "corpus" and
"animus." However, more important than the question
of trinity or duality is the question of "harmonious
suiting." Kleineke was obviously correct insofar as
concerns the thought that the soul shapes the body,
but one can hardly call that a new discovery of chivalry. However, if the use of the term should postu-
late an equation of the two quantities of body and
soul, such a thought is very far from Gower. Even
the context of the cited verses urges caution. Lines
1077-80[44] state that all mankind's possessions stem
from God and that nothing belongs to man as his own.
Thus from the outset the noble body is deprived of
inherent value. The passage referred to is followed
by a section that, borrowing from Neckam, indicates
the transitoriness and questionable nature of physical beauty,[45] and that ends with the distich:
Non tibi forma deum set mens sincera meretur,
Iusticie soli vita beata datur. 6.1089-90
[Not your beauty but a pure spirit is worthy
of God. A blessed life is granted to righteousness alone.]
This clear and plain appraisal of relative values pre-
cludes harmonious suiting as a balance of physical and
ethical values. It is the same ratio of values that
Gower employs for nobility of origin and nobility of
virtue:
Mores namque bonos veneratur curia celi,
Et celum iustus, non generosus, habet. 6.1023-24
[Indeed, the court of heaven reveres good conduct, and the upright man, not the nobly born,
reaches heaven.][46]
With that we come to the second point, the value of
noble lineage.

    With it Gower touches on a theme that had ac-
quired topical political significance in the 1370's.
In the waning Middle Ages the demand for a thorough
social reform appeared occasionally in connection
with the thought that men had originally been social
equals. The thought in itself is neither new nor

revolutionary.[47] It receives a politically aggressive
turn in England in the years before the Peasants'
Rebellion in the "Song of Adam and Eve":
    When Adam delved and Eve span,
    Who was then a gentleman?
The program expressed in the song was probably understood communistically only by radical leaders, and
even with regard to them one must reckon with the
possibility that a biased writing of history has
distorted their image for us.[48] At any rate, the
nobility's right to exist was then for the first
time doubted in principle, and the divinely-ordained
Christian class arrangement assailed through a shib-
boleth likewise sprung from a Christian source. Of
the poets of the time, Chaucer, as might be expected,
did not take a position on the problem. Supposing
that he was at the time working on TROILUS AND CRISEYDE,
he did not in any case find it necessary to include a
"degree speech." Langland singled out a part of the
problem when he turned against the doctrine of the
common ownership of property (in the B-Text of PIERS
PLOWMAN, composed ca. 1378-79):
    Enuye herd this and heet freres to go to scole,
    And lerne logyk and lawe and eke contemplacioun,
    And preche men of Plato and preue it by Seneca,
    That alle thinges vnder heuene oughte to ben in
                                            comune.
    And yit he lyeth, as I leue that to the lewed so
                                            precheth,
    For god made to men a lawe and Moyses it taughte,
    Non concupisces rem proximi tui.   B 20.271-76
Of course, Langland oversimplifies when he contrasts
the communism of pagan philosophers with the Ten
Commandments' protection of property. It was not
a question of a discrepancy between antiquity and
Christianity. The Stoic doctrine that there is no
private property according to natural law was domes-
ticated early by Christianity and transmitted to the
Middle Ages by Isidore.[49] It was, rather, a question
of interpretation. One usually distinguished between
communism before the Fall and its curtailment by
private ownership after that event, and thus escaped
the dilemma. Of course, when Gower writes, "Sunt nam
communes omnibus orbis opes" (6.360) [For the treasures
of the earth are common to all], he is thinking

                        147

neither about a paradisal state of affairs nor a communistic program. Rather, he is thinking of the indiscriminate distribution of earthly possessions that makes their value seem dubious and their possession hardly worth the effort.[50]

Langland does not discuss the more significant aspect of the question of human equality insofar as it concerns not property but class. Gower, however, discusses this problem in detail. The chief passage in the Mirror for a Prince is a series of verses that he appropriated from Peter Riga:[51]

Disceque cunctorum quod sit communis origo,
Ortus et occasus vnus, et vna caro.
Nobilis est mentis quisquis virtute refulget,
Degener est solus cui mala vita placet;
Mores namque bonos veneratur curia celi,
Et celum iustus, non generosus, habet. 6.1019-24
[And learn that there is a common origin for all men, and that there is one birth, one death, and one flesh. Anyone who is illustrious because of goodness of spirit is noble, and anyone who likes an evil life is base. Indeed, the court of heaven reveres good conduct, and the upright man, not the nobly born, reaches heaven.]

There are added Gower's own words to Richard, with which he challenges the royal youth to double his hereditary nobility with the nobility of virtue, that is, to harmonize in his person the principles of inheritance and accomplishment:

Si te nobilitas generosaque nomina tangunt,
In genus exemplum fer magis ipse tuum:
Nomine perspicuo cum sis generosus auorum,
Equipares stirpis moribus acta tuis.
Hoc in honore dei communi voce precamur,
Vt gemines animi nobilitate genus. 6.1011-16
[If nobility and noble names impress you, carry your own example of even greater nobility down to posterity. Even though you may be noble because of the illustrious name of your forefathers, you should match your ancestral deeds through your own good behavior. With one voice we pray in God's name for this, namely, that you unite your high birth with nobility of spirit.]

That true nobility is based on virtue, not birth, is

148

a Stoic-Christian commonplace. In the AURORA citation
Gower proves to be in accord with patristic tradition
as it was particularly nurtured in the monastic orders, whose internal peace could be easily destroyed
through emphasis on social distinctions.[52] The second
passage, which immediately follows the panegyric to
the Black Prince, has a more courtly character,[53] since
on this question the Mirror for a Prince is generally
much more moderate than the MIROUR.[54] Gower holds
fast to the principle of the nobility of virtue, yet
is very benevolently disposed towards nobility of
birth and attempts a synthesis of the two. Kleineke
regarded such cases as overlappings of the Christian-
Stoic and the courtly-chivalric ideals of the prince.[55]
Gower would hardly have been conscious of them. To
harmonize the nobilitas generis with the nobilitas
animi was the natural endeavor of a courtly-oriented
poet who, unlike members of the monastic orders--
especially the mendicants--had a quasi-professional
attitude towards inherited nobility.[56] The tradition of the Latin panegyrists had paved the way for
him there. These had also, in their attempt to portray the ideal ruler, confronted the dilemma of inherited and virtuous nobility. The influence of
antiquity is wholly sufficient to explain the many
layers exhibited in courtly literature by the theme
of nobilitas. Among Gower's contemporaries, for
example, Walter of Peterborough--in a poem about
Prince Edward's Spanish campaign composed after 1367--
linked hereditary nobility and the performance principle in the following model portrait:

Magnus avis, major animis, modo maximus armis,
  Nomen quodcunque magnificare potest.
. . . . . .
Quis dux, quis dominus majores progenitores
  Aut habet, aut habuit? saecula longa lege.
. . . . . .
Lumen conventu, leo conflictu, lyra cantu;
  Ergo prudens, ergo probus, ergo pius.
Per tot signa sacra probat Edwardus genitores,
  Et plus quo senior praedicat ipse patrem.
Semper enim sanguis vester, de semine divo,
  Narrat si quid habet, notificatque patres.[57]
[Great by ancestry, greater by spirit, greatest
                                    by arms,

He can glorify any name at all.
. . . .
What leader, what lord either has, or has had
   Greater progenitors? Read through the long ages.
. . . . . .
A light in the assembly, a lion in the conflict, a
                        lyre in the melody;
   Therefore prudent, therefore virtuous, therefore
                        pious.
Through so many holy signs Edward proves his ances-
                        tors,
   And as an older man himself he shows his father.
For always your blood, from divine seed,
   Tells if it has anything, and makes known the
                        father.]
Had Claudian written these lines, the Latin would
doubtless have been more tolerable; the content, however, would not have been essentially different. The
juxtaposition of a demand for nobility of virtue and
a positive estimation of noble derivation, therefore,
probably has its beginnings in a literary genre rather
than in Gower's inability to keep separate cultural
values of different origin.

One could rather fault Gower's indiscriminate
syncretism with the ideas that derive from the SECRETUM
SECRETORUM. They surface frequently in Chapters 13
and 14, which have just been discussed. If medieval
complexes of ideas could be interpreted clearly in
the sense of their origins, one might conclude that
here the oriental-despotic portrait of the ruler is
combined with the Christian-Stoic and courtly-chivalric
ideals. The valuation of "fama," "laus," and "gloria,"
for example, inclines sometimes to the Stoic-Christian
side, and sometimes conforms to the SECRETUM or to
chivalric views. The Christian view is prominent at
the point where, in connection with the theme ubi
sunt qui ante nos, the transience of earthly glory
is discussed:[58]
Ecce diu res nulla manet mortalibus, ecce
Nullus honor prohibet, gloria nulla mori:
Non prosunt quicquam preconia vana sepultis,
Torquent famosos tartara sepe reos.   6.1113-16
[Behold, nothing endures long for mortals. Behold, no honor, no glory staves off death: empty

praises are of no use to the interred. Hell puts
the guilty to frequent torture, even though they
are famous.]
It is also prominent a little later: Gloria nulla
potest in mundi rebus haberi (6.1129)[59] [No fame in
worldly concerns can be retained]. The chivalric view
appears to me to prevail especially where thoughts of
fame and agon are combined, particularly in the chapter concerning the Black Prince (see 6.977 f.):
Acta patris vince, maiorque vocaberis illo,
Totaque vox clamet laudis honore tue.
[Surpass your father's deeds and you will be
called greater than he, and every voice will
shout in honor of your glory.]
In other places the more utilitarian conception of
the SECRETUM shines through, especially in the interesting passage at 6.811-32. Here Gower hándles the
theme of largitas or liberalitas, and interprets it
in the Christian sense as almsgiving. He begins with
the word "larga," which proves in the course of the
first verse to be an epithet for elemosina: Larga
tuis meritis inopes elemosina curet [Through your
merits, let your generous aims take care of the poor].
And he ends on a purely Christian note:
Est ancilla dei simplex elemosina, mortis
Antidotum, venie porta, salutis iter:
Disputat aduersus dantis peccata, perorat
Auctori, redimit probra, precatur opem. 6.827-30
[A sincere alms is the handmaiden of God, the
antidote to death, the gateway to grace, the path
to salvation. It contends against the sins of the
giver, it pleads for its author, it redeems the
worthy, it supplicates for the rich.]
In between, however, are the SECRETUM's reflections
upon the cautions with which largitas or liberalitas
should be exercised. They are the same reflections
that Gower repeats with reference to Aristotle, without any of the Christian trimming, in Book VII of
the CONFESSIO AMANTIS.[60] In this context largitas
does not serve the goal of redemption, but is a means
of acquiring fame, and, according to the view of the
SECRETUM, fame is the proper goal of any lordship:
. . . fama ergo est quod principaliter et per se
ipsum appetitur in regimine, quia regimen non
appetitur propter se, set propter bonam famam.

151

[. . . therefore it is fame that preeminently and
for itself is desired in ruling, because ruling
is not desired for itself, but for fame.]61
The CONFESSIO AMANTIS combines the two points, the
end and the means of largitas, in a Latin distich in
a chapter superscription:
Fama colit largum volitans per secula Regem,
Dona tamen licitis sunt moderanda modis.
WORKS, III, 287
[Fame flying through the ages favors a generous King,
Nevertheless, gifts are to be distributed moderately.
The verses are then explained in detail in the text
(CONFESSIO 7.2014 ff.). No doubt the like formulations
of the Mirror for a Prince also derive from the SECRETUM:
Da tua non parce, cui des tamen aspice caute;
Crede, satis res est ingeniosa dare:
Non perit hec probitas que dona rependit honeste,
Namque piam laudem res data dantis habet. 6.815-18
[Do not give sparingly; rather, consider carefully
to whom you give. Believe that it is quite enough
to give intelligently. The goodness which expends
its gifts creditably does not come to nothing, for
a gift brings worthy praise to the giver.]
The extent to which Gower departs from the Christian
point of view is made clear by such sententious remarks as Munera tempus habent, fama perhennis erit
(6.824) [Gifts endure for a time, but fame will be
everlasting], which recalls the SECRETUM's
. . . acquisitio largitatis est gloria regis
et perhennitas regnorum [. . . the possession
of largess is the glory of the king and the per-
petuity of kingdoms].62
And yet the borrowings from the SECRETUM do not appear as intrusive elements from an alien value system.
They are, even though awkwardly, so etched into the
portrait of the Christian ruler that they can be
understood as an expression of the double nature of
the royal position with regard to this world and the
next. Largitas secures the prince fame in this world
and forgiveness of sin in the next, just as iustitia
similarly secures him the earthly and the heavenly
kingdoms.63

Gower does not adopt the SECRETUM's characteristic views on methods of conducting brutal warfare,

crafty diplomacy, and methodical intimidation of subjects, in which the oriental element is prominent. In the question of conducting war, he instead develops the theory of the bellum iustum with the customary Christian modifications;[64] in the question of how best to insure the obedience of subjects, he decides emphatically in favor of amor against terror.[65] One must in general bear in mind that the version of the SECRETUM Gower used already had strong Christian impulses,[66] and was sanctioned by the name of Aristotle. The medieval user had no suspicion of its oriental extraction.

The last chapters of the Mirror for a Prince (from the end of Chapter 14 through Chapter 17) are tightly connected thematically and as far removed from the SECRETUM's ideal king as they are from chivalry's ideal life. They proceed from the proposition that God has set self-understanding and love of his creator as rules of life for the king:

Noscere te studeas et amare deum, duo namque
Hec sunt, que tibi, rex, scire necesse iubet.
Hec est condicio sub qua tibi contulit esse
Viuendique modum conditor ipse tuus. 6.1035-38
[You should strive to know yourself and to love God, for these are the two things, O king, which He decrees indispensable for you to know. This is the condition under which your Maker has conferred existence and your way of life upon you.]

This divine goal-setting has nothing to do with the ethic of rule per se, but is, as Gower describes it in Book VII with reference to the creation of man, the life task of every man.[67] It has to do with monarchic ethics only insofar as they are a more important form of individual ethics, and because the consequences of the king's moral failures threaten the entire people.

Now knowledge includes sapientia, which is a gift from God and which is furthered by sustained contemplation of the vanity of earthly life. The Mirror for a Prince illustrates the first point with the story of Solomon's successful prayer for wisdom,[68] a narrative of paradigmatic significance for every ruler that appears in all three of Gower's major works.

153

The second point is treated in Chapters 16 and 17.
According to the medieval view, any moral philosophy
without a thorough discussion of the vanity of worldly
goods and the transitoriness of all things lacks importance and makes impossible the first step towards
self-knowledge. Thus Vincent of Beauvais begins his
SPECULUM MORALE with the biblical text, In omnibus
operibus tuis memorare novissima tua, et in aeternum
non peccabis (Ecclesiasticus 7.40) [In all thy works
remember thy last end, and thou shalt never sin].
Thus Lorenz, the Dominican royal father confessor,
prefaces with an ars moriendi the section of his
SOMME LE ROI that discusses the virtues.[69] Thus
Gower also begins the general observations that frame
his class critique with the Solomon-like vanitas
theme (II, Chapter 1), and concludes them with a detailed contemplation of death (VII, Chpts. 9-19).
It appears to me that the medieval predilection for
the theme of death differs from similar manifestations
of the baroque in that the didactic intent remains
most important even in the most realistic description, and in that there is inherent within it a tendency that is completely positive and directed towards this life. The keynote is optimistic rather
than macabre when, for example, the theme is stated
in the anonymous MYROUR OF SYNNERS:[70]

> Biholde now frende how profitable a myrrour it is
> for synners inwardly biholdyng of this hije sen-
> tence [sc. Ecclesiasticus 7.40]: that is wolde
> god that men sauereden and understonden and pur-
> ueiden for the laste thingis; for jif thou ofte
> biholde thiself in this myrrour and jif thou
> bisily studye to set thus thi self bifor thi
> silf, douteles thou schalt be strengere than
> sampson, more war than dauith, and wiser thanne
> salomon.

Meditations on death of this kind appear rather in-
frequently in mirrors for princes. The only examples
I know of are Waltenham and Gower.[71] It is almost
inconceivable in Gower's case that such meditations
were occasioned by the person of the addressee.
Richard II was fiteen in 1381; he was, therefore,
eleven to fifteen years of age during the time of
composition of the VC's Mirror for a Prince. And
yet these last chapters may have seemed to Gower

154

most fitting, for they lead to the true self-knowledge
that the ruler cannot acquire early enough in order
to choose the right way between virtue and vice. His
free will and his free choice then determine the weal
and woe not only of his own person, but of the state
entrusted to him:
  Fac ea que tibi vis, bona vel mala, sic et habebis,
  Te tamen in melius dirigat oro deus. 6.1157-58
  [Do what you will, either good or bad, and such
  will you have for yourself, but I pray that God
  may direct you toward the better.]
With that the Mirror for a Prince ends. The epilogue
(Chpt. 18) shall be treated in the next chapter in
the context of the VC's history of origin, or better,
history of development.

     When one attempts to evaluate Gower's Mirror
for a Prince as a whole, it becomes evident that its
value does not lie in a rational philosophy of govern-
ment. Gower had neither practical political experience
to employ, nor systematic studies to utilize. However,
he did have a strongly pronounced perception of the
ethical foundation of the state. With passionate
emphasis he discusses the problem of iustitia and the
ideal of the rex iustus. Certainly his Mirror for a
Prince is a mirror of virtue; however, it is virtue
far removed from moral narrow-mindedness. It por-
tends welfare and prosperity for the ruler as well
as his subjects.

Notes to Chapter Four
     1 G. R. Owst, LITERATURE AND PULPIT IN MEDIEVAL
ENGLAND (Cambridge, 1933), Chpts. 5-7, " The Preaching
of Satire and Complaint." On Gower see pp. 230 ff.
     2 The pope appears to have been interpolated
belatedly; cf. above, pp. 13 ff.
     3 These are the clerus, miles, and cultor; cf.
3.1 f. and Book III, Prologue.
     4 Prologue III passim; cf. esp. 103 f., which
possibly alludes, in the phrase "trina series," to
three projected books (III-V?).
     5 Cf. the prose summary of Book VI, Chapter 5:
Hic loquitur quasi per epistolam Iudicibus illis di-
rectam, qui in caduca suarum diuiciarum multitudine
sperantes, deum adiutorem suum ponere nullatenus

dignantur. [Here he speaks as if in a letter directed to the judges who put their trust in their transitory heaps of riches. In no way do they deem it fitting to establish God as their helper.] Cf. also the end of the chapter, 413 ff.: Iudicibus populi vanum tamen est quod in ista/ Materia scripsi; perdita verba dedi. [But it is in vain that I write of these matters to the people's judges; I have uttered wasted words.]

6 It is designated "metra" in 6.1191, "scripta" in 1194, "epistola" in the prose summary of Chapter 8.

7 Cf. below, pp. 195 f.

8 Cf. George L. Hamilton, "Some Sources of the Seventh Book of Gower's CONFESSIO AMANTIS," MP, 9 (1911/12), 323-45.

9 See below, pp. 151 ff.

10 It appears in John of Salisbury's POLICRATICUS, Books 5 and 6 in the freer edition, in a more concise form in the first chapter of Roger of Waltenham's speculum principis, and also in Vincent of Beauvais' SPECULUM HISTORIALE, Book VII, Chapters 24 ff. The extraordinary popularity of the INSTITUTIO in the High and Late Middle Ages is probably due to the fact that the organic conception of the state--which was in itself not new and which was related to the New Testament conception of the nature of the church-- offered so many possibilities for arranging details and toying with proportions.

11 SPECULUM HISTORIALE, ed. D. Nicolinus (Venice, 1591).

12 COMPENDIUM MORALE DE VIRTUOSIS DICTIS ET FACTIS EXEMPLARIBUS ANTIQUORUM, MS. Fairfax 4, Bodleian.

13 SUMMA PRAEDICANTIUM, s.v. "regimen."

14 DE CIVILI DOMINIO, ed. R. L. Poole (London, 1885), p. 125.

*The translation is that of George Holland Sabine and Stanley Barney Smith (Columbus, Ohio, 1929; rpt. Indianapolis, n.d.), p. 129. Trans.

15 A similar passage occurs in the CONFESSIO AMANTIS 7.2695-2701, where the same stylistic device of a series of questions is employed for the same train of thought:

> What is a lond wher men ben none?
> What ben the men whiche are al one
> Withoute a kinges governance?

What is a king in his ligance,
Wher that ther is no lawe in londe?
What is to take lawe on honde,
Bot if the jugges weren trewe?
[16] Cf. R. W. and A. J. Carlyle, A HISTORY OF
MEDIEVAL POLITICAL THEORY IN THE WEST, 6 vols. (Edin-
burgh, 1903-36), I, 161 ff. I have gratefully used
the rich collection of materials from these volumes
over and over in this chapter.
[17] The problem of the legal basis of the mon-
archy is not yet acute for Gower at the time of
Richard II and is therefore only slightly touched on
in the VOX CLAMANTIS. After the accession of Henry
IV, Gower treats the question in more detail, naming
three claims for Henry's kingship: the right of the
conqueror, the claim of legitimacy, and the choice
of the people:
Vnde coronatur trino de iure probatur,
Regnum, conquestat, que per hoc sibi ius manifestat;
Regno succedit heres, nec ab inde recedit;
Insuper eligitur a plebe que sic stabilitur:
Vt sit compactum, iuris nil defuit actum.
                    CRONICA TRIPERTITA 3.332-36
[Why he was crowned is approved by threefold
right: he conquered the realm, and because of
this, right is clearly on his side; he succeeded
as heir to the kingdom and has not abdicated from
it; in addition, he was chosen by the people and
thus firmly established. In order that there
might be agreement, no legal measure was omitted.]
[18] In 587 he styles it "normam scriptis de pluribus ortam" [a rule of conduct taken from many writings]
[19] According to scholars of the Romance languages,
the term has an innate, definite meaning. The definition of the DIGESTS reads: Regula est quae rem quae
est breviter enarrat [a rule is that which succinctly
states something which is], and . . . non ut ex regula ius sumatur, sed ut ex iure quod est regula fiat
[a law ought not to be derived from a rule, but let
that become a rule which is derived from a law]. PAUL
DIG. 50.17.1.
[20] S. v. "regimen," art. I: . . . Quantum ad
primum illorum [sc. regnatium] regula est duplex: una
que a deo datur, alia que a Cypriano, que a priori
non discordat, sed magis illam explanat [. . . As

157

far as the first of those [sc. rulers] the rule is
two-fold: one which is given by God, the other by
Cyprian--which is not at odds with the first, but
amplifies it].
21 Henricus de Bracton, DE LEGIBUS ET CONSUE-
TUDINIBUS ANGLIAE, ed. George E. Woodbine (New Haven,
1915), II, 33: Ipse autem rex non debet esse sub
homine sed sub deo et sub lege, quia lex facit regem.
Attribuat ergo rex legi, quod lex attribuit ei,
videlicet dominationem et potestatem. Non est enim
rex ubi dominatur voluntas et non lex. Et quod sub
lege esse debeat, cum sit dei vicarius, evidenter
apparet ad similitudinem Ihesu Christi, cuius vices
gerit in terra. [The king himself, however, ought
not to be subject to men, but to God and the law,
because the law makes him king. Let the king therefore allot to the law what the law allots to him,
namely power and might. For he is not king when
governed by will and not law. And that he ought to
be subject to the law, since he is God's substitute,
appears more clearly through the similitude of Jesus
Christ, whose office he holds on earth.]
22 It is unimportant for our purposes how it is
actually to be understood; cf. Theodor Mommsen,
ROEMISCHES STAATSRECHT, 3rd ed. (Leipzig, 1887), II,
751 f.
23 Cf. also the CONFESSIO AMANTIS 7.2718 f.:
            And natheles upon som side,
            His [the king's] pouer stant aboue the lawe.
Of contemporary English poets, Chaucer did not take a
position on this question. Langland's interpretation
is similar to Gower's; see below, pp. 143 f.
24 SENT. 3.51: Justum est principem legibus
obtemperare suis. Tunc enim jura sua ab omnibus
custodienda existimet, quando et ipse illis rever-
entiam praebet. Principes legibus teneri suis,
neque in se posse damnare jura quae in subjectis
constituunt. Justa est enim vocis eorum auctoritas,
si quod populis prohibent, sibi licere non patiantur.
[It is just that the prince observe his own laws.
For then he may consider his law ought to be observed
by all, when he himself offers it reverence. The
prince should hold to his laws, and not by his own
act damn the laws to which his subjects adhere. For
just is the authority of their voices if they do not
allow to themselves what they deny to the people.]

158

Gower appends some related considerations to
the catalogue of lawgivers in Book VII of the
CONFESSIO AMANTIS:

> And so ferforth it is befalle
> That lawe is come among ous alle:
> God lieve it mote wel ben holde,
> As every king therto is holde;
> For thing which is of kinges set,
> With kinges oghte it noght be let.
> What king of lawe taketh no kepe,
> Be lawe he mai no regne kepe.
> Do lawe away, what is a king? 7.3067-75

26 6.611-20:

> Dum tibi cuncta licent, ne queras cuncta licere,
> Res etenim licite noxia sepe ferunt:
> Tu super es iura, iustus set viue sub illis,
> Spesque tui nobis causa salutis erit.
> Est mors ira tua, potes id quod non licet, et te
> Prestita vota tamen ducere iuris habent:
> Quod licet illesa mentis precordia seruat,
> Omne tamen licitum non probat esse probum:
> Quod licet est tutum, set que potes illa sub arto
> Discute iudicio fultus honore tuo.

[While all things are permissible to you, do not
seek to permit yourself all things, for things
permitted to you often bring harm. You are above
the laws, but live as a just man under them, and
because of you there will be hope of welfare for
us. Your wrath is death; you can do what is not
allowed. Yet nevertheless, firm vows of justice
must guide you. Although it may keep your peace
of mind unimpaired, nevertheless the fact that
everything is permissible does not prove it to be
honorable. Granted that something is safe, you,
strengthened in your honor, must nevertheless determine with strict judgment the things which you
can do.]

27 Licere in the juridical sense appears in 611,
612, and 618; in a moral sense in 615 and 619. I am
unsure of its meaning in 617.

28 Gower's acquaintance with the writings of
Cassiodorus, be it direct or indirect, is evident
from the MIROUR, where he is cited under the name
Cassodre in 11770, 13920, 23059, and 24592. Here
Gower appears to have had in mind the following
passage from the VARIAE: . . . Imperiosa nimium res

est, patres conscripti, pietas nostra, quando propria
voluntate vincimur, qui alienis condicionibus non
tenemur. Nam cum deo praestante possimus omnia, sola
nobis credimus licere laudanda. [. . . O Senators,
piety is for us a concern of extreme importance, for
we are governed only by our own wills, we who are not
held in check by any other considerations. For although we can do everything with God's help, we believe that we should do only praiseworthy things.]
VARIAE 10.16. The antithesis of "posse" and "licere"
is not the only point of contact between Gower and
Cassiodorus. The use of such measures of value as
"laudanda" in Cassiodorus and "honor tuus" in Gower
links the two vis a vis Isidore's argument, which
concentrates more on the aspects of utility and
equity. A third point of contact lies in the importance which Cassiodorus attributes to the ruler's
pietas. In Gower's Mirror for a Prince, the epithet
"pius" is more frequent than any other in the apostrophe
to the king. In the CONFESSIO, "pite" as the moderator
of an inflexible justice is discussed in great detail.
   29 The duty of subjects is similarly enjoined in
the introduction to the Mirror for a Prince:
   Cumque sui Regis legi sit legius omnis
   Subditus, et toto corpore seruit ei . . . 6.581-82
   [Since every liege is subject to the law of his
   king and serves him with all his might . . .]
   30 Cf. MIROUR 26789-805; CONFESSIO AMANTIS
7.511-14; VOX CLAMANTIS 7.561-64, and esp. 573 ff.:
   Auctor enim rerum sic res decreuit, vt orbis
   Queque creatura consequeretur eum [sc. hominem];
   Vt seruiret ei factura, suumque vicissim
   Factorem solum consequeretur homo.
   [For the author of things has so decreed it that
   every creature of the world should wait upon man;
   that the creation should serve him and that he in
   turn should therefore wait upon only his creator.]
   31 See below, pp. 190 f.
   32 Cf. 6.1005 f. and 6.1197 f. (B-Text).
   33 Thus, for example, St. Augustine says in the
DE CIVITATE DEI 19.15: . . . Rationalem factum ad
imaginem suam noluit nisi irrationabilibus dominare
[sc. Deus]; non hominem homini, sed hominem pecori.
Inde primi iusti pastores pecorum magis quam reges
hominum constituti sunt, ut etiam sic insinuaret Deus,

quid postulet ordo creaturarum, quid exigat meritum peccatorum. Condicio quippe servitutis iure intellegitur inposita peccatori [Teubnerian]. [. . . He [sc. God] did not intend that His rational creature, who was made in His image, should have dominion over anything but the irrational creation,--not man over man but man over the beasts. And hence the righteous men in primitive times were made shepherds of cattle rather than kings of men, God intending thus to teach us what the relative position of the creatures is, and what the dessert of sin; for it is with justice, we believe, that the condition of slavery is the result of sin. Trans. Marcus Dods, THE CITY OF GOD (New York, 1948), II, 323-24.]
34 On the origin and tradition of this monarchic formula, see Jozsef Balogh, "Rex a recte regendo," SPECULUM, 3 (1928), 580-82.
35 Bromyard, s.v. "regimen": Sic ergo qui regis Israel intende ut per istas tres perfectiones tres partes compleas et perficias que in ethica continentur, vid. monasticam que docet de regimine suiipsius, iconomicam que docet de regimine domus et familie, et politicam que docet de regimine civitatis seu communitatis [Therefore you who rule Israel should direct your mind so that through these three perfections you complete and finish the three parts which are contained in ethics: namely monasticism, which teaches self-rule; economics, which teaches the rule of house and family; and politics, which teaches rule of the city or the community]. This is the old Aristotelean classification as one also encounters it, for example, in Bonaventura: Postremo, quia regimen virtutis motivae tripliciter habet attendi, scilicet respectu vitae propriae, respectu familiae et respectu multitudinis subiectae; ideo moralis philosophia triplicatur, scilicet in monasticam, oeconomicam et politicam [Next, because the reign of virtue has to be attained with a triple motive, namely with respect to one's own life, to the family, and to the ruled multitudes; therefore, the philosophy of morals is threefold, namely in monasticism, economics, and politics]. DE REDUCTIONE ARTIUM AD THEOLOGIAM, loc. cit., V, 321. Gower knows this classification himself and uses it in the seventh book of the CONFESSIO AMANTIS (1641 ff.) with a minor

161

variation in the nomenclature: he inserts the general notion "etique" in place of "monastica." In doing so he refers to Aristotle, that is, in this case to the SECRETUM SECRETORUM--incorrectly, as Hamilton (loc. cit., 326 f.) first remarked. Hamilton is of the opinion that Gower followed Brunetto Latini in the passage in question.

36 Bromyard, loc. cit.

37 Proverbs, 16.32: Melior est . . . qui dominabitur animo suo expugnatore urbium [He that ruleth his spirit is better than he that taketh cities]; Matthew 16.26: Quid enim prodest homini, si mundum universum lucretur, animae vero suae detrimentum patiatur [For what does it profit a man, if he gain the whole world, but suffer the loss of his own soul]?

38 I used the editio maior of W. W. Skeat, THE VISION OF WILLIAM CONCERNING PIERS THE PLOWMAN, etc., (Oxford, 1886), Vol. 1.

39 Thus E. T. Donaldson, PIERS PLOWMAN (New Haven, 1949), p. 91, understands the phrase.

40 C 22.303-5

41 C 23.29 f.

42 I employ the customary terminology, although Gower himself--at the point in the second book where he denies the existence of Fortuna--allows only dona naturae and dona gratiae; cf. 2.298-302.

43 W. Kleineke, "Englische Fürstenspiegel vom POLICRATICUS Johanns von Salisbury bis zum BASILIKON DORON König Jacobs I," STUDIEN ZUR ENGLISCHEN PHILOLOGIE, 90 (1937), 131.

44 O rex, quicquid habes dedit hoc deus, et nichil
a te
Est quod habes proprium, vel quod habere potes:
Esse creaturam te nosce dei, nec ab eius
Tu discede viis, si bene stare velis.
[O King, God has bestowed whatever you possess,
and nothing that you have as your own or can
have is from yourself. Know that you are a
creature of God, and do not withdraw from His
powers, if you wish to stand secure.]

45 Labile forma bonum, species inimica pudoris
Vtile virtutum sepe retardat iter:
Forma dei munus, etc. 6.1085 ff.
[Good looks are a fleeting gift; handsomeness
which is harmful to modesty often impedes the

proper path of virtue. Although beauty is
a gift of God, etc.]
[46] Adopted from Neckam, DE VITA MONACHORUM; cf.
Macaulay, Notes.
[47] Cf. Carlyle, op. cit., Vol 1, Chpts. 10 and
11; Bede Jarrett, SOCIAL THEORIES OF THE MIDDLE AGES,
1200-1500 (London, 1926), pp. 122 ff. The church,
without causing revolutions, constantly preached the
equality of men in the sight of death and God.
[48] Cf. G. M. Trevelyan, ENGLAND IN THE AGE OF
WYCLIFFE (London, 1909), 4th ed., p. 196, concerning
Froissart's account.
[49] Ius naturale commune est omnium nationum;
hoc iure communis est omnis possessio, et omnium una
libertas [ETYMOLOGIAE]. [Natural law is the same for
all nations; according to this law, property is common to all and freedom is the same for everybody.]
Cf., for example, Alexander of Hales on the passage
from Isidore: . . . dicendum quod iure naturali es-
sent omnia communia et omnium una libertas, hoc fuit
ante peccatum, et post peccatum quaedam sunt quibus-
dam propria et haec duo sunt per legem naturalem
[. . . it is said that by natural law all property
is common and there is one liberty for all; that was
before sin, and since sin certain things belong to
certain people and both of these are by natural law].
SUMMA III, Q. 27, M. 3, Art. 2, "Resolutio." Cited,
along with other instances, by Carlyle, V, 14.
[50] Quid petis argentum tibi? spem quid ponis in
aurum?
Sunt nam communes omnibus orbis opes.
Sepius ista dei data conspicis hostibus esse,
Ante deum nulla laus et habetur eis:
Ista paganus habet, Iudeus, latro cruentus;
Crede quod iratus sepe dat ista deus. 6.359-64
[Why do you seek silver for yourself? What
trust do you place in gold? For the treasures
of the earth are common to all. Quite often
you may perceive God's gifts given to His
enemies, yet they have no praise in the sight
of God. A pagan, a Jew, a bloody thief has
such gifts; you should believe that God has
given such things in anger.]
The valuation of earthly possessions is fundamentally
different in the MIROUR; cf. below, p. 201 n.3.

[51] Cf. Macaulay, Notes to 6.1019 ff.

[52] Bromyard, s.v. "nobilitas," gives the following citation from Bernard of Clairvaux: Quid gloriaris de parentela, ubi Christus non invenitur? Si Christus cum parentibus suis iustissimis in Hierusalem non inveniebatur, quando Maria et Joseph eum requirebant, Luc. 2, quomodo tu cum parentibus tuis usurariis vel raptoribus illum invenies? De qua parentela dici potest illud, Ezech. 22, Sordida nobilis, grandis interitu. Sordida quo ad animam, nobilis quo ad mundum. [Why do you boast about your ancestors, among whom Christ is not found? If Christ was not found to be with his most just parents in Jerusalem when Mary and Joseph sought him (Luke 2), how will you, accompanied by your usorious or ravenous parents, find him? About such ancestors it can be said (Ezechiel 22), thou filthy one, infamous, great in destruction. Filthy refers to the soul, infamous to the world.]

[53] It appears to have been influenced by a passage from Seneca that found its way into Waltenham's mirror for a prince, a passage which, however, I have been unable to identify among the fragments of the work cited, the DE MORIBUS. The same passage seems to me to be present in Thomas More's DISCOURSE CONCERNING THE WAY OF TRUE NOBILITY, which he inserted in his translation of the VITA of Pico della Mirandola. The Senecan passage in Waltenham reads as follows: Nobilitatis tue ab hoc menineris ut cum claritate generis morum sanctitate vel honestate contendas et cum nobilitate corporis seu generis animi nobilitatem assequaris. Pulcrum est enim nobilitati generis moribus contendisse [?], pulcrius genus humiliter [sic] moribus illustrasse [You should be mindful of your nobility in that you should strive to rival the fame of your family with holiness of conduct and seek with nobility of body or of family to attain the nobility of soul. For it is admirable to have rivalled nobility of family with behavior, but more admirable to have done honor to a humble family by behavior]. Roger de Waltenham, COMPENDIUM MORALE DE VIRTUOSIS DICTIS ET FACTIS EXEMPLARIBUS ANTIQUORUM, MS. Fairfax 4, Bodleian, fol. 10^v.

[54] Cf. Mirour 23377 ff., esp. 23401 ff.:
  Seigneur de halt parage plain,
  Ne t'en dois faire plus haltain,

Ne l'autre gent tenir au vil;
Tous suismes fils de dame Evain.
Seigneur, tu qui me dis vilain,
Comment voes dire q'es gentil?
Si tu le dis, je dy nenil:
Car certes tout le flom de Nil
Ne puet hoster le sanc prochain
De toy, qui te fais tant nobil,
Et du vilein q'en son cortil
Labourt pour sa vesture et pain.
[Lord of such a lofty lineage,
You should not act so superior,
Nor hold other people so base;
We are all sons of the lady Eve.
Lord, you who call me base,
How can I say to you that you are gracious?
If you say this, I will do the same:
For surely all the waters of the Nile
Cannot deny that the blood is the same
In you, who are so noble,
As in the peasant who
Labors for his clothes and bread.]
Or 23425 ff.:
He, quel orguil te monteroit,
Seigneur, si dieus fourmé t'avoit
D'argent ou d'orr ou de perrie,
Sique ton corps ne purriroit:
Mais certes n'est de tiel endroit,
Ainz est du vile tay purrie,
Sicome la gent q'est enpovrie.
[Well, what pride would elevate you,
Lord, if God had made you
Of silver or gold or precious stones,
So that your body would not decay:
But this certainly is not the case,
For you are as decayed by your baseness
As the people by their poverty.]
The aggressive tone is probably made possible because
the addressee is unspecified, whereas the personal
direct address to the king would demand another style.
55 Loc. cit., pp. 129 f.
56 An aggressive undertone is quite noticeable
already in Bernard of Clairvaux. The Dominican
Bromyard, however, expresses his opinion much more
sharply: Nobilitas est duplex: una quantum ad Deum

et animam, alia quantum ad mundum et carnem. Una
vera, et existens, et approbata in curia Dei; alia
falsa, apparens, et non existens, in curia quidem
mundi approbata, sed in curia Dei reprobata et
damnata, et peior quacunque corporali servitute.
[There are two kinds of nobility: the one important
to God and the soul, the other important to the
world and the flesh. The one true, and existing,
and approved in the court of God; the other false,
apparent, and non-existing, approved in certain
courts of the world, but in the court of God re-
proved and damned, and worse than any bodily ser-
vitude.] SUMMA PRAEDICANTIUM, s.v. "nobilitas."
    57 "Prince Edward's Expedition into Spain," ed.
Thomas Wright, POLITICAL POEMS AND SONGS, I, 98 f.
    58 The preceding lines read:
    Magnus erat Cesar totoque potencior orbe,
    Nunc quem nec mundus ceperat, vrna capit. 6.1107-8
    [Caesar was mighty, and more powerful than all
    the earth. An urn now contains the man whom
    the world did not contain.]
On the ubi sunt theme, cf. E. Gilson, LES IDEES ET
LES LETTRES, Chpt. 1.
    59 1. 789, Gloria nulla, precor, te, rex,
extollat inanis [Let no empty glory puff you up,
I beg of you, O King] does not belong in this context. "Inanis gloria" is a form of superbia.
    60 Cf. CONFESSIO AMANTIS 7.1-6. Generosity as
the second point of political ethics is discussed
at 7.1685-94, and illustrated with exemplary tales.
    61 Roger Bacon, SECRETUM SECRETORUM, in OPERA
HACTENUS INEDITA, ed. Robert Steele (London, 1920),
V, 45.
    62 Ibid., p. 44. Gower's text of the SECRETUM
appears to have been the French version of Jofroi de
Watreforde or its Latin prototype, since it uses an
extended interpolation concerning the cardinal virtues that occurs only there. Jofroi is available
to us in Yonge's English version, dating from a
generation after Gower. It is printed as the last
of three English texts of the SECRETUM in EETS ES 74.
I cited Bacon's text only to show how the Latin
termini agree.
    63 Cf. 6.1007: Lucratur populum que deum rex
iustus vtrumque [A just king wins both God and the
people].

⁶⁴ Cf. 6.971-74; above all, however, see 4.3-18 and 481-96.

⁶⁵ Cf. 6, Chapter 14, esp. 1025 ff. That "fratres amor" appears in lines 1025, 1026, and 1027--instead of the expected "plebis amor," which is demanded by the establishment of the problem in the beginning of the chapter--I would attribute to the influence of the biblical speculum principis, Deut. 17. It stresses in the beginning that the king should be elected from a circle of fratres, and at the end enjoins the king not to elevate himself above his brothers (Nec elevetur cor eius in superbiam super fratres suos. Deut. 17.20).

⁶⁶ One example, unimportant in itself but philologically attractive, which shows that Gower derived a biblical train of thought directly from the SECRETUM, occurs in Chapter 17 of Book VI of the VOX CLAMANTIS. There the Mirror for a Prince discusses the theme of memento mori. In these surroundings is accommodated a view of human life as an unending battle:

Est hominis vita quasi milicies reputata,
Bella super terram nam tria semper agit:
Rex qui per medium belli transibit inermis,
Sepius incaute stulcior ipse cadit. 6.1135-38
[The life of man is reckoned as a battle, for on earth it is always waging three wars. The king who would surpass the weak by means of war often recklessly comes to a foolish end.]

The passage begins with a quote from Job to the effect that all human life is a struggle (l. 1135); the struggle is threefold in nature (1136); the king who goes rushing off unarmed to war pays for his folly with death (1137-38). Everything is clear up to l. 1136's "tria bella," which are not even later explained. It appears as though a distich has been lost here. However, the triad is easily restored from the Bible, the liturgy, or from Latin hymns. They are the world, the flesh, and the devil. In order to give an approximately contemporary example, I wish to cite from a rimed English version of the sayings of Bernard of Clairvaux in the Commonplace Book of the Vernon MS. (EETS OS 117, p. 515):

Man, thou hast threo luther fon,
Heore nomes con I wel vchon
Gif I schal touchen alle:
Thyn oune flesch, the world, the fend . . .

What makes the SECRETUM seem to be Gower's direct
prototype is the similar course of the argument,
the only minor exception being that in the SECRETUM
Job appears at the end of the section rather than at
the beginning. The SECRETUM's design is also tripartite. Sentences coincide with thoughts and occasionally match one of Gower's distiches:

A. Gower: Est hominis vita quasi milicies reputata,
Bella super terram nam tria semper agit.
[The life of man is reckoned as a battle, for on earth it is always waging
three wars.]

SECRETUM: Al the day of oure lyfe in grete Perill
we byth, for thre enemys ws werryth,
dayes and nyghtes in vs hare assautes
makynge.

B. Gower: - - - - - - - - - - -

SECRETUM: The worlde that vs drawyth to cowetyse;
the fleshe vs chasyth to lecheri; the
Deuyl vs assaylyth by Pryde and envy.

C. Gower: Rex qui per medium belli transibit
inermis,
Sepius incaute stulcior ipse cadit.
[The king who would surpass the weak
by means of war often recklessly comes
to a foolish end.]

SECRETUM: Moche is he a fole and vncunnynge that
in so cruel a battaill noght dreddyth
ne helpe sechyth. There--for sayth
Jope, that chyualrie is manys lyfe in
erthe. EETS ES 74, p. 156.

Another image that may go back to the SECRETUM is the
comparison of the people to a garden which bears the
king fruit or thorns according to how he tends it.
Shakespeare is familiar with this metaphor and develops it with great art in RICHARD II. I have en-
countered it in the Middle Ages only in the SECRETUM
and in Gower's Mirror for a Prince. Thus it appears
to me more plausible to posit a direct dependence
rather than a topos. In Gower the image goes as
follows:

Plebs est regis ager, rex cultor qui colit agrum;
Si male, fert tribulos, si bene, grana parit.
6.1001-2

In the SECRETUM (loc. cit., p. 213), one reads:

168

"Thow shalt lewe well that thy subiectis bene lyke a gardyn, in wych bene dyuers maneres of trees, and thou shalt noght holde ham as londe berrynge thornes wythout frute." Whether Gower's advice to the young king (reminiscere facta paterna [remember your father's deeds] 6.919) is related to the SECRETUM's demand, "Alexandre, remembyr the of the dedis and werkis of thyne auncestres" (p. 143), can hardly be determined.

[67] See below, pp. 193 f.

[68] Book VI, Chapter 15, in imitation of the AURORA; the story occurs in I Kings 3.

[69] There are two English versions of the work in the 14th century: the AYENBITE OF INWYT of Dan Michel of Northgate (ca. 1340), and the anonymous BOOK OF VICES AND VIRTUES (ca. 1375).

[70] MS. Laud 174, fol. 93 ff., Bodleian.

[71] The material is treated in Waltenham's last chapter. For Gower, cf. also the CONFESSIO AMANTIS 7.4469 ff.:

> That every worthi Prince is holde
> Withinne himself himself beholde,
> To se the stat of his persone,
> And thenke hou ther be joies none
> Upon this Erthe mad to laste,
> And hou the fleissh schal ate laste
> The lustes of this lif forsake,
> Him oghte a gret ensample take
> Of Salomon . . .

Chapter Five
Gower's World Picture

A class critique springs from diverse roots
and comprehends diverse, or at least greatly differing, areas of human existence. It can either
attack the class organization of the state as such,
or censure the lapses of individual classes. It
can be oriented nationally or internationally,
terrestially or transcendentally.

As far as the first alternative is concerned,
the class-organized state surmounted by the monarch
is, for Gower as well as for the most of his contemporaries, a divinely ordained reality toward which
no criticism is directed. It is in its essence an
image of the hierarchical order of the cosmos, and
according to its history a divine arrangement of
force and an institution of salvation for bringing
about law and justice among a mankind morally weakened by the Fall.[1] The unequal distribution of
earthly goods likewise rests upon a divine arrangement and is therefore unassailable. But it has to
be understood correctly in its moral function. When
God subjugated the newly created world to the rule
of man, he thus established a kind of communal
property. The church fathers speak of it, although
traces of it are hardly ever to be found in Gower.[2]
He is interested in conditions after the Fall and
the inequality of possessions that then prevailed.
Earthly possessions have been lent their owners
ever since the exile from Paradise, not as an expression of a divine favoritism, but as a test and
trial of their sense of moral duty.[3] They have,
on the other hand, been withheld from the posses-
sionless, not out of prejudice, but in order to
facilitate for them, through earthly difficulties,
the way to heavenly bliss. Therefore, Gower does
not criticize the principle underlying the political or social order, but the deviations from this
principle of which the individual classes are guilty.

The question of whether Gower's class critique
is nationally or internationally oriented is difficult to answer. After we separated the Visio

171

from the original plan of the VOX CLAMANTIS, we saw
that the passages with a distinct national imprint
are confined to Books II and VII, that is, to the
frame of the class critique. If one ignores the
Mirror for a Prince, which according to its genre
belongs only conditionally to the class critique,
Books III-VI nowhere claim to describe specific
English conditions in the second half of the fourteenth century. There is absent any allusion to
the topical questions of contemporary politics, to
taxation and its apportionment, to the relationship of consuetudines to leges that one would expect in the sixth book (which treats of justice
and its functionaries). Not England but the world
furnishes the material for Gower's class critique.
Thus the prologue of the third book speaks of
"mundus" and "orbis," but not of "mea tellus":
  Fit mundique status in tres diuisio partes,
  Omnibus vnde viris stat quasi sortis opus,
  Et modo per vicia quia sors magis astat iniqua,
  Ponderet in causis quilibet acta suis:
  In quocumque gradu sit homo, videatur in orbe
  Que sibi sunt facta, sors cadit vnde rea. 3.Prol.3-8
  [And since the state of the world is divided
  into three parts, so that it seems like the work
  of fate to all men; and since our fate nowadays
  is quite adverse because of our vices, everyone
  ought to consider happenings in the light of
  their causes. No matter what rank a man is in,
  it would seem that fate turns out to be responsible for the things which happen to him in
  this world.]
Likewise, the goal of the work is the moral renewal
of all mankind, not just the English:
  Da loquar vt vicium minuatur et ammodo virtus
  Crescat, vt in mundo mundior extet homo. 3.99-100
  [Let me speak out so that henceforth vice will
  diminish and virtue flourish, in order that mankind may become purer in this world.]
Nor does the summary of the first chapter of the
class critique proper formulate a national question,
naming as its theme the "status et ordo mundi."[4]
Therefore the national issue is at first only peripheral, yet intensified so much under pressure of
the events of 1381 that, after the addition of the

172

Visio, the final version gave the overall impression, and was intended to as one may infer from Statement A, that it was nationally oriented.[5]

According to its line of sight, Gower's class critique is transcendental. He has no conception of the historical character and true nature of the state and one could hardly expect otherwise. The responsibility of individuals as well as of classes is not to the state but directly to God, with whom originates the principle of ordo and status.[6] Therefore the restoration of the relationships between God and mankind (affiliated by classes) is the prerequisite for political regeneration. Thus the transcendentally determined class critique develops necessarily into a homily. Its scope is the entire cosmos, which is implicated in the consequences of the conflict between man and God. Thus there results a breadth and depth of questioning that is impressive even though absolutely unoriginal in its whole and in its parts. It is a complete world picture in which all the parts are related to each other and in the midst of which stands man:

Hoc fateor vere, quicquid contingit in orbe,
Nos sumus in causa, sint bona sive mala. 2.629-30
[I truly acknowledge that whatever happens in the world, whether it be good or evil, we ourselves are the cause of it.]

The basic questions concerning the essence and destiny of man are discussed in Books II and VII of the VOX CLAMANTIS. Book II deals with the problem of fate and responsibility. The common view holds that Fortuna is to blame for the change of times and, therefore, is responsible for all present hardships. Here, from the periphery, Gower begins the thrust towards his true theme. He starts with Solomon's judgment regarding the vanity of earthly life and endows it with the traditional topoi of contemptus mundi literature (2.3-16). One distich ("if it is possible that one may be happy")[7] forms a transition to the contrasting pictures of a blissful national past and a gloomy present (2.19-36). Here the theme of the decline of the times is applied to a concrete historical situation and

173

is therefore more than a topos. Of course, Gower
does not achieve a detailed comparison of two historical epochs; however, he locates his golden age
neither in the beginning of human history nor in
the misty distance of an Arthurian antiquity, but
in the immediate past, and thus attains a certain
degree of realism.[8] Then, under the impress of the
subject of mutatio rerum, he poses the question of
blame. The common view holds that Fortuna is responsible for everything, while everyone considers
himself individually blameless:

> Se tamen inmunes cause communiter omnes
> Dicunt, vt si quis non foret inde reus;
> Accusant etenim fortunam iam variatam,
> Dicentes quod ea stat magis inde rea. 2.43-46
> [Nevertheless, all men commonly say that they
> have nothing to do with cause, as if no one
> were responsible for things. In fact, they
> now blame fickle Fortune, saying that she is
> responsible for them.]

If one considers Fortuna the cause of decay, one
thus acknowledges a limitation by external forces
upon the freedom of human will and action. What
sort of external forces these are is unimportant
to Gower. He reduces them to the common denomina-
tor Fortuna, probably because that conforms to the
literary mode and evokes in the reader familiar notions. In addition to fortune, he also refers to
"sors," "fatum," and "astra," without clearly dis-
tinguishing them.[9] We shall investigate them together as to whether and to what extent they limit
man's freedom of self-determination.

Behind Gower's superficial, slightly drama-
tizing treatment of the question, one occasionally
notices the formulations of theologians. It cannot, however, be said that Gower had his knowledge
at first hand. He could have consulted the entries
under "fatum" or "liberum arbitrium," "fortuna" or
"providentia" in anyone's theological summa, and
was sure to hit upon the relevant passages from
Boethius, Augustine, and Gregory. Of course, on
the question of the existence of fatum a considerable contradiction between Boethius on the one hand
and Augustine and his spokesman Gregory on the

174

other would have become immediately apparent.
Boethius affirms the existence of fatum and defines
it as an arrangement inherent in all moveable (that
is, changeable) things, by means of which divine
providence binds all that is individual with its
eternal laws of order.[10] "Fatum" and "providentia"
are two aspects of one and the same thing, namely
the divine control of the world. From God's point
of view as the undivided whole implicit in the unity
of the divine ratio, the control is providentia;
from the point of view of the world, dispersed in
time and space, and with reference to individual
phenomena, it is fatum.[11] Augustine and his dis-
ciple Gregory, on the other hand, deny the existence
of fatum. Gregory states clearly, "sed a fidelium
cordibus absit ut aliquid esse fatum dicant [but
there is absent from the hearts of the faithful
that which others call fate],[12] and, as the surrounding text makes clear, identifies fatum with
the influence of the stars. Augustine allows the
word "fatum" if by it nothing other than divine
providence is understood, although he considers
such careless usage reproachable.[13] Now, when Gower
says of Fortuna, "Attamen ore meo te nichil esse
puto (2.86 f.) [In my opinion I still reckon you
as nothing], he aligns himself with Gregory, whose
Homily I, 10--from which the fatum citation derives--
he also uses elsewhere. That theological discussion
is not entirely foreign to him is apparent from such
formulations as:
    Cum solo causante deo sint cuncta creata,
    Num fortuna dei soluere possit opus? 2.595-96
    [Since all things were created solely through
    the agency of God, Fortune could not undo the
    work of God, could she?]
After the account of creation, he points out that,
    Fortune nichil attribuit, set solus vt ipse
                                        [sc. deus]
    Cuncta creat, solus cuncta create regit. 2.623-24
    [Fortune contributed nothing, but because He
    alone created everything, He alone rules all
    creation.]
The second distich, with its "Fortune nichil at-
ribuit," provides a proof of Fortuna's non-existence
similar to that which Francis of Hales adduces for

the non-existence of fatum: Providentia divina . . .
nihil relinguit in rebus futuris [Divine providence
. . . neglects nothing in the affairs of the future].[14]

It may be an influence of late antiquity that the
problem of fate and free will amost invariably becomes critical on the question of the extent to which
men are subject to the influence of the stars. In
Augustine and Gregory the star of Bethlehem is a
prime example in showing that the stars are subject
to man, and not vice versa.[15] Gower is not content
with that. He constructs around the star of Bethlehem a systematic catalogue of all creation and shows
how everything--from angels down to fish--exists to
serve the vir iustus.[16]

The examples that Gower cites are all of a mir-
aculous nature: Moses' passage through the Red Sea,
Daniel in the lions' den, Jonah in the belly of the
whale. Consequently he goes so far as to maintain
the extreme thesis that the homo iustus is not only
free of the influence of Fortuna, fatum, or the
stars, but that he also stands above the law of nature:
    Ac elementorum celestia corpora iustum
    Subdita iure colunt, et sua vota ferunt.
    In virtute dei sapiens dominabitur astra,
    Totaque consequitur vis orizontis eum. 2.237-40
    [And subject to the law of the elements, the
    celestial bodies favor the just man and carry
    out his prayers. The man who is knowing in the
    virtue of God will dominate the stars, and all
    the power of heaven attends him.]
Here, obviously, the assertion is overstated for the
sake of the effect.[17] In other passages in the VOX
CLAMANTIS, as well as in the CONFESSIO AMANTIS, the
laws of nature are considered incontestable, and not
the homo iustus but only the saintly man has the
power, in prayer, to breach them:
    Contra naturam fiunt miracula, vires
    Nature deitas frangere sola potest. 5.625-26
    [Miracles happen only contrary to nature;
    only the divinity of nature can go against
    its own powers.]
    Bot yit the lawe original,
    Which he [sc. God] hath set in the natures,

Mot worchen in the creatures,
That thereof mai be non obstacle,
Bot if it stonde upon miracle
Thurgh preiere of som holy man. CONFESSIO 7.658-63
It is not only polemical zeal against a blind fatal-
ism or fervid joy that motivates Gower to elevate
the homo iustus to the absolute ruler of creation;
it is above all an active conviction of man's majesty. One may not be immediately prepared for observations such as the following in a medieval mor-
alist and homilist:
O quam diues homo, quam magno munere felix,
Cui totus soli subditur orbis honor!
Felix pre cunctis, cui quicquid fabrica mundi
Continet, assurgit et sua iussa facit. 2.275-78
[O how rich, how happy is man in his great reward! All the honor of the world is granted to
him alone. He is happy above all others. Everything the fabric of the world contains arises
for him and performs his bidding.]
One has become too much accustomed to associating
quite the opposite picture with medieval thought,
as if the consciousness of the miseria humanae
condicionis had led to a narrow, pessimistic interpretation of the human situation. However, dignitas
and miseria are by their very nature not to be divorced from one another. They complement each
other and are in their duality the perfect expression for the disunity of human existence. When one
consults Bromyard, one thus encounters both aspects:
Hominis conditio est duplex. Una nobilis, quam
cogitare debet, ne peccatis vilescat. Alia fra-
gilis, quam cogitare debet, ne superbiat. [The
nature of man is two-fold. The one aspect is
noble, which he ought to consider lest he be
sullied by sin. The other is frail, which he
ought to consider lest he be proud.][18]
The first chapter of the pseudo-Bernardine MEDITA-
TIONES PIISIMAE DE COGNITIONE HUMANAE CONDITIONIS
is De Dignitate Hominis, the second De Miseria
Hominis.[19] Examples could be multiplied endlessly.
Gower therefore follows familiar ideas when he first
draws the majesty of man, that is, of the homo iustus,
in its full splendor and then contrasts it to the
misery of man, that is, of the homo peccator.[20]

Thus Chapter Five's catalogue of men whom the entire creation serves with joy is matched by a second catalogue in Chapter Six that describes the misery of fallen sinners. And just as emphatically as man's dignitas was made independent of Fortuna, fatum, and the stars, his miseria is now removed from the influence of fateful and natural powers and traced unmistakably back to moral causes:

> Non sors fortune poterat sibi talia ferre,
> Set pro peccatis contigit illud eis. 2.331-32
> [The lot of Fortune could not have brought such things upon them, but they happened to them because of their sins.]

Bromyard gives this train of thought an especially attractive and less fervid expression, which may be inserted here as an illustration contemporary with Gower:

> Ratione primi est sciendum, quod aliqui tribulationes pluvie et siccitatis huiusmodi attribuebant planetis et causis naturalibus. Unde diligenter inquirunt, quis planeta tunc regnet, et quamdiu regnabit, et huiusmodi questiones vanas et frivolas faciunt, quorum dictum videtur esse contra rationem et contra sacram scripturam et contra legem canonum . . . Potius ergo videntur tales pestilentie ortum habere et causari a causa voluntaria, i.e. a peccato quod ex mala oritur voluntate quam a causa naturali. Huic etiam videtur concordare sacra scriptura. Querendum est enim ab illis qui dicunt quod planeta hoc facit, quis planeta regnavit tempore diluvii . . . Quis autem planeta vel constellatio illius pluvie occasio fuit nisi peccatum? Illa enim planeta videlicet peccatum tunc regnavit et pluvias illas occasionaliter causavit. Optimus namque astrologus deus illam assignavit causam. . . .
> Qua in re pensandum est quod illi qui peccando deum derelinquunt et diabolo adherent, terram tempestatibus et vindictis et fame turbant. Et quod peccatum est planeta regnans qui nos conturbat.[21]
> [In the first place it is understood that some attribute tribulations such as flood and drought to the planets and to natural causes. Whence

they inquire diligently what planet then reigns,
and how it will reign, and pose all manner of
empty and silly questions which are seen to be
contrary to reason, to Sacred Scripture, and to
canon law . . . Therefore such pestilences are
seen to have their birth in and to be caused
by willfulness, that is, by sin that is born
from evil will rather than by natural cause.
For this is seen to agree with Sacred Scripture.
It should be asked of those who say that a planet
did it, what planet reigned at the time of the
flood? . . . Yet what planet or constellation
was the occasion of that rain but sin? For that
planet, namely sin, reigned then and was the
occasion of that rain. The very best astrolo-
gers assign the cause to God. . . .
Having thus considered the matter, it is those
who by sinning abandon God and join the devil
who disturb the earth with tempests and punish-
ments and famine. And that sin is the reigning
planet that disturbs us.

The passage shows its kinship with Book II of
the VOX CLAMANTIS in its emphasis on human free will
and the resultant responsibility of man not only for
his own fate but also for events in nature.[22] It
agrees with the VOX CLAMANTIS in its way of thinking
insofar as it holds that tribulatio--worldly misfor-
tune--must be explained on moral grounds and be re-
lieved by a moral regeneration; mankind's earthly
welfare is the focus of interest. That is characteristic of the second book of the VOX CLAMANTIS,
but not at all pertinent for the analogous parts
of the MIROUR. The VOX CLAMANTIS states:
Ex meritis vel demeritis sic contigit omne,
Humano generi quicquid adesse solet:
Sic vario casu versabitur alea mundi,
Dum solet in rebus ludere summa manus. 2.345-48
[So whatever happens to the human race, everything is wontedly due to merit or lack of merit.
Thus the die of the world will be cast with
varying luck, as long as the hand of the Most
High is wont to sport with our affairs.]
The focus is primarily concentrated on this world,
even with the very strong emphasis upon human free

will and self-determination.[23] The MIROUR, on the
other hand, is permeated by the idea of the close
tie between human existence in this world and in
that to come, and in the end does not make manifest
its kinship with confessional speculum literature.
It sees its main concern as the adjustment of man's
relationship to his creator and considers the bet-
terment of the world a by-product:
  Pour ce chascuns qui le mal fait
  S'amende, et ce serra bien fait,
  Car deux biens en puet rescevoir:
  L'un est q'il puet de son bienfait
  Le siecle, q'est sicomme desfait,
  Refourmer tout a son voloir;
  L'autre est que nous savons du voir,
  Cil qui bien fait du ciel est hoir;
  Dont m'est avis, puisq'ensi vait,
  Qe l'omme ad propre le povoir
  De l'un et l'autre siecle avoir;
  Fols est s'il l'un ne l'autre en ait. MIROUR 27205-15
  [For each one who does wrong
  And makes amends, that will be well done,
  For two good things he can receive:
  The one is that by his good deed he can
  Reform to his liking
  The world, which is undone.
  The other is that as truth we know
  That he who does good is heaven's heir:
  Therefore, I think since things are so,
  That man has the power
  In the one world and the other;
  He is a fool who has neither the one nor the other.
The close relationship of, but also the difference in
rank between, the earthly and heavenly siecles ap-
pears even more clearly in another part of the MIROUR.[24]
Both aspects of human life are taken into account, al-
though the focus is primarily on the world to come.

    One may consider the MIROUR unoriginal, pedantic,
and tedious for long stretches, but it is all of a
piece, a perfect whole. It shows man the vices and
virtues in their proprietates, that he might choose
correctly. It shows him the duality of his own nature in the antithesis of body and soul, will and
reason, that he might know his place and his duty.

                        180

Here man stands for the genus humanum, caught in the conflict between the forces of light and darkness.

This general section is followed by the application of concrete instances. Individual impressions of the different classes are presented in a psychmachia that reveals human deficiency all along the line. For the individual, the classes, the genus humanum, there is but one possibility: to follow the way of the prodigal son. Then from the restoration of his relationship with the Father follows reinstatement in that step of the cosmic hierarchy that God designed for man. The fatted calf was not the prodigal son's goal when he began his journey to his father from the regio longinqua, the place far from God: it was a sign of reconciliation. And thus the MIROUR also assesses worldly prosperity.

In the VOX CLAMANTIS, on the other hand, Gower begins with the decline of the times and searches for a remedy to a specific historical situation; he shows the prodigal son the fatted calf, which he can attain only through a reconciliation with the heavenly father. The difficulty is that the author himself, approaching from the literature of edification, does not take the fatted calf altogether seriously and wants to lead the reader now to earthly prosperity, now to renunciation, a renunciation that regards the goods of this world in the same manner it does the misfortunes. Thus there result inconsistencies such as the juxtapositon at the beginning of Book II of the vanitas theme and the melancholy glorification of a golden national past. Similar contradictions occur elsewhere. At the same time, however, therein also lies the charm of the VOX CLAMANTIS. It was comparatively simple in the fourteenth century to establish a complete theological/philosophical system that discussed the relations of man to his creator as an individual and as a genus, and that illustrated these relationships in its discussion. It was substantially more difficult, but also incomparably more attractive, to disclose this relationship and its consequences in a concrete historical situation; it was, as it were, the proof of the pudding. Gower attempted this task in vain to the

end of his life. That does not mean that the tas.
was incorrectly posed. It had to be put thus and
not otherwise as long as it was held self-evident
that the God of history was a living God, that the
justice of history was a moral justice, and that
the prosperity of the citizens, at which the state
aims, lies in a moral mode of life.

We must return now to the seventh chapter of
Book 2. Just as in the preceeding chapters Fortuna's
power over man was contested because his fate springs
purely and simply from his moral behavior, so now
she is doubted because of divine omnipotence. "Est
deus omnipotens?" begins Chapter Seven (2.34 ff.).
There follows a summary of the doctrine of the
Trinity (2.361 ff.), a passage on Christ (2.379 ff.),
another about belief and the thirst for knowledge
(2.437 ff.), and a last about idolatry, the cult
of the saints, and the adoration of the cross
(2.495 ff.). These sections are often not uninter-
esting as cultural and religious history; yet, one
cannot escape the impression that Gower lost sight
of his theme proper from time to time and inadver-
tently fell into the customary exposition of the
Credo and the Decalogue. The intellectual connection is clearly that the true ruler of human
destiny must be discussed after Fortuna's false
claims have been rejected.

With Chapter Nine Gower returns to his original
concern and demonstrates that the creation allows
Fortuna no scope. Because God has created all, all
is directly dependent upon His will.[25] There is
attached a short description of the Hexameron, half-
biblical, half-Ovidian, which ends with this rather
neo-Platonic distich:
     Ars operi dictat formas, opifexque figurat,
     Artificis sequitur fabrica tota manum 2.621-22
     [The Maker's skill lent form to the work and
     He fashioned it. The whole framework resulted
     from the Author's hand.]
With that Fortuna can be abandoned and the way is
clear for a critique of man, who bears unlimited
responsibility for his fate:
     Est nichil infelix, nichil aut de sorte beatum,
     Immo viri meritis dat sua dona deus.

Quicquid adest igitur, sapiens qui scripta reuoluit
Dicet fortunam non habuisse ream:
Hoc fateor vere, quicquid contingit in orbe,
Nos sumus in causa, sint bona siue mala. 2.625-30
[Nothing is fortunate or unfortunate because of
fate; rather, God bestows his gifts according to
man's deserts. The wise man who ponders the scriptures will therefore say that, whatever happens,
he does not hold Fortune responsible. I truly
acknowledge that whatever happens in the world,
whether it be good or evil, we ourselves are the
cause of it.]

    If one skips the class critique of Books III-VI,
the Mirror for a Prince of Book VI, the discussion
of the cardinal vices luxuria and avaricia, and the
historical/philosophical essay concerning Nebuchad-
nezzar's dream at the beginning of Book VII, one returns with Book VII Chapter 4 to the theme of Book
II, the question of who is to blame for the present
miseria humanae condicionis. The only difference
lies in the terminology. Just as popular opinion
blamed Fortuna in Book II, so now it accuses Lady
World (Mundus):
    "O mundus, mundus," dicunt, "O ve tibi, mundus,
    Qui magis atque magis deteriora paris!" 7.361-62
    ["O world, world," people say. "O woe unto you,
    world, you who spawn baser and baser things!"]
And again the author sees himself obligated to investigate the nature of this supposed force:
    Quid sibi sit mundus igitur, que forma vel eius,
    Que vel condicio, singula scire volo. 7.363-64
    [I therefore wish to know everything--what the
    world is in itself, or what the essential nature
    is, or what its condition.]
Can Book VII be nothing more than a repetition of
Book II with different terminology? Or does Gower
borrow generously from his own MIROUR? In the
MIROUR, Fortuna plays a subordinate role: Siècle,
the equivalent of Mundus,[26] is allegedly to blame
for the ruin of man. However, the Siècle passages
of the MIROUR, according to their form (a predilection for increpatio) and content, are more like
the Fortuna than the Mundus sections of the VOX
CLAMANTIS. Are we therefore to conclude that in

the VOX CLAMANTIS Gower allowed for reasons of
symmetry a double appearance, with slightly altered
name, of that power to which man generally attributed
the responsibility for all hardship and which he himself had introduced in the MIROUR under the name
Siècle? Or did he divide it into two aspects, which
he examined as Fortuna in the introduction and as
Mundus in the conclusion? One would think that the
elimination of Fortuna and the concomitant demonstra-
tion of man's responsibility for his fate had once
and for all cleared the way for Gower's class critique. But that is obviously not so. The question
of responsibility is probed once more, as if Book II
had never been written. Men wish to hold Mundus
responsible.[27] Why?

To anticipate somewhat, the result of the investigation is the acquittal of World. Just as it was
demonstrated in Book II that the nature of fate depends on the moral conduct of man,[28] so it is now
shown that the nature of the world is dependent upon
the moral nature of man.[29] The posing of the same
question with the same conclusion twice within the
same work is suspicious, especially when the question occurs the second time, strictly speaking, post
festum. A class critique of the VC's sort presupposes man's responsibility; it must therefore be
discussed in the introduction, not in a postscript.
And thus we come again to the problem of the genesis
of the work. Before we take this up for the last
time, however, we will occupy ourselves with the
contents of the seventh book.

The fifth chapter contains a long and pene-
trating discussion of the transitoriness of all
earthly things. It does not concern itself with
mutatio rerum in that narrow, sentimentally-colored
sense of a depraved present contrasted to the good
old days, but with a fundamental cosmic principle
that is binding on man as well as the entire creation. The insight in this principle leads to two
results: a depreciation of earthly existence and
a query about the originator of such changes.

The individual themes that Gower employs here

are traditional; however, they are presented with great urgency and genuine concern. It is hardly worthwhile in every instance to ask about the topoi and their origin. Without effort one can hear Horace, Ovid, Seneca, and Boethius; one could with even greater justification point to the Bible and the church fathers. However, what appears important to me is not so much the fact that Gower here, as elsewhere, employs ready-made forms of expression and commonplace trains of thought, but the intensity with which he expresses the perplexed awareness that everything slips away from man, that nothing truly belongs to him. It is familiar as dogma to the Christian from youth on. Yet the dogma, or the fact, can be considered from two sides. It can increase gratitude to God, the giver of all gifts, or it can produce the bitterness of material and spiritual poverty. It is this second aspect, in which man perceives himself as deprived, not divinely bestowed, which Gower works out with full force. He is very deeply affected by it and repeats the theme over and over in different variations. In Chapter 5 he analyzes it in component images: the changing of the times, the ages of man, the transitoriness of spiritual and material possessions, the transfigura- tion of the earth, dread. Everything is not only in flux, but drives toward destruction:

Discite quam prope sit et quam vicina ruina,
Talis enim nullum que releuamen habet:
Discit quam nichil est quicquid peritura voluptas
Possidet et false vendicat esse suum. 7.371-74
[Learn how close and near destruction is, such
destruction, indeed, as has no remedy. Learn
that whatever a fleeting pleasure embraces and
falsely claims to be its own, it is as nothing.]

The two forces that govern the life of man are sor- row and dread, "dolor" and "metus."[30] For Gower they are one and the same: metus governs the future, dolor the present. Sorrow is the reaction to pre- sent hardship, dread the reaction to present pros- perity, behind which lurk transitoriness and im- minent destruction. Thus fortune and misfortune alike are cause for sorrow. Gower parades an en- tire series of material and spiritual goods before the eyes of the reader, only to belittle and dismiss

185

them again at once with the refrain "hinc doleas":

Si te nobilium prouexit sanguis auorum,
Hinc est quod doleas, degenerare potes. 7.431-32
[If the blood of noble ancestors has exalted
you, you should therefore lament the fact that
you can degenerate.]
Si tibi persuadet vxorum fama pudicam,
Hinc eciam doleas, fallere queque solet. 7.435-36
[If fame persuades you that your wife is chaste,
you should also lament accordingly that every
woman is accustomed to deceive.]
Si tibi perspicue pollet sapiencia mentis,
Vt merito doleas, in Salomone vide.
Si facies niuea rubicundo spersa colore
Splendeat, hinc doleas, curua senecta venit. 7.449-52
[If you possess the forceful wisdom of a keen
mind, look upon Solomon so that you may grieve
for your worth. If your complexion, tinged
with a rosy hue, gleams white as snow, you
should accordingly grieve that crooked old age
is approaching.]

Thus all the world's offerings are vanities, tarnished
by dolor and metus:

Sic inmunda suis de fraudibus omnia mundus
Polluit, et nullo tempore munda facit:
Iste per antifrasim nomen sibi vendicat vnum,
Quo nullo pacto participare potest. 7.505-8
[Thus the world corrupts everything through its
wrongdoings, and at no time makes everything
pure. Through a contradiction it claims for itself the name [of being pure], in which it by no
means can share.]

Thus the essence of the world is recognized and revealed, and Gower turns anew to the question of blame.

Book II discusses the problem of mankind's responsibility from the point-of-view of the possible
infringement upon human free will by the external
forces that were combined in the notion of Fortuna.
Book VII investigates the origin, nature, and scope
of this responsibility:

O si vera loquar, quicquid sibi mundus iniqum
Gestat, homo solus est magis inde reus. 7.509-10
[O, if I were to speak the truth, whatever wickedness the world contains, man alone is guilty of
it.]

186

Responsibility arises for man out of the role that God had originally intended for him when He created man in His own image.[31] The Genesis acount expresses this likeness by means of "imago" and "similitudo,"[32] which were distinguished in medieval theology in that imago was associated with knowledge, similitudo with love.[33] Imago and similitudo do not appear in Gower, although the two faculties of cognitio and amor, which are based upon them, and the duty of man to know and love God, do: Vnde creatorem noscat ametque suum (7.518) [Whence he may come to know and love his creator]. Man's dignitas consists in his likeness to God, which is also the reason why the creation is subject to him: Mundus eum sequitur et famulatur ei (7.520) [The world serves and waits upon him].

There follows an account of the creation of man,[34] the climax of which is the moment when the newest and noblest part of creation awakens wondering to a consciousness of himself. The section is unusually good and impressively shaped. Here Gower, who in this part of his work usually employed the artistic only as a means to enliven a little the purely didactic content and to preserve the reader from monotony, knew how to describe convincingly something of the first man's wonder in the beginning of the world:

Stat formatus homo, miratur seque suosque
Gestus, et nescit quid sit et ad quid homo:
Corporis officium miratur, membra moueri,
Artificesque manus articulosque pedum.
Artus distendit, dissoluit brachia, palmis
Corporis attractat singula membra sui:
In se quid cernit sese miratur, et ipsam
Quam gerit effigiem non videt esse suam:
Miratur faciem terre variasque figuras,
Et quia non nouit nomina, nescit eas.
Erexit vultus, os sublimauit in altum,
Se rapit ad superos, spiritus vnde fuit:
Miratur celi speciem formamque rotundam,
Sidereos motus stelliferasque domos:
Stat nouus attonitus hospes secumque revoluit,
Quid sibi que cernit corpora tanta velint.
Noticiamque tamen illi natura ministrat;

Quod sit homo, quod sunt ista creata videt:
Quod sit ad humanos vsus hic conditus orbis,
Quod sit ei proprius mundus, ep ipse dei.
Ardet in auctoris illius sensus amorem,
Iamque recognouit quid sit amare deum. 7.545-66
[Man stands created and marvels at himself and
his movements, and does not know what he is and
for what purpose he exists. He marvels at the
role of his body, that his limbs have motion,
at the skills of his hand, and at the joints of
his feet. He stretches his limbs, relaxes his
arms, and touches every limb of his body with
his hands. He marvels at whatever he beholds
in himself, yet he does not see that the likeness which he bears is his very own. He marvels
at the face of the earth and at the various
shapes, and does not recognize them, since he
does not know their names. He lifts his face,
he raises his voice to the heights, he trans-
ports himself to the heavenly hosts, whence
his spirit came. He marvels at the beauty and
rounded shape of the sky, at the sidereal movements and the starry mansions. His new friend
stands astonished, and ponders with him what
the many [heavenly] bodies he observes may intend for them. Nature, however, serves notice
to him that he is man, that these are created
things which he sees, that this earth is established for human use, that the world belongs
to him and to God. His feelings flame into
love for the author of it, and he now has recognized what it is to love God.]
His astonishment proceeds from the things nearest
at hand, his own body and its functions, and forges
ahead in a wider and wider circle--in an astonished
and incessant expansion of the horizon. The gaze
of man, awakened from the sleep of creation, passes
from his own person to the yet virgin, yet unnamed
earth,[35] and finally to heaven. The three stages
of the perceptual occupancy are indicated each
time by an expression of astonishment or bewilder-
ment (7.545 f.; 551 f.; 554; 559 f.). The underlying notions are "mirari" (545, 547, 551, 557) and
"nescire" (546, 554), which are varied and subsumed
in the last line (559): Stat nouus attonitus hospes

secumque revoluit [His new friend stands astonished and ponders with him].

The conclusion is at the same time a new beginning, marked by the anaphora "stat nouus . . ." (to "stat formatus homo," 1. 545). After man has assimilated the three domains of the universe and passed from admiration to bewildered questions about their meaning, he has progressed far enough that Nature can help him along to understanding. Nature, that is, the innate ratio of man, is sufficient in this instance.[36] Then, from an understanding of the creation and his own creatureliness, springs man's love of the creator. Again the development is in three stages: admiratio--cognicio--amor, forming an intentional crescendo that ends in the distich:

Ardet in auctoris illius sensus amorem,
Iamque recognouit quid sit amare deum. 7.565-66
[His feelings flame into love for the author
of it, and he now has recognized what it is
to love God].

The train of thought is traditional.[37] Gower's achievement is that he shapes a personal experience of the first human out of a doctrinaire abstraction.

The next (seventh) chapter occupies itself with the relation of man to the world, that is, it pursues the theme of man's dignitas from its creation to its consequences.[38] The entire creation is subject to him and stands at his service so that he for his part may serve his creator. This mastery, naturally, is meant only for man as God conceived him, for prelapsarian man. Accordingly, the chapter is formally addressed to Adam and Eve, beginning with an apostrophe:

Dic, Adam, dic, Eua parens, dic vnus et alter,
Dic tibi si desit gracia plena dei. 7.567-68
[Tell me, Adam, tell me, Mother Eve, tell me
both one and the other, tell me if you lack
God's abounding grace.]

The contents do not completely suit the form, since the last section (11. 619-36) ranges in time far beyong the situation in Paradise and speaks of the Fall and of the incarnation of Christ. Technically, this conclusion is unquestionably a part of the theme,

since Christ's labor of redemption represents the
last chapter in the history of mankind's creation
ad imaginem et similitudinem dei. After man's similarity to God was reduced by the Fall to an unlos-
able natural likeness--while the supernatural likeness was lost--the creation of a new man in Christ
was necessary in order to complete the original
divine program:[39]
  Set pietate prius qui condidit omnia solus,
  Ille reformauit et reparauit opus.   7.629-30
  [But He who single-handed founded all things
  through His goodness restored and amended His
  work.]
Thence follows a new and greater duty of love and
obedience upon which the happiness of man is based.
The conclusion of the seventh chapter is a repetition and intensification of the conclusion of
Chapter 6.

     The eighth chapter introduces a new concept
into the argument, that of man as a microcosm.
Gower is hardly affected by the complicated development of the idea of the microcosm in Scholastic
thought. Of the various possibilities according to
which man can be understood as a microcosm, he uses
only the most familiar. The one, of which he made
abundant use in the MIROUR,[40] derives from the doctrine of the elements. The other, widespread, he
got from Gregory, according to the evidence of the
CONFESSIO AMANTIS.[41] It is based on the correlation
of man's existence with that of every single member
in the hierarchy of creation, and occurs in the
MIROUR, in the VOX CLAMANTIS, and in the CONFESSIO.
According to it, man shares the faculty of cognition
with the angel, the five senses with the beast,
growth with the plant, and being with the stone.[42]
Thus he stands, in being and essence, in an indis-
soluble connection with the entire cosmos. If man
is corrupt, he infects, with the inevitability of
a natural law, the whole creation:
  Si tamen inmundus est, que sunt singula mundi
  Ledit, et in peius omne refundit opus.   7.649-50
  [If he is impure, however, he is injurious to
  everything which pertains to the world, and redirects its whole fabric for the worse.]

Qui minor est mundus, fert mundo maxima dampna,
Ex inmundiciis si cadat ipse reus:
Qui minor est mundus, si non inmunda recidat,
Cuncta suo mundi crimine lesa grauat. 7.653-56
[One who is a microcosm brings the greatest mis-
fortune upon the world, if he falls because guilty
of impurities. If one who is a microcosm does
not check his impurities, he weighs heavily upon
everything in the world, which is impaired by
his wickedness.]
The same thought occurs in the prologue of the CON-
FESSIO AMANTIS (ll. 957 ff.):
And whan this litel world mistorneth,
The grete world al overtorneth.
Here the nature of the effect of human sin upon the
entire creation is described more minutely than in
the VOX CLAMANTIS:
For ferst unto the mannes heste
Was every creature ordeined,
Bot afterward it was restreigned:
Whan that he fell, thei fellen eke,
Whan he wax sek, thei woxen seke;
For as the man hath passioun
Of seknesse, in comparisoun
So soffren othre creatures. CONFESSIO, Prol.910-19
In these verses Gower understands the influence of
human corruption on the condition of the world as a
disease that spreads from man to creature in rather
the same manner as the fall of Adam contaminated the
entire human race,[43] or as the lapses of a ruler con-
found an entire people.[44] Besides the involvement
of the creatures, however, there is something like
an active revolt of creation against man when he rebels against his creator. This is caused with reference to the duty of obedience by the parallelism
of the equation: creature:man::man:God. The conception is so familiar that Gower only hints at it
in the VOX CLAMANTIS: Celum deiecit set et odit
terra superbum (7.621) [Heaven cast down the proud
one and earth despises him]. He works it out more
precisely in the CONFESSIO:
The Lond, the See, the firmament,
Thei axen alle jugement
Ayein the man and make him werre:
Therewhile himself stand out of herre,
The remenant wol noght acorde. Prol.959-63

The idea is important in two ways. It is characteristic of the voluntaristic conception of nature,
and it reaches beyond the immediate issue into the
realm of politics. Naturally there can be no question of its originality.[45] However, it is good to
make clear again with such an opportunity that not
only the historical, but also the natural event was
clearly ethically determined for the average man of
the fourteenth century.

The Old Testament had presented the history of
the chosen people as a continual manifestation of
God. Augustine and Orosius had based the Christian
view of history on the same principle. It is not
poetry, but an interpretation of history when in
the Visio Gower describes the events of 1381 in
apocalyptic form. Such interpretation does not attempt to inquire into events as they have actually
taken place, but to illuminate the causes that have
motivated God's will to such a manifestation and
to recognize the means that lead to the mitigation
of divine wrath. The two factors that determine
the course of history are the will of God and the
moral behavior of man. The course of natural events
depends on the same factors. Thus the fate of man
and the world lies in man's own hands. His dignitas
surpasses that of all other creatures. What task
arises for him out of this majesty?

Conuenit ergo satis, humili quod corde rependat
Digna creatori dona creatus homo:
Restat vt ipse sui factoris querat amorem,
Restat vt ipse sciat quid sit et vnde venit.
                                        7.661-64
[Therefore, it is most fitting that man born
of the creator return Him worthy gifts with
humble heart. It remains for him to seek the
love of his maker; it remains for him to realize
above all that he alone is said to be a micro-
cosm, because of the high degree of his fame.]
Noscere te studeas et amare deum, duo namque
Hec sunt, que tibi, rex, scire necesse iubet.
Hec est condicio sub qua tibi contulit esse
Viuendique modum conditor ipse tuus. 6.1035-38
[You should strive to know yourself and to love
God, for these are the two things, O king, which

He decrees indispensable for you to know. This
is the condition under which your Maker has conferred existence and your way of life upon you.]
We touched earlier on the problem of self-knowledge;
now we must go into it in greater detail. It is the
central problem of Gower's three major works and it,
more than anything else, unites the MIROUR, VC, and
CONFESSIO. The two passages cited derive from the
seventh book and from the Mirror for a Prince. Self-
knowledge and love of God are accordingly the two
basic demands which God makes of mankind as well as
the prince. In the first quotation they are termed
a dona of man's creaturely gratitude, in the second
a vital law of human existence. Lines 7.661 ff. remind one slightly of a passage from Bernard of Clairvaux, knowledge of which Gower betrays in the second
book of the VOX CLAMANTIS.[46] Bernard's concern, however, is only with the obligation of grateful love.
How the apparently heterogeneous pair come about in
Gower requires investigation.

That self-knowledge is not an end in itself
for a medieval author is obvious. The two cited
quotations classify it in the broader context of
the relationships between man and God. Yet, self-
knowledge has several functions. Because it is a
part of human knowledge, one must first ask about
the purpose of knowledge generally. In the medieval
school system the student learned to enumerate four
or five objectives, of varying ethical value, for
the sake of which man acquires knowledge. In a
notebook from the school of Gilbert of Porre, the
anonymous SENTENTIAE DIVINITATIS, they are stated
in the following manner:
. . . Quidam enim sunt, qui ad hoc legunt et
discunt, ut sciant, quod curiositas est. Alii,
ut sciantur, quod vanitas est. Alii, ut vendant,
quod simoniaca pravitas est. Alii, ut aedificent,
quod caritas, alii, ut aedificentur, quod prudens
humilitas est.[47] [There are those who read and
discuss to the end that they might know; that
is curiosity. Others, that they might be known;
that is vanity. Others, that they might sell;
that is foul simony. Others, that they might
teach; that is charity. Others, that they might
be taught; that is wise humility.]

Knowledge as an end in itself, knowledge from ambition, and knowlege as a means of enrichment are
rejected. Only two kinds of thirst for knowledge
are morally justifiable: that which leads to the
instruction of others as a form of brotherly love,
and that which leads to self-knowlege as a way to
humility.[48]

Bernard of Clairvaux grants first place to
self-knowledge, first because it constitutes the
prerequisite for all further knowledge, above all,
however, because it is the most useful form of
knowledge.[49] Self-knowledge leads to humilitas,
to humiliatio, and to dolor, a progression which
is often verified in medieval texts with Ecclesiastes 1.18: Qui addit scientiam, addit et dolorem
[He that addeth Knowledge, addeth also labor].
And the value of this self-knowledge is that it
impels man towards divine forgiveness, for humil-
iatum cor et contritum non despicies [a contrite
and humbled heart, O God, thou wilt not despise]
(Ps. 50.19). It is the most important step of the
human soul along the path of redemption. It is so
highly regarded for that reason that Augustine can
say: Summa ergo philosophia est seipsum cognoscere
[Therefore the highest philosophy is to know your-
self].[50] Next to it all other knowledge is vain
and transient.[51]

The best way to attain self-knowledge is to
contemplate the impermanence of mankind:
    Est tibi nil melius igitur, quam prouidus illam
    Prospicias mortem, que tibi finis erit. 7.711-12
    [Therefore, there is nothing better for you than
    to provide for that death which will be your end.]
For that reason Gower links the themes of self-knowledge and contemplation of death and discusses
death and judgment for eleven chapters (9-19). What
he had only briefly suggested in the Mirror for a
Prince he here paints in broad and vivid strokes.
Their portraits in death and decay are held up to
the envious and wrathful man, to the miser, slug-
gard, glutton, and lecher. The sense of these detailed descriptions is the same as that stated in
the portrayal of bodily decomposition in the MYROUR
OF SYNNERS:

Bihold now brother, this is an horrible syht
but it is a ful profitable myrour. Oo ful happy
is he that besyly biholdith himself in this
myrour. Ffor there is no crafte, medycyne ne
techyng that so soone distroyeth vices and
plaunteth vertues as doth inwardly byholdyng
thus of a mannys laste thinges.[52]
After death comes judgment, in the description of
which Gower uses every stylistic means to engender
solemnity. Then, with Chapter 20, we reach the
point at which Bernard's convertetur ad lacrimes,
convertetur ad Dominum [he will be converted to
tears, he will be converted to the Lord] can be
employed:

Non poterit melius hominis caro viua domari,
Quam quod mente gerat mortua qualis erit.
Fletibus assiduis, est dum data gracia flendi,
Penituisse iuuat estque salubre satis:
Nec deus ethereus hec crimina vendicat vlli,
Que confessa dolens non residiua facit. 7.1119-24
[Man's living flesh cannot be better subdued than
by the fact that he bear in mind what it will be
when dead. It is helpful and quite beneficial
to have repented with continual weeping, as
long as opportunity for weeping is granted.
God on high does not punish any man for those
crimes which he does not repeat, once he has
confessed them penitently.]
One would expect that Chapter 24, which returns from
the universal necessity for man to rue and repent
to specifically English circumstances, would have
been joined directly to this introduction of a new
theme. However, Gower inserts here three chapters
about the decay of the times as it is documented
in the failure of all classes. The inspection
seems inappropriate or superfluous after the reader
has already worked through three extensive books of
class critique. It could simply be repetition; however, there is another conceivable explanation to
which we shall presently return.[53]

Chapter 24 begins with an acknowledgement of
involvement in the national misfortune that is one
of Gower's best pieces:

Singula que dominus statuit sibi regna per orbem,
Que magis in Cristi nomine signa gerunt,

Diligo, set propriam super omnia diligo terram,
In qua principium duxit origo meum.
Quicquid agant alie terre, non subruor inde,
Dum tamen ipse foris sisto remotus eis;
Patria set iuuenem que me suscepit alumpnum,
Partibus in cuius semper adhero manens,
Hec si quid patitur, mea viscera compaciuntur,
Nec sine me dampna ferre valebit ea:
Eius in aduersis de pondere sum quasi versus;
Si perstet, persto, si cadat illa, cado.
Que magis ergo grauant presenti tempore, saltem
Vt dicunt alii, scismata plango michi. 7.1289-1302
[I love all the kingdoms which the Lord has es-
tablished for Himself throughout the world and
which bear standards in Christ's name. But a-
bove all I love my own land, in which my family
took its origin. Whatever other lands may do,
I am not shaken by it, as long as I stand apart
at a distance from them. But if the native land
which bore me as a young child, and within whose
realms I always remain fixed--if she suffers anything, my innermost feelings suffer with her, and
she shall not be able to suffer her misfortunes
apart from me. I am almost overwhelmed by the
weight of her adversities. If she stands firm,
I stand firm; if she falls, I fall. Therefore,
I bewail the schisms which, at least so others
say, are so oppressive at this present time.]
In Book II Gower spoke, referring to the prosperous
national past, of the special election of the English
people.[54] His expression of patriotism here is entirely free from the notion of "God's own people";
on the contrary, the restrained passion of his love
appears to increase under the threat of God's anger.
As in Book II, the author again contrasts the golden
past and the depraved present, which has corrupted
even nature in the land (1417 ff.). Gower had already explained earlier that nature withholds her
services from the sinner, and thus nothing is more
natural than that the fields bring forth thorns
and thistles and that the precious metals of the
land be exhausted. The only way out of the present
situation is sinful mankind's self-awakening and
return to God:
Prospera qui veteris vult temporis esse renata,
Reddat et emendet facta priora nouis. 7.1417-18

[Let the man who wishes the prosperity of old
restored give up his former ways and repair them
by his new ones.]
Thus the book ends with a prayer for forgiveness,
which with the restoration of the correct relationship between God and man will lead to a better future for the nation:
Nos, deus alme, tui serui, quamuis modo tardi,
Te, non fortunam, credimus esse deum:
Scimus te solum super omnes esse colendum;
Sic nostri solus tu miserere, deus! 7.1439-42
[We, Thy servants, dear God, even though we are
dilatory at present, believe that Thou, not Fortune, art God. We know that Thou alone art to
be cherished above all, so Thou alone take pity
on us, O God!]

Finally, we have yet to clarify a few questions
connected with the structure of the VC. They concern the two versions of the last chapter of the
Mirror for a Prince, the internal relationship of
the Fortuna and Mundus themes, and the concise repetition of the class critique in Book VII.

We attempted to demonstrate in an earlier chapter that Gower had already conceived the plan of the
VC before the Peasants' Rebellion (1381) and with
the highest likelihood before the Great Schism (1379),
and, be it in whole or in part, had already executed
it. In doing so we depended chiefly on divergencies
in the manuscript tradition. Now the last chapter
of the Mirror for a Prince (VI, Chpt. 18) in the
A-Text is in form essentially different from that
in the B-Text.[55] The passage in question is the
last part of the letter to the young king. The
B-Text presents the greater part of the chapter in
the objective form of the third person singular and,
until l. 1184, speaks simply of the "rex." Richard
II is first addressed personally in the last section,[56] in order to show him the alternatives with
which he is confronted:
Hec tibi, rex, scribo pro tempore nunc que futuro;
Semper in ambiguo sors variatur homo. 6.1199-1200
[O king, I now write these things to you both for
the present and the future. Fate is ever changing
on this fickle earth.]

197

The earlier tradition, which fashions the last
chapter of the open letter into an epilogue, differs. It opens with an invocation to God in typical prayer style, a doxology in five relative
clauses comprising four distiches.[57] There follow
benedictions, likewise in four distiches, two of
which direct themselves to God, two to the young
king.[58] Now the direct address to the king begins,
and in eight fervid distiches the author expounds
on his hopes for the ruler.[59] The conclusion is
again four distiches long. It deals with the relationship of author to poem to king:

Ac decus imperii, Rex, ista tui metra scripsi
Seruus ego Regni promptus honore tibi.
Hec tibi que, pie Rex, humili de corde paraui,
Scripta tue laudi suscipe dona dei:
Non est ista mea tantum doctrina, sed eius
Qui docet, et dociles solus ab ore creat.
O iuuenile decus, laus Regia, flos puerorum,
Vt valor est in te, sic tibi dico vale. 6.1191-98
[I, a servant of the realm and eager for your
honor, have written these verses to you for the
glory of your rule, O king. Receive these
writings, which I have composed with humble
heart for you, good king, as gifts of God for
your praise. For this instruction is not so
much mine but His. He alone teaches and makes
men well taught by His words. O youthful
glory, royal honor, flower of youths, since
there is goodness within you, I bid you goodby.]

Gower obviously devoted painstaking care to the epilogue of the A-Text. The proportionate relationship
of units of verse and thought is well balanced: 4+4:
8:4. The corresponding chapter of the B-Text, on
the other hand, is neither balanced nor unified.
The play of words on "valor" and "vale" in the
last pentameter of the A-Text indicates the two-
fold character of the concluding "vale." It
comprises more than a simple farewell; it is at the
same time a benediction. However, the element of clo-
sure is not diminished as a result. The poet presents his verse to the king and takes his leave.
It is conventional to do both at the end of a work;
midway in Book VI of the VOX CLAMANTIS, however, it
is extraordinary. Unless the open letter and dedi-

cation are fictions, Gower expects the king to seek out a treatise respectfully presented to him in the midst of a more than substantial work. There are two possible explanations for the epilogue of the A-Text. Either Gower had an older work, a speculum principis composed for Richard and presented to the king upon an earlier occasion--perhaps his accession-- which he transferred without essential change to the sixth book of the VOX CLAMANTIS, or the VC originally ended with the Mirror for a Prince.

That Gower, unlike Chaucer, courted the favor of the reigning monarch his whole life long is shown by the original dedication of the CONFESSIO to Rich-ard and of the BALADES to Henry IV, by the poem on Henry IV's accession that borrows the invocatio from the epilogue of the Mirror for a Prince (A-Text), and by the importunately flattering conclusion of the CRONICA TRIPERTITA. Nothing can be said about the MIROUR in this respect, since it lacks begin-ning and end. The idea of introducing himself to the new monarch with a Latin work may therefore have suggested itself to Gower toward the end of the 70's. It is quite conceivable that, considering the king's youth, Gower would pursue his didactic bent and at the same time think to fulfill a moral mission. Be-cause it was an occasional poem, moreover, one can hardly blame him for seizing upon material that he had already treated in the MIROUR. The choice of Latin as linguistic medium may have been determined by the specialness of the occasion. Political writ-ings to princely addressees tended to be written in Latin. A speculum principis in the vernacular--be it Anglo-Norman, be it English--could easily have given rise to a suspicion that the addressee was illiterate, or stamped the contents as light reading. One may assume that Gower, in joining the Mirror for a Prince to a substantial class critique, departed from the class critique's usual arrangement (as discussed in Chapter 4) in order that the open let-ter would appear as the end and climax of the work. He also distinguished it formally from the other sections by going from the markedly general treat-ment of the other classes to a personal address, from an objective form of report to a subjective

form of epistle. The goal of the work was obviously
to instruct the royal youth about the condition of
the state in its class divisions and to explain to
him the duties which devolved upon him out of the
general situation and his own position. The Fortuna
book may have been an accommodation, even though
superficial, to courtly taste and the literary mode
of the day. Gower packs in it as much as possible
of the siècle argument of the MIROUR that was so
important to him. If the title VOX CLAMANTIS already
belonged to this original complex, it too could have
been chosen with regard to Richard. For John the
Baptist appears to have been something like the
special patron saint of the king. There is a poem
from the year 1393 that celebrates the reconciliation of the king with the citizens of London. The
author, John of Maidstone, describes processions,
entertainments, and living pictures in honor of the
king. Among other things had been erected a zoolog-
ical garden, in the midst of which stood John the
Baptist. And on this occasion it was said of the
Baptist that Richard II venerated him especially
ardently before all other saints.[60]

I am inclined to view as a later addition everything in the VOX CLAMANTIS that follows the Mirror
for a Prince. It must remain an open question
whether this material constitutes a special composition, after the manner of de contemptu mundi literature, that Gower incorporated into the work when he
added the Visio, or whether the rest of the sixth
and the entire seventh book were written ad hoc when
Gower felt, after the convulsion of 1381, the need
to sound a last great warning cry to the educated
classes of the nation. The short survey of the
estates in the seventh book, which appears superfluous after the substantial class critique of Books
III-VI, speaks for the first supposition. Also, the
considerable overlappings of the Fortuna book and
the Mundus argument are thus most easily comprehensible. For the second supposition can be ad-
duced the close of the seventh book, which, however,
could be a piece of touching up that was intended
to fit the passage to the VOX CLAMANTIS. Be that
as it may, what is new and important in the work as

it stands before us in the B-Text version is an alteration of the poem's character that results from
the change of the addressee and of the contemporary
situation. From a princely vade mecum it became a
substantial work of edificational literature that
differs from similar efforts only in that it undertakes to explain a concrete historical situation,
the Peasants' Rebellion, in its metaphysical bases
and earthly consequences.

The change-over from the original plan to the
final form was facilitated because the Mirror for a
Prince belongs by its nature to the realm of ethics
rather than political theory, and itself has strong
edificational inclinations. The profit that accrued
to the VOX CLAMANTIS from the expansion of 1381 is
considerable. The trite subjects--Fortuna, class
critique, speculum principis--receive new life from
the thrust of events. The author's genuine concern gives his verses a restrained power in the
newly added parts, and the homilist reveals himself not as the prophet of a cheap morality, but as
a man who shows his people, with the means at his
disposal, a way out of the chaos of their time--to
a moral regeneration without which a political regeneration is inconceivable.

Notes to Chapter Five
1 See above, pp. 135 f.
2 See above, pp. 146 f.
3 Cf. MIROUR 23221-32:
    N'est pas pour ce que dieus n'avoit
    Assetz du quoy dont il porroit
    Avoir fait riches chascuny,
    Q'il les gens povres ordinoit;
    Ainz fuist pour ce que dieus voloit
    Essaier les seignours ensi,
    S'ils ussent leur corage en luy:
    Car qui q'est riche et joust auci,
    Laissant le tort pour faire droit,
    Il ad grant grace deservi,
    Qant pour les biens q'il fait yci
    Les biens sanz fin puis avoir doit.
    [It is not because God hadn't
    Enough of that of which he could

201

Have made each one rich,
That He ordained people poor;
It was that God wished
To test men in this way,
To see if they had their trust in him:
For whoever is rich and plays thus,
Leaving wrong in order to do right,
He deserves great grace,
For as many good things as he does here
He ought to have good things without end.]

4 Hic tractat qualiter status et ordo mundi in tribus consistit gradibus, sunt enim, vt dicit, Clerus, Milicies, et Agricultores, de quorum errore mundi infortunia nobis contingunt. [Here he treats of how the state or order of the world consists of three estates. They are, as he says, the clergy, knighthood, and peasantry. Through their going astray, the misfortunes of the world befall us.]

5 See above, pp. 4 f.

6 That the classes are responsible for each other is self-evident; thus, for example, the people have to suffer the consequences of the king's sins (cf. 6.609 f.). For all that, the people may not call the ruler directly to account.

7 Si tamen esse potest quod felix esset in orbe,
Dudum felices nos dedit esse deus. 2.17-18
[Long ago, God granted that we be happy, if it is possible that one may be happy on earth.]

8 One would probably not be wrong in assuming that the brilliant period of Edward III and the Black Prince is intended. It appears to lie just in the past (l. 26 "nuper") and to have been of short duration (19 ff.). The enthusiastic tone matches that of the eulogy to the Black Prince (7, Chpt. 13). The same kind of historical view occurs in the song "Seldom Seen is Soon Forgot" (cf. above, pp. 42 f.).

9 The approximation of "fatum," "fortuna," and "casus" may go back to Boethius, DE CONSOLATIONE IV, prosa 6-8. I have used the edition of Adrianus a Forti Scuto (London, 1925).

10 DE CONS. IV, prosa 6: . . . fatum vero inhaerens rebus mobilibus dispositio per quam prouidentia suis quaeque nectit ordinibus [. . . but Fate is a disposition inherent in changeable things, by which Providence connecteth all things in their due order (Trans. I.T.)].

[11] Ibid.: Prouidentia namque cuncta pariter, quamuis diuersa, quamuis infinita, complectitur; fatum uero singula digerit in motum, locis, formis ac temporibus distributa; ut haec temporalis ordinis explicatio in divinae mentis adunata prospectum prouidentia sit, eadem vero adunatio, digesta atque explicata temporibus, fatum uocetur [For Providence embraceth all things together, though diverse, though infinite; but Fate putteth every particular thing into motion being distributed by places, forms, and time; so that this unfolding of temporal order being united into the foresight of God's mind is Providence, and the same uniting, being digested and unfolded in time, is called Fate (Trans. I.T.)].

[12] HOM. IN EVANGELIA, Book I, Hom. 10. Migne, PL 76:1112.

[13] DE CIV. 5.1: Prorsus divina providentia regna constituuntur humana. Quae si propterea quisquam fato tribuit, quia ipsam Dei voluntatem vel potestatem fati nomine appellat, sententiam teneat, linguam corrigat (Teubnerian) [In a word, human kingdoms are established by divine providence. And if any one attributes their existence to fate, because he calls the will or the power of God itself by the name of fate, let him keep his opinion, but correct his language (Trans. Marcus Dods)].

[14] SUMMA THEOLOGICA, pars 1, inq. 1, tract. 5, sect. 2, quaest. 3, tit. 1: De Fato, cap. 1: . . . providentia divina est cognoscitiva eorum quae sunt futura. Praecognitio autem Dei nihil relinquit in rebus futuris . . . quare si fatum, sicut dicit Boetius, est "dispositio in mobilibus" relicta ex divina providentia, cum nihil aliud a providentia relinquatur in rebus futuris: aut fatum simpliciter nihil erit vel non erit aliud a divina providentia. [. . . divine providence is knowledgeable of those things which are in the future. However, God's foreknowledge forsakes nothing in the affairs of the future . . . wherefore if fate, as Boethius says, is "a disposition inherent in changeable things" forsaken by divine providence, at the same time that none of the affairs of the future are forsaken by providence, then fate is either simply nothing or it is something not from divine providence.] Quaracchi edition (1948), IV, 304.

203

[15] Gregory, HOM. IN EVANG. I, 10: Sed inter haec sciendum quod Priscillianistae haeretici nasci unumquemque hominem sub constitutionibus stellarum putant; et hoc in adjutorium sui erroris assumunt, quod nova stella exiit cum Dominus in carne apparuit, cuius fuisse fatum eamdem quae apparuit stellam putant. Sed si Evangelii verba pensamus, quibus de eadem stella dicitur: Usque dum veniens staret supra ubi erat puer, dum non puer ad stellam, sed stella ad puerum cucurrit, si dici liceat, non stella fatum pueri, sed fatum stellae is qui apparuit puer fuit. Sed a fidelium cordibus absit ut aliquid esse fatum dicant. Vitam quippe hominum solus hanc conditor qui creavit administrat. Neque enim propter stellas homo, sed stellae propter hominem factae sunt. [But they among those knowing that heresy of the Priscillianists thought each man to be born under the regulation of the stars; and this they claimed in swearing to their error, that a new star ascended when God appeared in the flesh, whose fate they thought to have been the same as the star that appeared. But if we consider the words of the Gospels, in which it is said about the same star, "all the while coming that it might stand over where the boy was," since the boy did not hasten to the star but the star to the boy, the star, if one is permitted to say so, was not the boy's fate but this boy who appeared was the star's fate. But far be it from the hearts of the faithful to think that fate is anything real. Certainly the founder who created human life alone administers it. For man was not made because of the stars, but the stars because of man.] Migne PL 76:1111 f.

[16] 2.237-74. The same catalogue appears with slight variations in the MIROUR 26989-27072. However, the MIROUR speaks for the most part simply of "homme"--once of "prodhomme"--while the VC seeks to develop, with great emphasis, the idea of the homo iustus.

[17] The CONFESSIO handles the question of free will and belief in the stars with more reserve. 7.633-63 contrasts the views of the "naturien" and the "divin" and ends with a compromise. In a later passage (1281 ff.), the influence of the stars is categorically accepted: [the sterres] . . . worchen

manye sondri thinges/ To ous, that ben here under-
linges.

18 SUMMA PRAEDICANTIUM, s.v. "homo."
19 Migne, PL 184:485 ff.
20 2.281-348.
21 SUMMA PRAEDICANTIUM, s.v. "tribulatio."
22 Gower leaves this second part of the problem
unexplained at this point, since it does not pertain
directly to his theme, the national misfortune. He
returns to it in the seventh book of the VOX CLAMAN-
TIS and in the CONFESSIO; cf. below, pp. 190 ff.
23 Cf. 2.201 ff.
Set fortuna tamen nichil est, neque sors, neque
                                          fatum,
Rebus in humanis nil quoque casus habet:
Set sibi quisque suam sortem facit, et sibi casum
Vt libet incurrit, et sibi facta creat;
Atque voluntatis mens libera quod facit actum
Pro variis meritis nomine sortis habet.
[But in spite of this, Fortune is nothing, and
neither destiny nor fate nor chance has anything
to do with human affairs. But each man fashions
his own destiny and opposes chance as he pleases
and creates his own fate. And indeed, a free
mind considers what it voluntarily does for its
own benefit as done in the name of fate.]
24 MIROUR 27121-29:
    He, homme, molt es benuré,
    Sur toutes bestes honeuré,
    Que dieus t'ad fait lour capitain,
    Et si bien fais ta dueté,
    Apres la mort t'ad ottrié
    Du ciel la joye plus haltain:
    Du double bien tu es certain,
    Si bien governes le mondain,
    Le ciel avras enherité.
    [Well, man, you are most blessed,
    Honored above all animals,
    For God has made you their captain,
    And if you do your duty well,
    After death there will be bestowed on you
    The highest joy of heaven:
    You are certain of double good fortune:
    If you control the earthly good,
    You will inherit that of heaven.]

205

[25] 2.581 ff.

[26] The word "world" originally had a temporal character and served as a translation of "mundus" as well as of "saeculum"; in this second sense it is still contained today in the liturgy: "world without end"--in saecula saeculorum. An exchange of the terms was thus possible.

[27] A charming illustration of Gower's lines occurs in Bromyard, s.v. "tribulatio." He speaks of how David ended the tribulations of his people by admitting his guilt (I Kings 24), while today each pushes guilt off upon the other: Sed heu in modernis tribulationibus omnino contrarium est, quia illi qui sunt causa tribulationis peccata propria non confitentur nec facta iudicant nec sibi ipsis cum David tribulationis causam imponunt sed aliis . . . Adam culpam imponit Evae et Eva Adae ad excusandas excusationes in peccatis, quod neuter sine culpa est . . . Si in aliquo recognoscant tales tribulationes propter peccata incidere, dicunt: mundus est malus et falsus vel illi sunt tales; mundum et alios accusant et aliena confitentur delicta. [But, alas, everything is different in today's tribulations, because those who are the cause of the tribulations do not confess their own sins nor judge their own deeds, nor do they with David blame themselves for tribulations, but instead blame others . . . Adam placed the blame on Eve and Eve on Adam in declining by excuses into sin, because neither was without blame . . . If they do recognize in anything that tribulations occur on account of sin, they say: "the world is evil and false," or they are such that they accuse the world and others and confess another's fault.]

[28] Debet enim semper sors esse pedisseca mentis (2.207)[For fate ought always to be the handmaiden of the mind].

[29] Cf. 7.646-60:
Est homo qui mundus de iure suo sibi mundum
Subdit, et in melius dirigit inde status:
Si tamen inmundus est, que sunt singula mundi
Ledit, et in peius omne refundit opus:
Vt vult ipse suum proprio regit ordine mundum,
Si bonus ipse, bonum, si malus ipse, malum.

Qui minor est mundus, fert mundo maxima dampna,
Ex inmundiciis si cadat ipse reus:
Qui minor est mundus, si non inmunda recidat,
Cuncta suo mundi crimine lesa grauat:
Qui minor est mundus homo, si colat omnipotentem,
Rebus in humanis singula munda parit:
Qui minor est mundus, si iura dei meditetur,
Grande sibi regnum possidet ipse poli.
[The man who is pure in his own right subjects
the world to himself, and accordingly guides its
circumstances for the better. If he is impure,
however, he is injurious to everything which
pertains to the world, and redirects its whole
fabric for the worse. He rules his world by his
own command as he wishes: If he is good, it is
good; if he is evil, it is evil. One who is a
microcosm brings the greatest misfortunes upon
the world, if he falls because guilty of impurities. If one who is a microcosm does not
check his impurities, he weighs heavily upon
everything in the world, which is impaired by
his wickedness. [But] if one who is a microcosm worships the Omnipotent, he is the source
of everything pure in human affairs. If one
who is a microcosm meditates upon the laws of
God, he will possess the great kingdom of
heaven for himself.]
   30 Cf. 7.497-98:
Quo se vertit homo, dolor aut metus incutit ipsum;
Excipitur nullus qui sit in orbe gradus.
[Wherever a man turns, grief or fear strikes
him; no rank on earth is exempt.]
   31 7.513-20:
"Nos faciamus," ait [sc. deus], "hominem, qui nos
                                          imitari
Possit; et vt nobis seruiat atque colat,
Inspiremus ei sensum racionis, amorem,
Vim discretiuam, quid sit et vnde venit:
Inspiremus ei factoris cognicionem,
Vnde creatorem noscat ametque suum,
Quis suus est auctor, quis ei dedit esse vel vnde:
Mundus eum sequitur et famulatur ei.
[Let us make man, who can be like us. And in or-
der that he may serve and worship us, let us
breathe into him the sense of reason, love, the

power to distinguish what he is and whence he
is come. Let us breathe into him the knowledge
of his maker, whence he may come to know and
love his creator, and may come to know Who his
author is, Who gave him essence, or for what
reason the world serves and waits upon him.]
32 Genesis 1.26: Et ait: Faciamus hominem ad
imaginem et similitudinem nostram [And he said:
Let us make man to our image and likeness].
33 Hugh of St. Victor summarizes the evidence
quite concisely: Factus est homo ad imaginem et
similitudinem Dei, quia in anima . . . fuit imago
et similitudo Dei. Imago secundum rationem, similitudo secundum dilectionem; imago secundum cog-
nitionem veritatis, similitudo secundum amorem
virtutis. [Man is made in the image and likeness
of God because in regard to his mind . . . he was
the image and likeness of God. Image according to
reason, likeness according to love; image according to recognition of the truth, likeness according to love of virtue.] DE SACRAMENTIS. Migne,
PL 76:264.
34 7.525-66.
35 One is reminded slightly of the old magical theory about language, according to which the
giving of a name amounts to acquisition of the object named, in l. 553 f. and its complement in the
following chapter:
Te caput esse dedit rerum, rebusque locatis
Nomina te cunctis queque vocare dedit [sc. deus].
7.605-6
[The author of things caused you to exist, and
once things were set in order, He caused you to
summon up names for everything.]
The notion was readily employed in the exegesis of
Genesis 2.20 f.; cf. Hugh of St. Victor: Nam idcirco ipse creator non a se . . . singulis quibus-
que animalibus, sed ab homine nomina formari voluit,
ut manifeste ostenderet quod singulorum naturam et
usum et officia ex insita sibi ratione homo agnovit.
Quae enim propter illum creata erant, ab illo re-
genda et disponenda erant, et idcirco horum omnium
Deus illi scientiam tribuit et providentiam reli-
quit. [For that reason the Creator Himself wished
the names of each and every animal to be formed

not by Himself but by man, so that He might manifestly show that man perceived by his innate reason
the nature and use and office of each. For those
things which were created on account of him are
governed and disposed of by him, and for that
reason God gave him knowledge of them all and re-
linquished authority.] DE SACRAMENTIS, loc. cit.,
col. 271.

[36] Cf. "Merci Passeth Alle Thing," a poem from
the Vernon MS., ll. 129-32:

And whonne we breken Godes heste,
Ajeynes kuynde we ben un-trewe:
Ffor kuynde wolde that we him knewe
And dradde him most in ure doing.

[37] Cf., for example, Vincent of Beauvais,
SPECULUM MORALE, lib. 1, pars 1, dist. 10 on the
question of whether knowledge is the prerequisite
to love.

[38] 7.567-636.

[39] Cf. Col. 3.10; 2 Peter 1.4; and esp. Rom.
8.29 and 2 Cor. 3.18.

[40] Cf. MIROUR 26617 ff.

[41] CONFESSIO AMANTIS, Prol.945.

[42] Cf. VOX CLAMANTIS 7.637-44.

[43] Bromyard, s.v. "homo," may again serve as
an illustration: In natura . . . aptum est, quod
moriente corde, a quo est omnium membrorum vitale
principium, moriuntur et membra, sicut etiam vene-
nata. . . . sic per unius delictum, immo peccatum,
et omnes homines in condemnationem, et per inobed-
ientiam unius hominis peccatores constituti multi.
[In nature . . . it is fitting that after the heart
is dead, from which comes the life principle of all
the members, the members also die, just as if poi-
soned. . . . Thus through the fault of one, nay
rather the sin, and all men are condemned, and
through the inobedience of one man are many sinners determined.]

[44] Bromyard, s.v. "regimen": Quorum [sc. male
regentium] error licet in proprium periculum re-
dundet eternum, tamen interim in damnum redundat
subditorum . . . Est enim in talibus respectu ad
subditos . . . sicut de stomacho respectu ad membra, et sicut de sole in medio planetarum; quorum
si stomachus et cor bene disponantur, membra sunt

sana. Sed ubi hec male disponuntur et ubi sol ec-
clipsatur, necesse est alia membra esse indispos-
ita et alias stellas ecclipsari. [Granted that
their [sc. wicked rulers] error abounds to their
own eternal danger; nevertheless, in the meantime
it abounds to the damnation of the subjects . . .
as the stomach to the limbs and the sun in the midst
of the planets; if the stomach and heart are well-
disposed, the limbs are healthy. But when they are
indisposed, and when the sun is eclipsed, then the
other members are necessarily indisposed and the
other stars eclipsed.] Gower designates the rex
iuste the salus of his subjects.
    45 Cf. by way of example the powerful passages
in the "Sermo de Miseria Humana" ascribed to Bernard
of Clairvaux: O homo! . . . Omnia propter te fecit
Deus; et tu propter omnia relinquis eum. Propter
omnia quae occurrunt tibi, dimittis Deum; ed idcirco omnia dimittunt te. Propter creaturas relinquis Creatorem; et ideo contra te insurgent omnes
creaturae. Quia offendendo Creatorem offendisti
omnem creaturam: ideo creaturae quae factae sunt
in ministerium et utilitatem tuam, convertentur
in vindictam et poenam tuam. [O man! . . . God
made all of you, and all forsake Him. Because of
all that happens to you, you abandon God, and for
that all abandon you. You forsake the creatures
of the Creator and therefore all the creatures rise
against you. Who offends against the Creator offends against all the creatures; therefore, the
creatures who were made for your servants and
helpers become your rod and punishment.] Migne,
PL 184:1111.
    46 Quid rependam domino pro omnibus his non
habeo? Nam quicquid sum, erit sicut stella ad
solem, stilla ad flumen, pulvis ad montem; quid
ergo retribuam domino pro omnibus que retribuit
mihi nisi ut ipsum diligam? [What shall I repay
the Lord for all this which I do not possess?
For whatsoever I am it is like a star to the sun,
a drop to a river, a handful of dust to a mountain;
what therefore shall I repay the Lord for everything that He gives me but that I love Him?] I
have not identified the passage, but take it from
the LAVACRUM CONSCIENTIE OMNIBUS SACERDOTIBUS

SUMME UTILE AC NECESSARIUM (Cologne, 1501), fol.
44^r. Cf. Gower, 2.475 ff.:
   Vna quid ad solem sintilla valet, vel ad equor
   Gutta, vel ad celum quid cinis esse potest?
   Vult tamen a modicis inmensus, summus ab ymis,
   Vult deus a nobis mentis amore coli.
   [What does one spark avail the sun, or one drop
   the sea, or what can our ashes be worth to
   heaven? Nevertheless, God wishes to be worshipped by us with a loving spirit, the Infinite wishes to be worshipped by us insignificant
   ones, the Most High by the lowest.]
   47 Ed. B. Geyer, Diss. Münster 1907, p. 8.
   48 Similar enumerations occur in Bernard of
Clairvaux, "Sermo XXXVI in Cant. Cant.," Migne, PL
183:968; John of Salisbury, POLICRATICUS, VIII,
Chpt. 15; Hugh of St. Victor, ERUD. DIDASC., Migne
PL 176:798; Vincent of Beauvais, DE ERUDITIONE
FIL. REGIS, Chpt. 13.
   49 Volo proinde animam primo omnium scire se
ipsam, quod id postulet ratio et utilitatis et
ordinis. Et ordinis quidem, quoniam quod nos sumus
primum est nobis; utilitatis vero, quia talis scientia non inflat, sed humiliat, et est quaedam
praeparatio ad aedificandum. Nisi enim super humilitatis stabile fundamentum, spirituale aedificium
stare minime potest. Porro ad se humiliandum nihil
anima invenire vivacius seu accommodatius potest,
quam si se in veritate invenerit . . . Convertetur
ad lacrimas, convertetur ad planctus et gemitus,
convertetur ad Dominum, et in humilitate clamabit:
Sana animam meam, quia peccavi tibi (Ps. 40.5).
[Accordingly, I wish first of all to know the mind
itself, because it demands reason and utility and
order. Order because what we are is foremost to
us; utility because such knowledge does not puff
up but humbles and is preparation for building.
For unless it rest upon a firm foundation of humility, a spiritual building is unable to stand. Furthermore, humility by itself is unable to enter the
mind permanently or suitably, because it enters
with the truth . . . He will be converted to tears,
he will be converted to laments and sighs, he will
be converted to the Lord and in humility he will
shout, "heal my soul, for I have sinned against

211

Thee (Psalm 40.5).] At the end of the sermon, Bernard establishes the connection between self-knowledge and the knowledge and thus the love of God: Ego quamdiu in me respicio, in amaritudine moratur oculus meus. Si autem temperabit mox amaram visionem mei visio laeta Dei . . . Tali itaque experimento et tali ordine salubriter innotescit Deus, cum prius se homo noverit in necessitate positum, et clamabit ad Dominum, et exaudiet eum, et dicet: Eruam te, et honorificabis me [Ps. 99.15]. Atque hoc modo erit gradus ad notitiam Dei cognitio tui. [As long as I look upon myself, my eye lingers in bitterness. However, the joyous vision of God will soon temper for me the bitter vision . . . And thus by such a trial and such an arrangement God becomes more soundly known, when man previously in distress will have recognized the place he will shout to the Lord and rejoice in Him and say, "I have strayed from you and you will honor me [Ps. 99.15]. And in this way your knowledge will be by stages to the knowledge of God.] Migne, PL 183: 969 f.

50 Cited in Bromyard, s.v. "sapientia."

51 Cf. 7.699-704:
Quid penetrasse iuuat studiis archana Platonem,
Natureque suos composuisse libros? etc.
[What help was it for Plato to have penetrated
mysteries through his studies, and to have
compiled his books of natural philosophy? etc.]
This is obviously a variation upon the ubi sunt qui ante nos theme.

52 MS. Laud 174, fol. 96^v, Bodleian.

53 See below, pp. 200 f.

54 Cf. 2.17 ff.

55 Two MSS., L and L$_2$, have the two versions back to back.

56 O rex, ergo tui detergas crimina regni, etc. (6.1185 ff.) [Therefore, O King, you should wipe out crime in the kingdom, etc.].

57 6.1159-66.

58 6.1167-74.

59 6.1175-90.

60 Astitit his medius sanctus Baptista Joannes,
Indicat hic digito, agnus et ecce Dei!
Inspicit attente rex hunc, quia quem notat
iste,

Illius ut meminit mitior inde fuit.
Nam quia devotus colit hunc constanter,
                                    eidem
Prae reliquis sanctis porrigit ipse preces.
Hujus ad intuitum, si quid sibi manserat irae,
Extitit exstinctum protinus usque nihil.
[In the midst of these people stands St. John
                                the Baptist,
He proclaims with a finger, behold the lamb
                                    of God!
The king views him attentively, because the
                            One he points to
Was gentler, as he remembers, than the Baptist.
Therefore he worships him devotedly and pours
Out prayers to him before the relics of the
                                        saints.
If any anger is still in him, it immediately
Vanishes from then on while he looks at him.]
John de Maidstone, "The Reconciliation of Richard II
with the City of London," ed. Thomas Wright, POLITI-
CAL POEMS AND SONGS (London, 1859), I, 294.

Chapter Six
Gower's Narrative Technique

The prolific Gower's ability to tell a tale manifests itself in a characteristic narrative directness and tautness that lead to a striking tempo. He both avoids the bareness of excessive moral concern, into which the exempla style frequently degenerates, and simultaneously avoids a solemn pomposity and verbose thinness of meaning that Chaucer himself does not always escape. I will begin my illustration of the special characteristics of Gower's narrative technique with an example that does not put him in competition with Chaucer. It is the story of Acteon (Ovid's Actaeon) in the CONFESSIO AMANTIS,[1] not one of Gower's best tales, hardly, indeed, one of his better. However, for that very reason it seems appropriate as an illustration of the strength of his techniqe and at the same time of its limitations and dangers. It has the advantage of being suitably brief, and it also prevents the reader from applying inappropriate criteria derived from a comparison with Chaucer. Finally, the tale stems from a Latin author whose own narrative art follows such totally different paths that one does not run the risk of investigating the characteristics of the model rather than the specifically Gowerian.

The contentual relationship of Gower's story to Ovid's can be defined in a few words.[2] In Ovid the story requires 115 verses, in Gower 45. Gower therefore reduces the narrative to a bare third, if one considers the quantitative relationship of the Latin hexameter to the iambic tetrameter of the CONFESSIO, a relationship which, of course, is in part further balanced by the greater syllabic conciseness of English. Yet only the description of the action is shortened, not the action itself, which is rendered in toto. A substantial economy is achieved in the character apparatus, which Gower reduces to the absolutely essential. That is apparent in both Acteon and Diana, the two chief figures. Ovid surrounds Acteon with a troop of hunters (11.144-54); Gower suppresses them. Ovid has Diana step into her bath surrounded by her

nympths, whose names and functions are individually
introduced (ll. 165-72); Gower foregoes the names
and disposes of the entire ceremony in one verse
(1. 365). A third reduction of character apparatus
concerns the pack of hounds. Ovid allows it no fewer
than twenty lines (206-25) and makes it the subject
of a highly skilled parody of heroic-epic technique.
The two champions are presented with monstrous solemnity, as if they here Homeric heroes on their way to
battle:

        . . . primumque Melampus
    Ichnobatesque sagax latratu signa dedere,
    Gnosius Ichnobates, Spartana gente Melampus.
                       3.206-8
    [. . . and first Melampus, and the good-
    nosed Ichnobates gave the signal, in full
    cry. Ichnobates was a Gnossian dog; Melampus
    was of Spartan breed.]
Signa dare, the epithet sagax, above all the solemn
ethnic note, are in imitation of epic style. The
names and characteristics of the rest of the pack
are gathered in a kind of Homeric hero catalogue--
extremely precious, well-nigh masterly. Gower has
no use for such artistry and reduces hounds and
hunters alike to a minimum. Names are, of course,
not used.

    So much for the simplification of character
apparatus. It causes a more powerful concentration
on the chief characters as well as on the action,
but it would hardly be remarkable in itself if
Gower had stopped with the quantitative change. He
goes considerably further. Ovid's story is bipolar.
The narrative begins with Acteon and the picture of
the heated hunting company lying down to rest (ll.
143-54). There then follows in narrative succession
what in reality is simultaneous: the figure of the
goddess preparing herself for a bath (ll. 155-72).
Each of these "scenes" is introduced by a description of the locality: Mons erat . . . (1.143); Vallis
erat . . . (1. 155). The parallelism is manifestly
conscious and intended, and any transition is most
painstakingly avoided. Thus the two main figures
stand--each in his or her own space--separate before the eyes of the reader until fate sets them
in motion towards each other in ll. 174 ff. and

destiny runs its course. Ovid therefore has two
carriers of the action, whom he introduces successively and independently of each other in order to
have them then collide. He employs this scheme
again after Acteon's metamorphosis, when he first
presents the stag transformation with the corresponding explanation, then the pack of hounds, in
order to loose the two finally upon each other and
so arrive at the tragic finale.

Gower follows a fundamentally different method.
He tells the story of Acteon, the story of a man
who, uncontrolled, allowed his gaze all too free a
course. Gower's moral position is clear. Ovid had
generously given full scope to fatum;[3] in his attitude of weighing and waiting he had interpreted
the story as the fatal, but in the last analysis
not culpable, collision between two elements that
must lead to a tragic end. This is reflected in
the construction of the narrative. Gower, because
he weights Acteon morally, creates an essentially
different structure for the story. For him Diana
has no inherent right to exist; she only serves
the purpose of making known Acteon's serious lack
of discipline. Consequently, it is only natural
that Gower does not proceed according to the Ovidean
scheme, but regards the entire action from beginning
to end from the same perspective. Like Ovid he begins with Acteon; however, there is no passage
like that in Ovid at 1. 155. Rather, Gower incor-
porates the locus amoenus, with which Ovid introduces the Diana episode, into the perspective of
Acteon. Thus Ovid's objective description becomes
something like Acteon's personal experience. The
marks of this can be pursued into the syntactic
construction, which also firmly retains Acteon as
the grammatical subject:

> On his hunting as he cam ride,
> In a Forest al one he was:
> He syh upon the grene gras
> The faire freisshe floures springe,
> He herde among the leves singe
> The Throstle with the nyhtingale:
> Thus er he wiste into a Dale
> He cam, where was a litel plein,
> All round aboute wel besein

With buisshes grene and Cedres hyhe;
And ther withinne he caste his yhe. 1.350-60
The landscape has no objective reality, occurring
rather in the gaze of the main figure. Gower thus
achieves three different effects: the description of
scenery does not interrupt the action, it does not
divert the reader, and it is itself incorporated
into the action. In this way the topos of the locus
amoenus is varied so that it supports a living function and no longer operates as a cliche. The landscape, personally experienced by Acteon, forms the
natural transition to the meeting with the goddess.

What is important in this meeting is the fact
that Acteon sees Diana nude. Ovid prepared the
climax carefully--one could say shrewdly--leading up
to it step by step. The goddess lays aside bow and
quiver, steps out of her sandals, slips the robe
from her shoulders. Ovid thus employs a kind of subtraction process that a modish public undoubtedly
relished. At the last moment, with masterful
piquancy, he does not reveal the vision of the un-
veiled goddess. The attendant nympths notice Acteon
and conceal with their own bodies the mistress, who
in divine nobility towers by a head over them. The
combination of lustfulness and hypocritical decency
in Ovid is not to be equalled. How does Gower deal
with the episode? He does two things. First, he
follows the eyes of Acteon and does not reveal Diana
to the reader until she appears in his field of vision:
Amidd the plein he syh a welle,
So fair ther myhte noman telle,
In which Diana naked stod
To bathe and pleie hire in the flod. 1.361-64
Thus the reader is not granted a furtive sneak preview.
And the second difference, which results from the
first, is that the youth's gaze and the goddess' complete nudity collide unexpectedly, without having
been modified or weakened. The changes in the aesthetic and moral atmospheres are so tightly interwoven here that one can hardly treat them separately.
The abruptness of the meeting is on no account at-
tributable to a primitiveness in Gower's style. Need-
less to say, one should not efface the difference in
rank between the two story tellers, yet Ovid's subtle
subtraction technique was not beyond Gower's stylistic

capabilities. His description of the house of
Morpheus in the "Tale of Ceyx and Alcyone" proves
that.[4] There, in order to show that nothing diverts
the senses and disturbs the sleeper, Gower evokes a
series of optical and acoustical images only in order to eliminate them again immediately and achieve,
through a process of subtraction, the sensation of
complete lethargy:

> Ther is no fyr, ther is no sparke,
> Ther is no dore, which mai charke,
> Wherof an yhe scholde unschette,
> So that inward ther is no lette.
> And forto speke of that withoute,
> Ther stant no gret Tree nyh aboute
> Wher on ther myhte crowe or pie
> Alihte, forto clepe or crie:
> Ther is no cok to crowe day,
> Ne beste non which noise may
> The hell . . .   4.2995-3005

The method is extremely effective and, as far as
this story is concerned, Gower's own improvisation.
Neither Ovid nor Chaucer chanced upon it, and it is
only later, in Spenser, that one finds a similar
approach.[5] It is not due to inability that Gower
foregoes the use of this technique in the story of
Acteon.

With that we come to the question of morality,
an unpleasant question, for since Chaucer there has
prevailed the notion of the "moral Gower."[6] The
usual explanation holds that prudery prevented the
"moralistic" author from following in Ovid's foot-
steps, and may add some general observations about
the lateness of the Renaissance in England and about
how Shakespeare's contemporaries were the first
Englishmen to have eyes for the beauty of the human
body. But did Gower really have moral scruples
along these lines? One would suppose, then, that
he would have taken offense not only at the piquancy
of Ovid's description, but at the story itself; if
he needed an exemplum for unbridled visual curiosity,
he could just as well have chosen the harmless tale
of Lot's wife. Instead, he freely chose Acteon.
And if he does not join in Ovid's sensual sublety,
yet he by no means veils the phenomenon of divine
nudity. On the contrary, he calls attention to it

twice in the course of a few verses,[7] while Ovid,
significantly, employs the epithet nudus only for
the nympths. Obviously Gower thought it important
that the unexpected encounter have a powerful, un-
diminished impact--on Acteon as well as on the
reader. It attains this again through the most extreme stylistic economy and through the intentional
concentration of events into Acteon's perspective.
Acteon remains the subject in action and syntax,
whereas in Ovid--who sees in the story only the fatal coincidence of unfortunate circumstances--he is
condemned to passivity in syntax and action. Not
for an instant does the august author inquire into
Acteon's reaction to the divine apparition, but
abandons him to a paralysis that leaves him only
when he becomes sentimentally and elegiacally conscious of his metamorphosis into a stag. Gower,
on the other hand, sharply emphasizes the question
of the decision with which the Diana experience
confronts the young man, because that is the essential point for the CONFESSIO. Acteon's sin lies
not in the encounter itself, but in his reaction
to it. He remains--and not only grammatically--
the carrier of the action even when he forgets to
act at all:
>But he his yhe awey ne swerveth
>Fro hire, which was naked al. 1.366-67
The goddess' anger concerns this failure, not the
accidental trespass on her forest privacy. In Ovid
Acteon's metamorphosis is an act of divine self-
defense; in Gower it is punishment for Acteon's
lack of discretion. It is comparatively unimportant
how he himself submits to this punishment, and therefore Gower tells the end of the story summarily,
without any emotion. One almost receives the impression that his interest in Acteon flagged and
that the clamor of the hunt occupied him more than
the youth's death. In any case, the conclusion is
strikingly weak, architectonically, stylistically,
metrically, syntactically--I almost venture to add
psychologically, for psychologically absolutely
nothing more happens after Acteon fails to do the
morally correct thing. Here the weakness of Gower's
narrative technique becomes apparent. He takes no
pleasure in the depiction of a situation and lacks
the imagination that develops an image for its own

sake. He is the "moral" Gower in the sense that he
pushes his heroes and stories with high-principled
directness towards a question of moral decision.
This point attained, he loses interest and becomes
mediocre, curiously inept, and--not infrequently--
dull. Even Gower's best stories suffer from these
sudden lapses of interest that follow the climax.[8]

To speak of a development of Gower's narrative
technique is dangerous insofar as we know nothing
about the chronology of the individual parts of the
CONFESSIO AMANTIS. When in what follows any statement is made about the development of technique, it
is with the reservation that nothing is being said
about the temporal order of the tales. Any such
statement should be viewed as an aesthetic judgment
with no claim to chronological correctness. In this
sense one can show a development of narrative technique in the Pygmaleon story of Book IV.[9] It moves
in the direction that the Acteon story showed to be
characteristic of the author: the action is tight,
the tempo quick, and the perspective unified. The
story thus gains a narrative intensity that matches
the intensity with which Pygaleon's passion grows.
Let us look at the story itself.

The immediate source is again Ovid.[10] It is
unlikely that Gower used in addition the OVIDE MOR-
ALISE.[11] The criterion of names, successfully employed to clarify Chaucer's relationship to French
poetry, fails because the differences in the forms
of the names here prove nothing. The distribution
of emphasis and, in connection with it, the moral
interpretation of the story are so different that
a dependence hardly appears likely. The author of
the OVIDE MORALISE interprets the tale after the
fashion of a Bernard Shaw: the nobleman elevates
to his station, by means of appropriate clothing and
instruction, a lower class beauty, perchance his
maidservant, whom he finds naked (=poor) and mute
(=uneducated), makes her his wife and has a son by
her. Gower's point, on the other hand, is a warning against false timidity in dealing with women:
        And if he wolde have holde him stille
        And nothing spoke, he scholde have failed.
                                    4.426-27

There is no difference this time in the length of Ovid's and Gower's narratives. Gower found the following in Ovid: a woman-hating artist creates the figure of a girl whose extraordinary beauty and vivacity fill him with desires. He conducts himself toward the object of his love as one would toward a courtesan: he flatters her and shows himself to be generous. His gifts include everything that can please a woman: jewels and precious stones, flowers, small birds, and costly gowns. At the festival of Venus the artist begs the goddess to give him the ivory maiden, or one like her, for a wife. His prayer is heard and the image awakens to real life. There follows a prayer of thanks, Venus blesses the marriage, and the result is the birth of the boy Paphos.

What Gower makes of the story is something entirely different. Because his story is supposed to illustrate the rewarded persistence of the lover, he cannot use a woman hater. A woman hater would be absurd in the role of a gallant who persistently woos against all likelihood of success. Thus Ovid's bachelor becomes Gower's "lusti man of yowthe" (4.373). The alteration appears of little significance, but it contains two important factors. It indicates the abandonment of the double aspect hinted at by Ovid, namely that not only is the statue transformed as a favor to the man, but also that the man, under the influence of beauty, undergoes a transformation-- there is a delicate interrelation of events, a latent symmetry, which tacitly forms the background of Ovid's story. Furthermore, it involves an alteration of the dynamic. Gower's "lusti man of yowthe" sets to work with a fresh, joyous unconcern; in Ovid love strikes like a devastating flame[12] and causes the utmost confusion.[13]

If Gower simplifies the story and renders it inoffensive after his fashion, however, he does not merely diminish it. He improves it in directness and tautness because he eliminates the subjective point of view, thereby bringing the beginning and end a little closer together. The directness is further reinforced because Gower again unifies the perspective: Pygmaleon is the grammatical subject

almost throughout. Ovid has several intrusions of
an objective character (ll. 250-52; 265 f.) and an
entirely new beginning with the festival of Venus
(ll. 270 ff.). Gower avoids the intrusions by inter-
weaving the objective description of the statue with
references to its creator Pygmaleon:

Riht as a lyves creature
Sche semeth, for of yvor whyt
He hath hire wroght of such delit,
That sche was rody on the cheke
And red on bothe hire lippes eke;
Wherof that he himself beguileth.   4.382-87

He expunges the festival of Venus entirely and presses
to the climax in a steady crescendo. Despite all its
outward similarities, this passage (4.388-414) contrasts most strongly with Ovid. In content it is
entirely after the manner of the courtly Middle Ages,
in form entirely after the manner of Gower. In Ovid
the denouement is sultry with eroticism. Physicality
is the dominant element, a physicality to which the
statue is delivered up, with no will of her own,
passive, and without any individual character. In
Gower, on the other hand, she has from the very beginning something like a soul, a human individuality,
not only a power of erotic attraction, that determines Pygmaleon's relationship to her:

For with a goodly lok sche smyleth,
So that thurgh pure impression
Of his ymaginacion
With al the herte of his corage
His love upon the faire ymage
He sette, and hire of love preide.   4.388-93

She is the mistress, Pygmaleon her humble servant.
Instead of an almost enraptured physicality and a
suppressed eroticism, we have in Gower a "pure impression of his ymaginacion"; instead of the statue's
passivity, a smile, a little personality in which the
process of becoming human quietly suggests itself,
even though she remains mute at first ("Bot sche no
word ayeinward seide" 4.394). Even her silence, moreover, appears to be made radiant by that mysterious
smile. It would be presumptuous to try and treat
her as a courtesan and bribe her with presents,
which Ovid allows to be done to his statue. Gower
expunges all the gay fripperies. The statue's presence alone is the sine qua non of life for Pygmaleon,

and therefore Gower allows her to share work, meal,
and bed with him (4.395-403). Here the lines are
run-on. They become shorter and choppier as passion
grows, and they employ anaphora to signal endlessly
repeated efforts. At last the ends of lines and
clauses coincide in a rhythmical succession of tetrameters that calls to mind the lover's breathing.
The subject of the passage remains always Pygmaleon,
nor is he allowed to rest for even one short verse:

> And after, whan the nyht was come,
> He leide hire in his bed al nakid.
> He was forwept, he was forwakid,
> He keste hire colde lippes ofte,
> And wissheth that thei weren softe,
> And ofte he rouneth in hire Ere,
> And ofte his arm now hier now there
> He leide, as he hir wolde embrace,
> And evere among he axeth grace. 4.402-10

Pygmaleon's restlessness and tortured agitation are
manifested stylistically as a mass of verbs that
hardly leave room for a substantive. Everything
centers on a constantly repeated he, always unac-
cented in order not to interrupt the action. Of
course, the English line was more susceptible to
verb expression than the Latin hexameter, but even
in Chaucer it seldom achieves such intensity as it
does here in Gower. The release of the tension
then follows in a few clauses that operate even
rhythmically as a pleasant relaxation from the
breathtaking tetrameters. That Gower grants Venus
only a modest role is connected with his point.
Had he over-emphasized the fact that the intervention of a goddess is necessary to arouse a stony
beauty to the humanness of love, the prospects for
the indefatigable lover would have been slim.

The dissimilar behavior of the two authors at
the moment when the statue awakens to life is again
characteristic. Ovid describes the incident ob-
jectively, while Gower, incomparably more effective,
transmits it through the medium of Pygmaleon:

> Be nyhte and whan that he worst ferde,
> And it lay in his nakede arm,
> The colde ymage he fieleth warm
> Of fleissh and bon and full of lif. 4.420-23

Thus is the climax attained. Gower does not spoil

it by going into detail. Ovid's account is not bad,
and perhaps necessary in order to allow his statue,
hitherto patently inert and unliving, to become convincingly alive:

> . . . dataque oscula virgo
> Sensit, et erubuit, timidumque ad lumina lumen
> Attollens pariter cum caelo vidit amantem.
>
> 10.292-94
>
> [. . . the maiden, too, feels the kisses given
> her, and blushes; and raising her timorous eyes
> toward the light of day, she sees at once her
> lover and the heavens.]

Such was not necessary for Gower. For him the before
and after are not unrelated conditions: the metamorphosis to humanness is present in nucleus from the
beginning on. What appears as a miracle in Ovid is
almost a natural process of development in Gower.
Not the "moral" Gower--Ovid is also thoroughly de-
cent here--but the practised, consciously-shaping
Gower ended just at the right moment. Of course,
for the sake of completeness the birth of Paphos
could not be excluded; however, it is unobtrusively
appended to the interpretation of the tale (4.431 ff.).
It is amusing to observe that the cunning Ovid speaks
of a marriage between Pygmaleon and the eidolon, from
which Paphos results. The "moral" Gower, on the
other hand, unconcernedly follows the precepts of
courtly love and allows the pair a night together
without making a middle class attempt to legalize
the affair.

With the "Tale of Pygmaleon" Gower has surpassed
by a good bit his "Acteon." There the unification of
perspective and the acceleration of action served
above all to focus attention on the moral problem.
The tempo at which Acteon moved towards Diana was
basically unimportant; on the other hand, it was important that no digressions diminish Acteon's responsibility for his conduct or divert the reader's interest from the question of decision. The same means
serve to increase the psychological depth in "Pygmaleon."
The unity of perspective effects a special intimacy in
the relationship between Pygmaleon and his eidolon.
The statue is rarely exposed directly to the gaze of
the reader; rather, it is seen through the medium of
Pygmaleon. The accelerating speed of the tempo is

the stylistic equivalent of the accelerating intensity of desire, whereby emotion is intentionally and
consistently expressed as action. Gower proves his
complete mastery, however, in breaking off the story
at the right moment.

As a third example I have chosen a story that
Gower as well as Chaucer attempted without having
altogether controlled. It is the tale of the knight
Florent,[14] who falls into the hands of his enemy and
can hope for pardon only if he learns within a year's
time the correct answer to a question--it contains,
therefore, a fairy-tale motif combined with other
elements, for the question itself belongs not to the
fairy-tale type, but rather to the province of the
French parliament of love. It is: what do women
most desire in the world? The knight seeks the
answer in vain, until, in a solitary place, he meets--
just before the expiration of the appointed time--an
ancient hag who professes to know the correct answer.
She will teach it to him if he will promise to make
her his wife after the happy outcome. He gives his
promise, the answer proves to be the right one, and
the knight's dilemma begins. After various compli-
cations, the loathsome hag becomes an enchanted
princess in the bridal bed.

Gower's story, like Chaucer's, is bound to a
specific milieu (in Chaucer so much that the story
almost seems an intrusion, in Gower not so conspicuously) from which it becomes by progressive action
more and more independent. Most disturbing in
Chaucer is the heteronomy of moods. He locates his
story in Arthur's court and in a magic world: the
knight belongs to Arthur's circle, the lady to the
fairy kingdom. That these two worlds were intrin-
sically related and could be artistically blended
with one another is obvious even if one forgets
about Spenser. Chaucer proceeds, therefore, from
a world removed from history, transfigured by magic,
in which the tale must run its course. Perhaps it
is still tolerable when he expects the reader to
include in this illusion an episode from the soph-
isticated frivolity of the French parliament of love.
However, when his fairy opens her mouth and begins
to speak with the incessant fluency of the Wife of

Bath, the illusion is seriously endangered. Her ef-
florescence, her sarcasm, her feeling of superiority,
are in themselves refreshing, but they explode the
unity of atmosphere. Irony and the mood of fairy
tale preclude each other. One sees Chaucer's delight
in experimentation, one sees his pellucid rationalism,
which never suffers for long the twilight of the
fairy tale mood. One sees his humor, and one sees
the huge profit, the psychological mastery, which
leads to the metamorphosis of the tale in the teller's
conception. Only when one, as in the present instance,
has reasons for divorcing the narrative from its
frame and considering it for itself can it not be de-
nied that the experiment has the character of a brilliant operation that the patient unfortunately did
not survive.

    Gower also divorces his story from the milieu
of its beginning, but he proceeds more slowly and
cautiously and with another goal in mind. Unlike
Chaucer's, his story takes place at the emperor's
court in a semi-historical, clearly defined sociological milieu. Florent is a model knight without
individual characteristics:
            He was a man that mochel myhte,
            Of armes he was desirous,
            Chivalerous and amorous,
            And for the fame of worldes speche,
            Strange aventures forto seche,
            He rod the Marches al aboute. 1.1412-17
In addition, he gets into his precarious position
through the caprice of Fortuna, not through personal
guilt:
            Fortune, which may every thred
            Tobreke and knette of mannes sped,
            Schop, as this knyht rod in a pas,
            That he be strengthe take was. 1.1419-22
His exemplary standing and his illustrious ancestry
are respected by his enemies, and, instead of putting
him to death they grant him a period of time in which
to find the answer to the question of what woman most
desire. If unsuccessful, he will die. He returns to
the emperor's court and a conference of philosophers
is convened; however, the question remains unsolved.

    So far Gower's narrative is proper, colorless,

and tedious. The chief figure does not step out of
the social milieu. His emotional reactions do not
appear to have occupied the author for a moment. As
long as Florent moves in a firmly outlined, familiar
setting, as long as he conducts himself as a member
of a specific social class according to the rules of
this society--in an extreme situation, indeed, but
yet in one for which social customs are alleged--he
has something automatic about him and the motive powers of individual actions or passions remain obscure.
Gower's art in general is insufficient to individualize
convincingly his figures within a social milieu; they
easily become types. Or perhaps it is more correct
to say that Gower never strove for a realism in
Chaucer's sense because differentiation within a
sociological reality did not attract him. His realism, if one wishes to apply the notion to him in a
general way, is psychological--one could almost say
moral. His characters remain types until they are
thrust into a situation that demands a moral decision.
Driven psychically into a corner, they lose their
typicality and become human beings. Of course,
Gower's psychological realism nowhere exhibits a
tendency towards the working out of the accidental.
Because all his stories contain exemplary characters,
there clings to them, even in the situation of moral
decision, a certain universal validity. All of his
characters have something about them of the chief
figure of a morality play: they represent the genus
humanum, be they called Acteon, Pygmaleon, or Florent.
What distinguishes them from types in this situation,
however, is the fact that they represent, in the
uniqueness of their painful personal experience, a
universally meaningful human problem. There appears
to be a law of that literature not yet fully developed in its means of expression--as long as it is
not of a dramatic nature--that psychological realism
test itself first on the description of painful experience, a law from which probably only great mast-
ers are exempted. Thus Gower's attempts at realistic
description are indebted in part to the pressure of
the situation. In other respects, however, they are
inherent in him, expecially in the means of expression that he employed.

The turning point from typus to individuum in

the "Tale of Florent" is located after 1. 1521. It
is the moment when Florent quits the emperor's court
to meet his fate. The stylistic means that effects
this transformation is the double use of the accented
word alone, an extremely simple means with a remarkable power of expression:

> And thus he wente forth his weie
> Alone as knyht aventurous,
> And in his thoght was curious
> To wite what was best to do:
> And as he rod al one so . . . 1.1522-26

Here the man is quite undramatically and yet with the
surest hand divorced from his social setting and put
on his own, at first only externally. However, the
external isolation is only the preliminary condition
or the mirror image of the inner solitude in which
fate and the author place the man in order to shape
him individually. It is not only so in this story.
One encounters isolation in Gower again and again as
the spiritual context in which all important events
take place. To the solitude is joined, moreover,
a retarding element: deliberation. So far Florent
has behaved correctly, competently, without hesita-
tion. He has signed a covenant, made a report, given
his testimentary instructions. There has been no
trace of relection. Now, because scarcely anything
remains to be done, the solitary knight suddenly
emerges:

> And in his thoght was curious
> To wite what was best to do.

There is no restlessness in it, nor angst, nor rebellion; rather, a bemused astonishment. Florent
rides on his way, considers his situation more passively than actively, and thus comes to his meeting
with the ugly old woman, the loathly lady.

For the time being we will not speak of her.
In Chaucer she immediately seizes the reins of the
action, just as she seizes the reins of the horse,
in order to accompany, or rather to lead, Florent
to the king's court. Not for another moment is one
free from her and her torrent of words. She is determined to dominate, and she dominates. Chaucer's
Florent proceeds unsuspectingly into a situation
over which he gradually loses control, and thus be-

comes more and more colorless. Gower leaves the
conduct of the action to his Florent, just as he
leaves him freedom of decision. Because the tale
is supposed to illustrate the theme of obedience,
we must examine the situation and this freedom
of decision before we can talk about active obedience. Gower foregoes the mass of tension-pro-
ducing elements that in Chaucer effectively bring
about the climax at the king's court.

Florent encounters the loathly lady, discovers
from her that she possesses the correct answer,
learns the price of this answer, and is faced with
a decision. Although the encounter took place in
direct address, here the narrative reverts to objective description. The dialogue, naturally a
dramatic element, is here oddly still, while the
neutral description is full of realistic vivacity.
The method is again frugal, the sentence structure
simple, and nowhere is there a trace of emotion.
The inner unrest is converted into external motion:

> Tho fell this knyht in mochel thoght,
> Now goth he forth, now comth ayein,
> He wot noght what is best to sein,
> And thoghte, as he rod to and fro,
> That chese he mot on of the tuo,
> Or forto take hire to his wif
> Or elles forto lese his lif. 1.1568-74

Again the doubling ("Now goth he forth, now comth
ayein"; "as he rod to and fro"; "Or forto take . . .
Or forto lese") causes an increase in intensity.
Moreover there is, in addition to Florent's restlessness and perplexity, yet another element in
the to and fro of his physical motion. One receives the impression of a bird in a cage, of con-
finement between two equally unacceptable alternatives, which are stated in the last two lines. The
parallelism between "Now goth he forth, now comth
ayein," and

> Or forto take hire to his wif
> Or elles forto lese his life

is a true reflection of the inner and outer motion.
The weight of his psychic burden is expressed in the
plainest way imaginable, in a simple statement of
quantity without any psychological differentiation
("Tho fell this knyht in mochel thoght") that is

later followed by an equally simple "he wot not" and
"and thoghte." Perhaps what is left unsaid is equally
important in this emphasized simplicity. The knight
does not sigh, as Gower's heroes are prone to do
otherwise. There prevails that anxious silence that
is more impressive than eloquent description. The
loathly lady does not observe him, nor does he pay
her any heed at this moment. That is to say that
Gower, in order to isolate completely his hero and
guarantee the freedom of painful decision, suspends
in this situation the relationship of the two figures which just now was manifested in the dialogue
and which is reestablished with the moment when
Florent arrives at a decision and breaks his silence.

Florent reaches his decision--with an inner
reservation, to be sure, but one which has no great
importance for the course of the action--and receives
the answer that should deliver him. With it he sets
out for his destination, while the loathly lady remains behind.

The threat of death in itself induced in Florent
nothing other than impersonal reactions. It belonged
to situations for which there was a class-bound,
formulaic approach. It isolated him only externally
and led him into solitude. The threat to his freedom through the voluntary-involuntary wedding, however matches no conventional pattern and requires
a personal inner strife. It presses heavily upon
the man, not the knight. Florent is different from
now on: "He goth him forth with hevy chiere" (1.1619).
He does know the correct answer, but it does not
make him free. It means only a short reprieve, after
which he must return to his real problem:
             Florent of his answere is quit:
             And tho began his sorwe newe,
             For he mot gon, or ben untrewe,
             To hire which his trowthe hadde. 1.1664-67
Unlike Chaucer, Gower confronts his knight for a second time with the decision with which he must already
have wrestled in the first encounter with the loathly
lady, and thus deepens that decision's moral intensity.
He gives Florent the opportunity to evade the consequences of his oath by not returning to her. Only

now does Florent accept his fate in its full significance. When he gave his oath there existed the
possibility either that an answer other than the one
thus purchased would save him, or that this answer
itself would prove to be a deception. Moreover, his
choice was made under the threat of death. Now Gower
gives Florent complete freedom of moral decision and
he must choose yet again. Also, the choice's alternatives have been changed in the meantime. At first
they consisted of death or an unwanted marriage, and
perhaps this choice was the easier because it dealt
with two very real matters. Now Florent is confronted with the question of an odious marriage or
dishonor, a dishonor that would possibly remain
secret since the loathly lady does not appear pub-
licly in Gower. One sees that what Gower lost in
dramatic power when he did not have the loathly
lady appear at court is clear profit psychologically.
He is thus in a position to present and develop the
problem of obedience in all its complexity.

Florent makes the right decision:
>Bot he, which alle schame dradde,
>Goth forth in stede of his penance,
>And takth the fortune of his chance,
>As he that was with trowthe affaited.
>1.1668-71

He achieves obedience—-an obedience that consists
for the time being in the joyless acceptance of the
penance that fate demands from him—-and prepares to
return to the ugly hag. Gower is sparing of direct
expression of emotion and says nothing of Florent's
feelings along the way. Yet, as he reaches his
destination,
>Florent his wofull heved uplefte
>And syh this vecke wher she sat. 1.1674-75

There are only two lines, but they remind one involuntarily of Auerbach's interpretation of Genesis 22.4
(from the story of the sacrifice of Isaac):[15] "Then
on the third day Abraham lifted up his eyes, and saw
the place afar off." Florent's arrival to the old
woman and Abraham's arrival at the place of sacrifice—-both under the pressure of an obligation of
obedience that strains their strength to the utmost—-
are of course only rough parallels. Yet, Florent's
raising of his head is to be understood in the same

fashion as Abraham's lifting of his eyes to Mount
Moriah: the weight of silent obedience, the burden
of impending sacrifice until then kept Florent's
eyes depressed. Of course, the young man raises
his eyes not in order to recognize his destination,
but to look upon the object of his grief.

At their first meeting Florent had been confronted with the phenomenon of repulsive ugliness
as a totality:

> In a forest under a tre
> He syh wher sat a creature,
> A lothly wommannysch figure,
> That forto speke of fleisch and bon
> So foul yit syh he nevere non. 1.1528-32

Here Gower renders an impression and foregoes a description of the ugly hag. Not so at Florent's return. The approach is again according to Gower's
technique of subjective experience. Now, however,
there ensues an inventory of all the repulsive particulars that produces an objective character:

> Florent his wofull heved uplefte
> And syh this vecke wher sche sat,
> Which was the lothlieste what
> That evere man caste on his yhe:
> Hire Nase bass, hire browes hyhe,
> Hire yhen smale and depe set,
> Hire chekes ben with teres wet,
> And rivelen as an emty skyn
> Hangende doun unto the chin,
> Hire Lippes schrunken ben for age,
> Ther was no grace in the visage,
> Hir front was nargh, hir lockes hore,
> Sche loketh forth as doth a More,
> Hire Necke is schort, hir schuldres courbe,
> That myhte a mannes lust destourbe,
> Hire body gret and nothing smal,
> And schortly to descrive hire al,
> Sche hath no lith withoute a lak;
> Bot lich unto the wollesak
> Sche proferth hire unto this knyht.
>   1.1674-93

The old hag is not only the ugliest woman that Florent
ever met, but the ugliest creature that ever came
under a man's gaze. Thus within a passage the narrative quietly changes from subjective ("Florent syh")

to objective ("That evere man caste on his yhe").
Yet one can just as easily consider the catalogue
of details that follows the result of Florent's observation as the objective proof of the generalizing
relative clause (11. 1676 f.). It seems to me there
is artistic intent in this uncertainty of reference.
Florent proceeds slowly, adding up the overwhelming
sum of ugliness with which he must share his life
in the future. The idea of ugliness, until now
vague in its generality, becomes clear to him in
its drastic details.

The catalogue of ugliness itself is noteworthy
because of a realism such as Gower never achieved
in the description of beauty. Had he wished to
follow the conventional catalogue of beauty provided by poetics, with reverse symptoms so to speak,
he certainly would not have found it difficult to
use grotesque or repugnant objects of comparison
instead of the objects of value that poetics furnished for the praise of beauty. One could let
lips be withered tree bark instead of coral, convert eyes into guttering candles instead of twink-
ling stars. The negative catalogue of beauty certainly does not first appear in England with
Shakespeare,[16] but it belongs to a non-narrative
genre. There exist two satirical love poems of
this type from the early 15th century, the one by
Hoccleve ("Of my lady, wel me reioise I may"[17]),
the other attributed to Lydgate ("My fayr lady so
fresshe of hew"[18]). In addition, two anonymous
satirical verse letters by a pair of lovers survive in a manuscript that belongs paleographically
to the second half of the 15th century.[19] Because
it is a small omnibus manuscript, the pieces could
conceivably have been written considerably earlier,
but not, of course, before Chaucer had become the
recognized model of style.[20] In all these poems
the negative catalogue of beauty is employed with
parodic intent. In his opening lines Hoccleve,
like Shakespeare later, adheres closely to the
customary scheme:

> Of my lady, wel me reioise I may:
> Hir golden forheed is ful narw and smal;
> Hir browes been lyk to dym reed coral;
> And as the Jeet hir yen glistren ay.

Later on he improvises more freely (11-12):
        Hir nose a pentice is, that it ne shal
        Reyne in hir mowth thogh shee vp-rightes lay.
The anonymous author offers the following variations
on the theme:
        The Goodlynesse of your persone is esye to
                                                endyte
        For he leuyth nat that can youre persone
                                               appayre
        So comly best shapyne of feture most fayre
        Most fresch of contenaunce euyn as an Oule
        Ys best and most fauoryd of ony odyr foule
        Youre manly visage shortly to declare
        Your forehed mouth and nose so flatte
        In short conclusyon best lykened to an hare
        Of alle lyvyng thynges saue only a catte.
                                            I, 3-11
In the second poem he makes a two-fold point in the
following detailed simile:
        Youre caumsyd nose with nose-thryllys brode
        Vnto the chyrch a noble Instrument
        To quenche tapers brennyng afore the roode
        Ys best apropred at myne avysement. II.22-25
Even when an author writes with the intent to parody, however, he cannot compress loathsomeness with
complete success into a catalogue of similes, since
the grotesque simile mitigates as it objectifies.
Because these poems do objectify, they all mention
plain, realistic features--in the fourth stanza of
Hoccleve; in I, stanza 4 and II, stanza 6 of the
anonymous pieces.

        Now Gower had to shun parody at all events if
he wished convincingly to shape Florent's inner
turmoil by such a sight. Therefore, with the exception of 1. 1686, he foregoes simile. He gives
the overall impression (1. 1676 f.) that he resolves
the sight into its components with naturalistic precision and dryness (11. 1678-89); that is, he presents its physical details as if in close-up and
only sums it up at the end in the one striking
image of the wool sack (11. 1690-3). The wollesak
works so much more effectively than Hoccleve's
foot-bal[21] because it is active and asserts a claim
upon Florent:

> Bot lich unto the wollesak
> Sche proferth hire unto this knyht.

Hoccleve's simile, on the other hand, is static and
but one among many. Perhaps, however, it was not
only his fear that simile would bring an unwanted
comic element into the tension of the situation
that determined Gower's realistic description. Perhaps the convincing impression of ugliness can only
be attained through naturalistic precision, whereas
there appears to be inherent in beauty a latent connection with an absolute value that either illumin-
ates the lovely subject transcendentally or challenges it to competitive comparison with other lovely
subjects.

However, we must return to the story. The old
woman takes the knight at his word, the horse by the
reins, and sets the action once again in motion.
Florent thinks that his heart must break (ll. 1700 ff.).
In order to clarify the knight's mental condition,
Gower employs in this passage one of his infrequent
lengthy similes, and in it a change takes place.
From now on Florent accepts his fate; the uncertainty,
the dreadful burden of decision, are past:

> Ia Loke, how a sek man for his hele
> b Takth baldemoine with Canele,
> c And with the Mirre takth the Sucre,
> Ryht upon such a maner lucre
> Stant Florent, as in this diete:
> IIc He drinkth the bitre with the swete,
> b He medleth sorwe with likynge,
> a And liveth, as who seith, deyinge.
>   1.1703-10

The image is based on antitheses. The first three
lines present them in material form, the next two
relate the object of comparison to the subject of
comparison (they are something like a formal axis
around which the metaphor revolves), and the following three lines, which repeat the antitheses in
a slightly more abstract form, constitute the conclusion. Formally the construction is very attrac-
tively done, not too schematic, but pleasing, with
an unexaggerated but nevertheless clearly perceptible balance and with a reciprocal relationship to
content, syntax, and meter. The two groups of
antithetical verses are situated around the axis,

11. 1706-7, in such a way that they form an expanded chiasmus. In one designates the two groups I and II, then the arrangement Ia, b, c matches the arrangment IIc, b, a. Proceeding from the axis, that means that Ic ("Mirre . . . Sucre") is answered by IIc ("bitre . . . swete"), and Ib ("baldemoine . . . Canele") less stringently by IIb ("Sorwe . . . lyking"). The parallelism of the contents is reflected in syntactical similarity, which, though it does not lead to a complete similarity of sentence structures, nevertheless clearly removes the two groups of verses from the different constructions of the surrounding lines and binds them to each other. The paired antitheses are metrically paired because they appear each time in the same position in the line. The relationships between Ia and IIa are much less evident, are, in fact, merely hinted at in the similarity of the images: "sek man . . . hele" (Ia) and "liveth . . . deyinge" (IIa). It is as if the more rigorous scheme of correspondence relaxes the further one moves away from the axis, a sign of a wholesome freedom that is able to renounce mechancial symmetry in favor of lively ease.

One could conclude that the accentuation of the antitheses must reflect Florent's inner strife, as do the antitheses in ll. 1568 ff. That is not at all the case. In fact, a change is at hand. For the antitheses here are no longer merely juxtaposed to each other, as in "Now goth he forth, now comth ayein"(1. 1564), but are joined together: "he drinkth the bitre with the swete." Clearly Florent is still a long way from an organic synthesis, but in his conduct he does overcome the apparent irreconcilables. And the choice of images proclaims a positive conclusion. Florent is the sick man who must take bitters for his recovery, but at least one is able to speak of recovery. Thus the new phase of the tale begins under positive omens.

Florent keeps his promise conscientiously and the wedding takes place. Gower devotes some space to detail, while Chaucer, to good effect, cuts the ceremony short. In return, Gower makes amends with the description of the bridal night, which is one

of his really good pieces. He introduces it with
an overstatement topos in plainest form:
> So wo begon was nevere knyht
> As he was thanne of mariage. 1.1762-63

Alongside it he puts the following couplet, which
contrasts in mood and in vivacity of expression:
> And sche began to pleie and rage,
> As who seith, I am wel ynowh. 1.1764-65

Then the climax slowly begins. She wishes to be
kissed, while, on the other hand,
> His body myhte wel be there,
> Bot as of thoght and of memoire
> His herte was in purgatoire. 1.1774-76

Purgatoire recalls the earlier used penance and has
a two-fold aspect. The cleansing fire is indeed
agonizing as a place of residence, but it also has
the character of a transitional stage. Gower probably wishes to call forth both associations simultaneously, painful torment with reference to Florent's
present situation, suggestive promise for the further
course of the story.

The next step is for him to go to bed with the hag.
Chaucer compressed the situation into a single couplet:
> He walweth and he turneth to and fro.
> . His olde wyf lay smylynge evermo.
> Wife of Bath's Tale, 1085-86

The contrast between the tortured restlessness of the
knight--which is above all distinctly marked in the
monosyllables at the ends of lines and in the slight
alliteration of the tenues--and the smiling superiority of the old woman--whose person is emphasized
by the caesura, whose well-being is stressed by the
smooth flow of the last half of the second verse--
is first-rate. But Chaucer's terseness permits no
elaboration of the scene, no possibility of a climax.
The rest is direct address, but didactic address,
not dramatic dialogue. Gower develops the situation
for its own sake, not as an occasion for moralizing
observations. He looks, and allows the reader to look:
> And whan thei were abedde naked,
> Withoute slep he was awaked;
> He torneth on that other side,
> For that he wolde hise yhen hyde
> Fro lokynge on that foule wyht.

        The chambre was al full of lyht,
        The courtins were of cendal thinne. 1.1781-87
Florent, who tries in vain to hide his eyes for shame;
the room, which is so bright that the diaphonous bed
curtains cannot create a softening semi-darkness; the
oppressive and humiliating consciousness of uncon-
cealed nakedness; the inescapable conclusion that the
loathly lady draws from the situation ("For now, sche
seith, we ben bothe on," l. 1743); and Florent's
deathly despair ("And he lay stille as eny ston,"
l. 1794)--all that is masterfully done. All emotion
is shunned; the curve of the psychological experience
appears clearly and distinctly. "Wo begon," "purgatoire,
"stille as eny ston," mark the three stages that lead
Florent to a kind of inner death. Earlier he had accepted the marriage as an unavoidable bond; now he
must accept it as a fait accompli:
        He herde and understod the bond,
        How he was set to his penance. 1.1798-99
Because he finds himself in a state of lethargy after the death of his physical pride, he acts "as it
were a man in trance"--but he acts. He turns to the
old woman--and finds her transformed.

        Gower does not say in so many words that the
knight's inner change occasions or causes the loathly
lady's outer transformation, although this is basically the theme of his story. Rather, he maintains
that Florent's submissive reply to a vexatious question is the deciding factor. That was part of the
story as Gower and Chaucer found it and neither has
actually altered it much. The story betrays its
courtly origin by the kind of question and answer
on which Florent's life depends in the first part.
The question is: what do women most desire? It requires an answer in the spirit of courtly love cul-
ture: mastery in love ("Sovereynetee," says Chaucer,
Wife of Bath's Tale, 1038); "Be soverein of mannes
love," says Gower, 1.1609). This answer, however,
must not only be recognized and acknowledged, but
also experienced. Therefore, the second part ties
the transformation of the ugly old woman into a
dawn-lovely princess to the willingness of the knight
to submit himself unconditionally to the loathly
lady. This willingness is tested with a second
question that is put to the knight on the evening

of the forced wedding. He must choose whether he
would rather have his wife young and beautiful or
ugly and faithful (as in Chaucer); or whether he
would rather see his beloved young and beautiful by
day but old and ugly by night, or, vice versa,
beautiful and young by night but ugly and old by day
(as in Gower).

Florent passes the test because he leaves the
decision to the lady, and thus acknowleges her
"sovereynetee." Now it is curious that this point
is elucidated so altogether differently in Chaucer's
and Gower's versions. Gower prepared so well psychologically that the decision seems almost to be
anticipated and the correct answer to the test
question loses some significance. Thus in Gower
Florent already demonstrated obedience in a much
more bitter sense when he went back to accept the
loathly lady, in all her ugliness, as bedfellow.
According to the logic of the story, the transformation occurs at this moment. Florent's readiness
to submit himself to her decision--whether she will
be ugly only by day or only by night--has by far
the lesser effect and in Gower affects only the
permanence of the transformation. Thus the force
of the spiritual transformation impairs the originally sensational effect of the point. Likewise,
the denouement then degenerates utterly. It is
technically necessary to complete the plot, but it
contains no further moral problem and thus Gower
reels it off with little sympathy.

Chaucer does not anticipate the transformation.
Yet, he endangers the point with another element,
namely with the lecture that the old hag gives the
knight after she has put the test question to him.
The alternatives in Chaucer are young, lovely, and
faithless, or old, ugly, and true. The loathly
lady points to the answer--old, ugly, and true--with
every rhetorical and dialectical means, and with an
unequalled loquacity. In the event that the content
of the lecture is not intended ironically, then one
would expect that Florent would derive profit from
it and now, without further ado, be in a position
to give the correct answer. Yet suddenly the reader
discovers to his considerable astonishment that the

240

correct answer consists in the renunciation of decision. A slight flaw in the logic is the result. It is to a certain extent compensated for by the moment of surprise that the unexpected denouement causes. This combines with the subsequent unexpected, final transformation of the loathly lady for a cumulative effect such as Chaucer loved.

When one weighs this phase of Gower's and Chaucer's stories, one must for a moment consider the different wording of the test question. It has been supposed that the choice with which Chaucer confronts his knight is of greater moral significance than the choice between beauty by day or by night with which Gower confronts Florent. That is no doubt correct. But in so siding one fails to see that the choice qua choice is unimportant since it remains unchosen; instead of decision, the story demands submission to the will of the lady. With this submission the goal of the story is attained. One cannot avoid the impression that Chaucer's narrative frame impaired the value of the story at this point, for the demand for submission accords all too well with the character of the teller, the Wife of Bath, and is thus flavored with a barely concealed irony. It almost seems as if the self-characterization of the Wife of Bath is Chaucer's chief concern. In this he succeeded incomparably, but the story suffers as a result. Florent shares the inglorious fate of the aforesaid lady's five husbands when he laconically and submissively accepts his new-found conjugal bliss.

Chaucer's narrative is the story of the loathly lady, or, indirectly, of the Wife of Bath. He works with the coarser means of conflict of moods, an occasional brilliance of expression, and irony. Gower makes his task less simple, and actually tells the story of Florent. He is not as concerned with the moment of surprise and the happy ending as he is with what matters above all to him, proper conduct in a situation of moral decision. If we may employ the idea of development yet once more in the context of Gower's narrative art, this story is new in that the moral decision does not

241

ensue suddenly--as in "Acteon," where everything
seems pointed to the one end--but passes through
more phases. In this way the tale receives a grad-
ual intensification and a psychological deepening
that necessitate a new descriptive technique. In
the other two tales Gower tightened the action and
quickened the tempo; in "Florent" he takes as his
artistic task the shaping of the retarding moment.
Gower sacrifices surprise to the greater credibility of his knight's inner development and often
achieves astonishing results with economical means,
although Chaucer deals with his material in a superior manner. Gower pursues the moral and psychological problem with great care, and is superior
in this area even to the 16th century novel. He
scarcely heeds what lies to the right and left of
the way, and may sometimes for that reason appear
pedantic and tedious. One cannot expect in him
a fullness of life, but he undertook earnestly
and persistently, as did hardly any of his contemporaries, the attempt to understand and describe
man from the moral motives of his behavior. His
narrative art is the living expression of this
endeavor.

Notes to Chapter Six
    [1] CONFESSIO AMANTIS 1.333-78.
    [2] Ovid, METAMORPHOSES, ed. Rudolf Merkel, 2nd
ed. (Leipzig, 1904), 3.138-252. [The English translations of Ovid are throughout those of Henry T.
Riley, THE METAMORPHOSES OF OVID, Bohn's Classical
Library (London, 1851). Trans.]
    [3] See ll. 141-42:
        At bene si quaeras, fortunae crimen in illo,
        Non scelus invenies, quod enim scelus error
                                            habebat?
        [But, if you diligently inquire into his
        case, you will find the fault of an accident,
        and not criminality in him; for what crim-
        inality did mistake embrace?]
and l. 176: . . . sic illum fata ferebant [thus did
his fate direct him].
    [4] CONFESSIO AMANTIS 4.2927-3123.
    [5] The cave or grotto of Morpheus appears in
Ovid, MET. 11.592 ff.; in Chaucer, BOOK OF THE DUCH-
ESS, 153-65; in Spenser, FAERIE QUEENE, 1.1.39 ff.

[6] Chaucer, TROILUS AND CRISEYDE, 5.1856 f.:
"O moral Gower, this book I directe/ To the . . ."
[7] See ll. 363 and 367.
[8] Compare the end of "Mundus and Paulina,"
l. 761 ff.
[9] CONFESSIO 4.371-436.
[10] MET. 10.243-97.
[11] After comparing eleven stories, I am unable
to establish a single conclusive correspondence between the CONFESSIO AMANTIS and the OVIDE MORALISE.
[12] MET. 10.252-53:

> . . . miratur, et haurit
> Pectore Phygmalion simulati corporis ignes.
> [. . . Pygmalion admires it; and entertains,
> within his breast, a flame for this fictitious
> body.]

[13] MET. 10.254: Saepe manus operi temptantes
admovet [Often does he apply his hands to the work].
Ibid., l. 258: Et metuit, pressos veniat ne livor
in artus [And is fearful lest a livid mark should
come on her limbs when pressed].
[14] Gower, "The Tale of Florent," CONFESSIO
AMANTIS 1.1407-1861; Chaucer "The Wife of Bathes
Tale," in THE COMPLETE WORKS OF GEOFFREY CHAUCER,
ed. F. N. Robinson, 2nd ed. (Boston, 1957).
[15] See Erich Auerbach, MIMESIS (Berne, 1946),
p. 14.
[16] Compare Shakespeare, Sonnet 130.
[17] EETS OS 73, 37 f.
[18] Ed. J. O. Halliwell, A SELECTION FROM THE
MINOR POEMS OF DAN JOHN LYDGATE, Percy Society
(London, 1842), II, 199 ff.
[19] Ed. R. H. Robbins, "Two Middle English
Satiric Love Epistles," MLR, 37 (1942), 415 ff.
[20] See l. 8 of the second poem: "The Ynglysch
of Chaucere was nat in youre mynd." Loc. cit., 417.
[21] l. 13: "Hir comly body shape as a foot-bal."

INDEX

244

245

Layamon, 39
Le Clerq, J., 104, 123, 127
Lewis, C. S., 73; ALLEGORY OF LOVE, 118
Literary Prayer, 98-100
Lorenz, Dominican Cardinal, SOMME LE ROI, 154
Macaulay, George M., ix, 1, 2, 7, 8, 15, 18, 19, 57, 59, 64, 65, 118, 119, 122, 164
Medieval Allegorical Poetry, 29, 46
Medieval Biblical Exegesis, 30, 35, 50, 52
Medieval Doctrine about Possessions, 145
Medieval Preacher, 70, 86-89, 104-7, 123-5; discussion of proper preaching, 126-9
Medieval Prologues (form), 91-4
Medieval Sermon (tradition and form), 69, 71, 74, 83, 98-102, 104-13, 116, 122
MIROUR DE L'OMME, 1; stylistic character, 14-18; 24, 26, 38, 57, 74, 76, 77, 79, 119; as class critique, 131-3; 140; psychomachia, 145, 146; 149, 160, 163, 164, 179, 180, 183, 184, 190, 193, 199, 201, 202, 204, 205, 290
MIROUR DES PECHIEZ, 102
Mirror for a Prince, 6, 10, 17, 26, 78-80, 119; open letter form, 131-4; law and justice in the state, 134-8; ruler's function, 137, 138; ruler's rela-

tionship to law, 139, 140, 158, 159; ruler's relationship with God, 140, 158; definition of a Prince, 141-3, 151; virtue, 145, 155; "dona naturae," 145, 162; "dona fortunae," 146, 148-50, 162; rules for life of king, 153-55, 167; 172, 183, 194, 197, 199-201
MORALIA IN JOB, 122
Morality (Gower's), xi, 219-221, 228, 240-2
"Mundus" (theme), 183, 184, 197, 200, 201, 206, 207
"Mutatio rerum," 184, 185
MYROUR OF SYNNERS, 154, 194, 195
"Natura denatura," 36
Nobility (Nobles), 3, 4, 43
"O Deus Immense," 81-3
"Ordo" (divinely ordained hierarchy), 34, 36, 37, 41
Orosius, 192
Ovid, 28, 48, 49, 52, 58, 185; TRISTIA, 29, 57, 58, 64, 65; INTEGUMENTII OVIDII, 30; METAMORPHOSIS, 64;
OVIDE MORALISÉ, 30
Owst, G. R., PREACHING IN MEDIEVAL ENGLAND, 116, 122, 132, 155
Paphos (in "Actaeon"), 222, 225
Peasants, 4, 12, 13,15;